GEO-ECONOMICS

The Interplay between Geopolitics,
Economics, and Investments

Joachim Klement, CFA

Statement of Purpose

The CFA Institute Research Foundation is a not-for-profit organization established to promote the development and dissemination of relevant research for investment practitioners worldwide.

Biography

Joachim Klement, CFA, is a research analyst and former chief investment officer with 20 years' experience in financial markets worldwide. He spent most of his career working with high-net-worth individuals and family offices, advising them on investments and helping them manage their portfolios. He has also managed equity portfolios for banks and independent asset managers.

Today, Joachim heads the Strategy, Accounting, and Sustainability team at Liberum Capital Limited, where he focuses on stock markets and helps investors navigate not only traditional financial and economic risks but also risks emanating from environmental, social, and governance issues as well as geopolitics.

Joachim studied mathematics and physics at the Swiss Federal Institute of Technology (ETH) in Zurich, Switzerland, earning a master's degree in mathematics. During his time at ETH, he experienced the technology bubble of the late 1990s firsthand and grew interested in finance and investments. Joachim then studied business administration at the University of Zurich in Switzerland and the University of Hagen in Germany, graduating with a master's degree in economics and finance.

Joachim entered the financial services industry just in time for the run-up to the 2008 global financial crisis. His friends advise him to never switch fields again, because a few years later, the entire industry tends to collapse.

Contents

PL Qualified Activity — CFA Institute — This publication qualifies for 9 PL credits under the guidelines of the CFA Institute Professional Learning Program.

Foreword

In 1970, Susan Strange threw down a gauntlet to the disciplines of international relations (IR) and economics. Then a research fellow at the Royal Institute for International Affairs, she would later become the first (and so far only) woman to hold the Montague Burton Professorship of International Relations at the London School of Economics and Political Science. Her article, "International Politics and International Economics: A Case of Mutual Neglect" (*International Affairs*, Vol. 46, No. 2, April 1970), is now recognized as the origin point of a literature that would grow into the subdiscipline of IR called international political economy (IPE).

The tradition of Adam Smith and David Ricardo notwithstanding, the larger discipline of economics has never really considered the prefix of "international" a terribly meaningful or differentiating one. To be sure, economists study areas such as trade, foreign exchange, and cross-currency monetary theory, but the discipline defines these subjects as subfields of economics rather than a collection constituting a new field called "international economics."

Alternatively, although IR is likewise a subfield of politics or political science, it has been starkly differentiated from its parent discipline by both its subject matter and its name. Predominantly the study of the relationships between sovereign states, IR has a long and rich history that begins, as does nearly every undergraduate IR curriculum, with the Melian Dialogue from Thucydides' *History of the Peloponnesian War*. And, because a state of conflict and war between sovereign states has historically been the most common condition of international relations, it is not surprising that most IR scholarship relates directly or indirectly to conflict and war.

Strange was proposing in 1970 that IR scholarship needed to pay more attention to what was even then a growingly interconnected *economic* world. And although her plea may have been directed to both the IR community and the economists, it ultimately gathered momentum only among IR practitioners. There are a variety of reasons for this result, not the least of which was then-prevailing positivism in the discipline of economics—that is, an approach that seeks to determine *how* things work, not how they *should* work. Nevertheless, a burgeoning group of IPE scholars, including Robert Cox and Peter Katzenstein, soon began producing groundbreaking work that culminated in Robert Gilpin's magisterial description of the field in *The Political Economy of International Relations* (Princeton University Press, 1987).[1]

In the first half of the present book, Joachim Klement makes yet another significant contribution to the literature of IPE. But he does this from the distinct perspective of an investor—that is, someone who assumes risk in the capital markets with the expectation of being compensated for assuming that risk. This perspective differentiates Klement's book from other IPE scholarship in several important ways.

First, although he possesses a firm command of the literature, he is not interested in engaging in theoretical debates regarding the academic apparatus of the field. Moreover, despite covering many of the same conceptual problems as other authors, his arguments unfailingly bring those issues back to the way in which they cause information to become manifest in market prices.

Second, whether discussing war, natural resources, or globalization, Klement dispenses with lengthy description of the phenomenon and moves directly to the manner in which these events affect both markets and market prices.

Finally, Klement applies the conceptual first half of the book to practical, real-world challenges in the second half. These include US–China competition, energy and natural resources, data and cyber security, and climate change. Before exploring these challenges, however, Klement first provides a powerful chapter on forecasting (acknowledging a substantial debt to Philip Tetlock) along with a compelling rationale for the title of his book being *Geo-Economics* rather than *International Political Economy*.

A close if slightly narrower synonym for IR is geopolitics, a word coined in 1916 by Swedish political scientist Rudolf Kjellén, a contemporary of several other geography-oriented IR scholars who came to define the literature of geopolitics. Among them were naval historian Alfred Thayer Mahan, geographer Halford Mackinder, and later, political scientist Nicholas Spykman. Each wrote about the deterministic nature of geography in the disposition of international politics. Mahan chose to focus on the choke points of the high seas—the Strait of Gibraltar, the Strait of Malacca, the Strait of Hormuz, the Bab el-Mandeb—asserting that whoever controlled these choke points controlled the sea lanes. For Mackinder, it was the heartland, which he identified as eastern Europe, that was dispositive: Whoever controlled the heartland controlled Eurasia, which he referred to as the "world island." Spykman considered control of the rimland, or Eurasia's coastal regions, to be dispositive.

---

[1]For a full history of IPE as an academic subdiscipline, see Benjamin Cohen, *International Political Economy: An Intellectual History* (Princeton University Press, 2008).

Debates about these powerful and sharply contrasting theories have dominated geography and geopolitical discussion for a very long time.

Klement takes a different approach, avoiding the geographical determinism of his forebears. By using *Geo-Economics* as the title of this book, he is reinforcing the shift in thinking first articulated in 1990 by Edward Luttwak in his article "From Geopolitics to Geo-Economics: Logic of Conflict, Grammar of Commerce" (*The National Interest*, No. 20, Summer 1990). Luttwak is a prolific scholar who has authored, among many other works, three separate books on the grand strategy of the Roman Empire, the Soviet Empire, and the Byzantine Empire, respectively. Like Klement, he is an acute observer of geopolitics. For both Luttwak and Klement, the significance of the geo-economics rubric is embodied by the brilliant subtitle of Luttwak's article: *the logic of conflict carried out in the grammar of commerce.*

Klement's focus on the logic of conflict is perhaps the most important part of his contribution to the literature of geopolitics and the second half of the book. In all of the specific challenges he takes up—US–China competition, energy and natural resources, data and cyber security, and climate change—he portrays the issues in terms of an essential conflict; the possible ways in which that conflict might resolve itself; the effect of those resolutions on economic variables; and, most importantly, the potential consequences of those changes in economic variables on markets and market prices.

This focused approach to four central international challenges in the book's second half is original, refreshing, and trenchant. Klement's arguments add a new dimension to contemporary debate and will be of keen and sometimes arresting interest to scholars of both IR and economics, as well as to investment management practitioners. The principal reason for his originality, I would argue, is that he is a practitioner who has produced a piece of scholarship rather than a scholar who, after a temporary stint as a practitioner, writes about practice.

Scholars have written some very powerful texts about the lessons of their practical experience: for instance, Henry Kissinger's *Diplomacy* (Simon & Schuster, 1994), Zbigniew Brzezinski's *The Grand Chessboard* (Basic Books, 1997), or John Taylor's *Global Financial Warriors* (W. W. Norton, 2008). These excellent books offer insight and historical perspective but never the kind of poignant, practical translation of the logic of conflict into the logic of the markets that Klement articulates here.

In 2004, the great political scientist Samuel Huntington coined the term "Davos Man." It was meant to be disparaging, describing someone so geopolitically naïve and self-possessed with their own progress and success that they had forgotten even their own nationality because it was only a hurdle to their further success. Huntington's article was "Dead Souls: The Denationalization of the American Elite" (*The National Interest*, Spring 2004). This naïveté is echoed today in the often-expressed desire to become a "world citizen," a phrase that is very ambiguous in its meaning.

Joachim Klement's *Geo-Economics: The Interplay between Geopolitics, Economics, and Investments* is the perfect antidote to revive those "dead souls" and ought to be required reading for all future Davos participants. The CFA Institute Research Foundation is delighted to present it.

Robert E. Kiernan III
CEO of Advanced Portfolio Management LLC (APM)
Senior Fellow at the Kennedy School of Government at Harvard University
Bronxville, New York
March 2021

Introduction: Geopolitics for Investors

Geopolitics is ultimately the study of the balance between options and limitations. A country's geography determines in large part what vulnerabilities it faces and what tools it holds.

—*Peter Zeihan*, The Absent Superpower

Narratives or Fairy Tales?

On 7 January 2017, Robert Shiller gave the presidential speech at the annual meeting of the American Economic Association.[1] The topic he chose was unusual. He titled his speech "Narrative Economics" and discussed the fact that economics (and, by extension, finance) has focused too much on quantitative methods and forgotten something important in the process: We humans have evolved to be storytellers. The stories we tell each other bind us together as families, communities, nations, and religions. These narratives define what it means to be a mother, a German, or a Jewish person.

And because we are natural storytellers, we also tell stories in economics and finance. Yet in economics and finance, we have been trained to ignore stories and narratives and to instead look at hard facts and data. On the one hand, some quantitative investors might even consider the narratives "fairy tales" because although the stories can contain a grain of truth, they are largely considered justifications for investors who cannot do the required math. Such critics often claim that economic narratives are for laypeople and are not a proper subject for economic analysis.

Shiller, on the other hand, laments that we might overlook a crucial driver of financial markets if we ignore the stories and narratives because, to quote the sociologist William Bruce Cameron, "Not everything that can be counted counts, and not everything that counts can be counted" (1963, p. 13). Luckily, thanks to technological advances, such as textual analysis software, we can increasingly bridge the gap between the things that can be counted and the things that count.

---

[1]See Shiller (2017). Robert J. Shiller, a Yale professor, won the 2013 Nobel Prize in Economic Sciences, which he shared with Eugene F. Fama and Lars Peter Hansen.

Exhibit 1 shows the results of a Google Trends search of different words and phrases (or narratives) on financial sites on the internet. The early years of the 21st century were dominated by the topic of globalization. China was emerging as an economic superpower, and other emerging markets, most notably the former communist countries in Eastern Europe, were opening up their economies and expanding the opportunity set for investors. But investor interest in these markets (as reflected in search volumes) was already in decline early in the century. Other narratives, such as the housing boom in the United States, were capturing investors' attention. Of course, that boom ended in tears, and between 2006 and 2008, investors around the world had to become experts in subprime mortgages, collateralized debt obligations, and other arcane financial innovations that had led the global economy to the brink of collapse.

The central banks of the world had to step in to rescue the global economy. In the years after the global financial crisis of 2006–2008, central banks and their unconventional monetary policy measures, such as quantitative easing, were the main drivers of financial markets. Even the near default of some eurozone countries did not derail global equity markets, nor did the technical default of the United States that was missed by a heartbeat in 2011. All that mattered were the actions of the Federal Reserve Board, the European Central Bank, and other central banks. This devotion of investors to the power of monetary policy lasted for many years, but recently, politics has taken center stage again.

Exhibit 1. Google Trends in Investment Narratives of the 21st Century

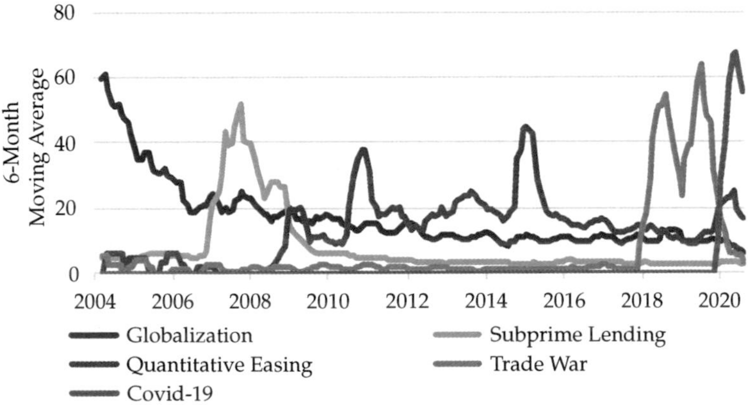

Source: Google Trends.

The election of Donald Trump as president of the United States led to a sudden and significant change in both foreign and domestic US policies. The trade war between the United States and China is probably the most prominent example of this renewed importance of politics in recent years, until the Covid-19 pandemic became the all-encompassing narrative of 2020.

Note in Exhibit 1 that two of the major investment narratives of the past 20 years (globalization and the trade war) were "geopolitical" in nature. Both globalization and the rise of populist policies that led to the trade war are political and driven by nations' strategic goals. As China has evolved from the workshop of the world to a country with an economy that rivals that of the United States, it has become more assertive on the global stage and thereby introduces some new political challenges for developed and developing countries. Meanwhile, the Covid-19 pandemic has upended the world in 2020.

To be clear, a pandemic is not, by definition, a geopolitical event. As we have seen with the intensifying tensions between the United States and China, however, the pandemic has accelerated existing geopolitical tensions. The trade war between the United States and China is on hold for now, thanks to the Phase 1 deal established in early 2020, but the political and economic relationship between the two countries is arguably worse today than it has been in the past 40 years.

Thus, today's investors need to understand geopolitical trends as a main driving force of markets. This book provides just that: an understanding of the interplay between geopolitics and economics and of the impact of that dynamic on financial markets. To that end, this introductory chapter will first briefly introduce geopolitics and the aspects of geopolitical research that are relevant for investors and then provide an overview of the individual chapters in the book.

I invite readers to read the entire book from front to back, but I would like to emphasize to the time-pressed reader that each chapter in this book can be read on its own because I have tried to put little nuggets of wisdom and lesser-known research findings in each chapter. Thus, even experienced investors and economists will find something in each chapter that they did not already know. So, sit back, relax, let the markets crash and the children scream—and enjoy this book.

What Is Geopolitics?

Traditionally, geopolitics was understood to be the study of how geography (the "geo" in geopolitics) influences the international policies of nations and societies (the "politics"). Flint (2006) thus defined geopolitics as a component of both human geography and international affairs.

Classical geopolitics can be traced back to Aristotle, who derived the political systems of Greek city-states from their climatic and geographical conditions. But the most common starting point for classical geopolitics is provided by Swedish geographer Rudolf Kjellén, who first used the term "geopolitics" in 1916, and by German geographer Friedrich Ratzel, who wrote in 1897 about how states receive their power as nations from the territory they occupy. Unfortunately, Ratzel combined his theory of geopolitics with elements of social Darwinism and postulated that every people strives to expand what he called *Lebensraum* ("living space"), the space occupied by a culture and civilization. He believed that different cultures and races had different levels of fitness; hence, higher cultures would rightfully replace lower cultures from their homelands. This concept of *Lebensraum* became an integral part of the ideology of Adolf Hitler and the Nazis and led straight to the gas chambers of Auschwitz.

Whereas the German school of classical geopolitics descended into one of the worst theories ever invented, the Anglo-American school focused on how geography determines a nation's military security and its options to project power. This school of thought was thus more about politics and identifying beneficial paths for international political action than was the European view. It came to prominence with the advent of the Cold War, when the United States and the Soviet Union were in a constant struggle to enhance their international influence. Combined with an invention from mathematics—game theory—geopolitics and the simulation of geopolitical scenarios with the help of war games became an indispensable tool for political and military decision makers.

Classical geopolitics was rather rigid, however, in its assumptions about the limiting factor posed by geography. A core assumption of many classical geopolitical studies was that geography is immutable and cannot be overcome. Hence, if a country occupies certain strategic territories or has access to crucial chokepoints in international waters, it will always be able to dictate its will to other nations and have a permanent political advantage. Halford Mackinder (1919) claimed, "Who rules East Europe commands the [Eurasian] Heartland; who rules the Heartland commands the World-Island; who rules the World-Island commands the world." If that were true, the Soviet Union—as the country that ruled Eastern Europe and the Eurasian heartland—should have won the Cold War.

Modern geopolitics does not see geography as immutable destiny but as a set of limitations and opportunities that influence the space of possibilities for decision makers. This geographical factor, together with the political options chosen, can lead to very different outcomes from region to region. Cohen

(1991), for example, differentiated between "gateways" and "shatterbelts." Gateways are regions where various societies and countries foster international cooperation and economic growth. Classic examples of a gateway are the European Union and the countries participating in China's Belt and Road Initiative. Shatterbelts are regions dominated by interregional conflicts and the rivalry of external powers for influence, something we observe in the Middle East.

Hence, Scholvin (2016) defined the three pillars of the modern geopolitical approach as follows:

- Geographical factors must not be seen as irreversible fate. They provide both opportunities and constraints, but these opportunities and constraints are not static.

- General patterns and long-term processes are substantially influenced by geographical factors, but understanding specific developments in international affairs requires taking into account nongeographical factors.

- For geopolitical scientists, revealing causal mechanisms and concentrating on the role of geography therein are helpful.

Bergesen and Suter (2018) provided an instructive example of this thinking when they argued that geopolitics follows long-term cycles in which periods of globalization and the removal of borders and geographical barriers alternate with periods of rising nationalism and the erection of (new) borders. **Exhibit 2** shows the Composite Index of National Capability (CINC) as calculated by the Correlates of War project for four major countries back to 1816.[2] The CINC is a combination of several factors—such as the share of the global population in a country, the size of a country's military, the military expenses of a country, and the energy consumption of a country. As such, it is not an economic measure but a measure of military power relative to that of other nations. The CINC is expressed as a country's share of global military capabilities.

As Exhibit 2 shows, the early to mid-19th century was a period of great globalization with a single hegemon—the British Empire. Within the British Empire, trade prospered, and borders were torn down. As the British Empire declined in the second half of the 19th century, it was increasingly challenged by rising powers in Europe and North America. This confrontation led to the era of "Great Power competition," wherein each of the rising powers expanded its colonies and tried to gain access to vital resources around

---

[2]Correlates of War is a research project by several US universities under the leadership of the University of California, Davis, and Penn State University that collects quantitative data on international relations and conflicts.

Exhibit 2. Composite Index of National Capability, 1816–2012

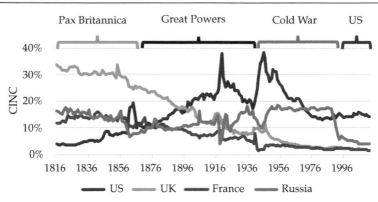

Source: Correlates of War.

the globe. The competition among the great European powers of the United Kingdom, France, Germany, Austria-Hungary, and Russia eventually led to the outbreak of the First and Second World Wars, which from a geopolitical perspective can be understood as one long, 30-year war.

At the end of the Second World War, the United States emerged as the sole global hegemon. It was (at least economically) challenged only by the Soviet Union during the Cold War. With the dissolution of the Soviet Union in 1991, the United States finally occupied a position similar to that of the British Empire in the first half of the 19th century, and a renewed period of globalization and the removal of national borders occurred.

Throughout these periods of globalization and Great Power competition, geographical factors such as access to natural resources played a key role in establishing and defending power. But as technology advanced over time—as coal was replaced by oil, for example—the benefits of access to some natural resources declined, allowing other countries to challenge the hegemons of the past. Today, technological progress seemingly makes geography irrelevant in many cases (think of the internet) but, as the reader will see, this situation does not herald the end of geopolitics. It simply shifts the power balance and benefits to some countries while leading to the relative decline of others.

From Geopolitics to Geo-Economics

This book is not about military power and political strategy, however, but about economics and investments. In an age of nuclear weapons and the possibility of destroying all of human civilization in a potential third world war, the projection of military power has to be limited. Instead, geopolitics increasingly uses economic means to project power. Luttwak (1990) coined the term "geo-economics" when he argued that power comes from "disposable capital in lieu of firepower, civilian innovation in lieu of military-technical advancement, and market penetration in lieu of garrisons and bases" (p. 17).

Scholvin and Wigell (2018) defined geo-economics as the application of economic means of power to achieve strategic objectives. And in this book, we adopt a similar definition. To me, geo-economics is the study of how geopolitics and economics interact in international relations.

A good example is the role Germany has played in international politics since the end of the Second World War. Germany, for understandable reasons, has been reluctant to use military force and, instead, uses its economic might to impose its preferences on other nations. When the eurozone faced an existential crisis in 2011 and 2012 with the near collapse of Greece and the potential spread of the eurozone debt crisis to Italy and other large economies, Germany was the leading advocate for the austerity measures imposed on Greece and other countries. Effectively, Germany promised to help bail out the weaker countries in the eurozone if they committed to strict fiscal discipline in the years to come.

Another example of geo-economics is the use of economic power by both China and the United States to impose international rules and standards on other nations. The International Monetary Fund (IMF), the World Bank, and the World Trade Organization are all institutions that were shaped largely by US economic preferences, and they have influenced global trade and global finance for the past seven decades. Meanwhile, China, with its Belt and Road Initiative and its Asian Infrastructure Investment Bank, is trying to project its own economic preferences globally. These topics will be covered in separate chapters in this book.

Today, the era of globalization of the past 30 years seems to be coming to an end. Nationalism is on the rise, and geopolitical and geo-economic risks increasingly take center stage. **Exhibit 3** shows the top five risks identified by global business leaders each year at the World Economic Forum (WEF). I have marked geo-economic risks in gray boxes and other risks in white boxes. Five to ten years ago, the risks perceived as most likely to come true were predominantly economic or social in nature—another financial crisis, a slowdown of the Chinese economy, rising unemployment, or inequality. The geo-economic risks that will be discussed in this book have dominated the list in recent years—from global terrorism, cyber attacks, and data fraud to natural disasters and extreme weather triggered by climate change.

Exhibit 3. Top Five Risks in Terms of Likelihood

	2010	2011	2012	2013	2014	2015	2016	2017	2018	2019
1st	Market Crash	Storms	Inequality	Inequality	Inequality	War	Migration	Extreme weather	Extreme weather	Extreme weather
2nd	China slows	Floods	Fiscal crisis	Fiscal crisis	Extreme weather	Extreme weather	Extreme weather	Migration	Natural disaster	Climate change
3rd	Pandemic	Corruption	Climate change	Climate change	Unemployment	Governance failure	Climate change	Natural disaster	Cyber attacks	Natural disaster
4th	Fiscal crisis	Biodiversity loss	Cyber attacks	Water	Climate change	State collapse	War	Terrorism	Data fraud	Data fraud
5th	Governance failure	Climate change	Water	Demographics	Cyber attacks	Unemployment	Natural disaster	Governance failure	Climate change	Cyber attacks

Note: Gray boxes indicate geo-economic events.
Source: WEF (2019).

The Things to Come

Plenty of books on geopolitics have been written by eminent experts in politics and international affairs. This book is not one of them.

First, I am neither a political scientist nor an expert in international affairs. I am an economist and an investment strategist who has been fascinated by geopolitics for many years. And this fascination has led me to the realization that almost all books and articles written on geopolitics are useless for investors. Political scientists are not trained to think like investors, and they are not typically trained in quantitative methods. Instead, they engage in developing narratives for geopolitical events and processes that pose risks and opportunities for investors.

My main problem with these narratives is that they usually do not pass the "so what?" test. Geopolitical risks are important, but how am I to assess which risks are important for my portfolio and which ones are simply noise? Because geopolitics experts focus on politics, they do not provide an answer to this crucial question for investors. What could be important for a geopolitics expert and for global politics could be totally irrelevant for investors. For example, the US wars in Iraq and Afghanistan have been going on for almost two decades now and have been an important influence on the political discussion in the United States. But for investors, the war in Afghanistan was a total nonevent, and the war in Iraq had only a fleeting influence, when it started in 2003.

Geopolitics experts cannot answer the question of which geopolitical events matter for investors and which do not. Unfortunately, some experts thus claim that all geopolitical risks matter and that these risks cannot be quantified but only assessed qualitatively. Nothing could be further from the truth. In the chapters that follow, I discuss geopolitical and geo-economic events from the viewpoint of an investor and show that they can be quantified and introduced as part of a traditional risk management process. I do this in two parts.

Part I: Reviewing How Geopolitics Influences Investments. The first part of this book focuses on geopolitics that matters to investors. It reviews the literature on a range of geopolitical events and shows which events have a material economic effect and which do not. To do so, **Chapter 1** briefly discusses how geopolitics can affect the economy and investments. As the reader will see, some geopolitical events have only a fleeting, short-term impact (or none at all), whereas others have a long-lasting impact that might be felt for years—if not decades. The impact depends on the economic variables that are affected by the geopolitical event.

Chapter 2 examines the types of events that probably first come to mind when we talk about geopolitics: wars and international conflict. Unfortunately, in many cases, wars do not really matter all that much for investors, but in some circumstances, wars can and do have a material influence on financial markets. This chapter will enable readers to differentiate between the two types and provides examples of how big the impact of international conflict has been on markets historically. Because the face of international conflict is also changing, this chapter covers not only traditional wars between nation-states but also the impact of international terrorism on the economy and financial markets.

The focus of **Chapter 3** is on one of the most important topics of geopolitics—namely, access to natural resources, such as oil and minerals. Crude oil is the lifeblood of the modern economy; thus, access to crude oil at affordable prices is of vital interest to any modern economy. A material disruption in the supply of natural resources has the potential to significantly slow economic growth and trigger inflationary spikes. How big these disruptions have to be before they have a material impact on the economy and an investment portfolio is the central topic of this chapter. The chapter also tries to help investors identify ways to hedge the geopolitical risks caused by a disruption in the access to natural resources.

Chapter 4 focuses on the opportunities created by geopolitical events, and in it, I note the benefits of globalization, free trade, and related processes for the global economy and financial markets. Globalization and free trade have received a lot of bad press in recent years, and some of this criticism is justified. Although globalization has provided many benefits, it has also had unintended consequences that have caused a political backlash. Rising inequality in developed countries and criticism of some of the policies the IMF has imposed on emerging economies are just two examples that are critically examined in this chapter.

Part II: Evaluating Current Geopolitical Trends. The first four chapters of this book consider geopolitical aspects that matter for finance and investment. The second part of this book puts the insights from those first chapters into practice by applying them to current geopolitical trends. In this second part, I stick my head out and examine the impact the geopolitical trends have on the economy and financial markets today and their likely development in the coming years.

Forecasting the future is difficult, however, especially with respect to geopolitical and geo-economic developments, which are subject to large errors. Hence, **Chapter 5** introduces the rules of forecasting that I have developed during my career and that provide guidelines for the subsequent chapters in this part of the book.

Chapter 6 focuses on the dominant geopolitical topic of our time—namely, the economic and political rivalry between the United States and China. As China has grown to be an economy similar in size to that of the United States, the country has become increasingly assertive on the global stage—for example, demanding more influence in existing international organizations such as the IMF and the World Bank. China is also in the process of upgrading its economy from a manufacturing base for low-tech products to a high-tech economy similar to that of Japan or South Korea.

Of course, the changes in China provide a direct challenge to the global economic influence of developed countries and have caused a lot of irritation in some places. An example reaction to China's demands for its rightful place at the table of great economic powers is the trade war initiated by the United States, but other, more subtle developments are taking shape today. How the trade war and the geo-economic competition between China and the rich countries of the West might develop is the focus of Chapter 6.

As noted in this introductory chapter, geography itself is not a permanent obstacle to the rise and fall of economies. Today, geopolitical and geo-economic rivalry is based less on access to natural resources (which is clearly dominated by geographical factors) and more on access to data (which is not). Data have often been dubbed the oil of the 21st century, and access to data is not always pursued by legal means. Cyber warfare and cyber terrorism have become tools that complement traditional warfare and terrorism. In our connected economies, the economic damage caused by successful cyber attacks can be tremendous, so **Chapter 7** focuses on the potential impact of a large-scale cyber attack. Could a successful cyber attack cause a prolonged blackout of a major city or even trigger another financial crisis? If so, how bad would it be? These are the questions I address in this chapter.

Chapter 8 shifts the focus to an emerging form of resource competition. As renewable energy is becoming an increasingly important part of our energy supply, access to the minerals used in batteries and solar cells, as well as the technology to build modern renewable energy applications, is becoming vital. The shift to renewable energy might also have some destabilizing economic effects on countries that rely heavily on the export of crude oil and other fossil fuels, triggering new geo-economic developments. How both oil exporters and oil importers can prepare for the rise of renewable energy and benefit from its opportunities is the focus of this chapter.

Chapter 9, the final chapter of the book, focuses on one of the most pressing global challenges for politics and humankind alike: climate change.

Climate change is already triggering more intense and more frequent extreme weather events—cyclones, floods, and droughts—than in the past. And these extreme weather events have a rapidly rising impact on the economy of the affected regions. As climate change progresses, investors need to deal with two major geo-economic developments: the likely economic impact of climate change and the societal consequences of climate change, such as famine, mass migration, and civil strife.

As I noted, each chapter can be read on its own, but the introductory chapters in each part (Chapters 1 and 5) provide a mental model for the reader that creates a guiding theme for each of the subsequent chapters. Of course, what will provide the most coherent economic narrative is to read all the chapters in order, which I invite the reader to do.

Bibliography

Bergesen, A., and C. Suter. 2018. "The Return of Geopolitics in the Early 21st Century: The Globalization/Geopolitics Cycles." In *The Return of Geopolitics*, edited by A. Bergesen and C. Suter, 1–8. Munster, Germany: Lit Verlag.

Cameron, William Bruce. 1963. *Informal Sociology: A Casual Introduction to Sociological Thinking.* New York: Random House.

Cohen, S. 1991. "Geopolitical Change in the Post-Cold War Era." *Annals of the Association of American Geographers* 81 (4): 551–80.

Flint, C. 2006. *Introduction to Geopolitics.* Abingdon, UK: Routledge.

Luttwak, E. 1990. "From Geopolitics to Geo-Economics: Logic of Conflict, Grammar of Commerce." *National Interest* 20 (Summer): 17–23.

Mackinder, H. J. 1919. *Democratic Ideals and Reality: A Study in the Politics of Reconstruction.* New York: Holt.

Scholvin, S. 2016. "Geopolitics—An Overview of Concepts and Empirical Examples from International Relations." FIIA working paper (April).

Scholvin, S., and M. Wigell. 2018. "Power Politics by Economic Means: Geoeconomics as an Analytical Approach and Foreign Policy Practice." *Comparative Strategy* 37 (1): 73–84.

Shiller, R. 2017. "Narrative Economics." *American Economic Review* 107 (4): 967–1004.

WEF. 2019. "Global Risks Report 2019." World Economic Forum.

Part I: Geopolitics that Matters

Not all geopolitical events matter for investors, and knowing which ones do and which do not is of critical importance for investors. In the subsequent chapters, I will review the empirical evidence on those instances that matter. To do this, I will focus in the Chapter 1 on the different pathways by which geopolitical events can affect the economy and crucial variables that determine financial markets; these include inflation, risk premiums, and the future cash flows of financial assets. This chapter will provide us with a mental model that we should have in the back of our mind when addressing specific geopolitical events and their potential impact on markets.

After this brief theoretical chapter, in Chapter 2, I will address armed conflicts in the form of wars and terrorist attacks and their impact on economic growth, economic sentiment, and financial markets. Next in Chapter 3, I will take a closer look at natural resources, in particular oil but also metals and water, and how commodity price shocks triggered by geopolitical events propagate through the global economy and financial markets. Finally, in Chapter 4, I will look at the impact of international economic cooperation in the form of free trade and globalization. Unlike the chapters on armed conflict and natural resources, this chapter shows that geopolitical events do not only create risks for investors but can create significant opportunities.

Because the focus is on geopolitics that matter *for investors*, the subsequent chapters are full of empirical results and hard data. The selection of studies in these chapters is necessarily subjective and incomplete. Covering all the relevant studies would fill several books. Thus, I have decided to focus on the main results that can be generalized to future events and developments and that investors can use as starting points to assess the potential impact of these developments. I have focused mainly on the impact of geopolitical developments on developed markets, as well as on the BRIC regions (Brazil, Russia, India, and China) as the most prominent examples of emerging markets. A plethora of additional studies is available covering all kinds of emerging and frontier markets that I could not discuss in this book. In fact, the material on the impact of geopolitical developments on emerging markets is so vast that it would warrant a book on its own.

Furthermore, the impact of geopolitical developments on financial markets can be exploited not only through traditional long-only investments in stocks, bonds, and other assets but also through derivatives and complex investment strategies. Because this book is written for a broad audience of investment practitioners, we do not have sufficient space here to explore the complex investment strategies that macro hedge funds and some other investors would implement to benefit from geopolitical developments.

Chapter 1: How Geopolitics Can Influence Markets

Political shocks command a risk premium despite being unrelated to economic shocks. Investors demand compensation for uncertainty about the outcomes of purely political events, such as debates and negotiations.

—Lubos Pástor and Pietro Veronesi

The Link between Geopolitics, Economics, and Investments

To understand how geopolitical events can affect financial markets, one must go back to basics and look at the valuation formula for financial assets. Astrophysicist Stephen Hawking wrote in the acknowledgments to his popular book *A Brief History of Time* that "someone told me that each equation I included in the book would halve the sales" (1988). Fortunately, this book is written for investment practitioners and available for free, so I do not have to worry about sales or an audience that is intimidated by equations. Nevertheless, only one equation appears in this book:

$$FV = \sum_{t=1}^{\infty} \frac{E[CF_t]}{(1+r_f+\pi+k)^t}.$$

Using the discounted cash flow (DCF) model, in this equation FV is the fair value of an asset (i.e., the present value of discounted future cash flows), $E[CF_t]$ are the expected future cash flows of the asset at each time t, r_f is the real risk-free rate, π is the rate of inflation expected over the life of the asset, and k is the risk premium. This equation governs the valuation of every financial asset that produces cash flows, whether it is a bond, stock, real estate, private equity, infrastructure, or something else. Only two major asset classes are not governed by this equation: currencies and commodities.

Because neither currencies nor commodities generate cash flows, they are difficult, if not impossible, to value. Commodity prices are determined exclusively by supply and demand, both of which can be affected by geopolitical events. Some commodities, such as crude oil and gold, are extremely sensitive to geopolitical events, which is why I discuss them in some detail in

Chapter 3 of this book. Currencies, on the other hand, reflect differences in inflation, interest rates, and other factors between two countries and hence are influenced by geopolitical events insofar as the effect they have on these variables. As a result, throughout this book I discuss the impact of geopolitical events on currencies only when clear evidence exists for a measurable effect. In particular, I focus in Chapter 3 on commodity currencies, such as gold.

Going back to the discounted cash flow model just presented, geopolitical events can affect each of the variables in the model in different ways. At the end of this chapter, I discuss a case study on the impact of defense spending on the fair value of investments. However, the most obvious and direct way for geopolitical events to influence the fair value of an asset is through a changing risk premium. Pástor and Veronesi (2013) investigated whether policy events in general are associated with a risk premium. Traditionally, one would expect only economic events to demand a risk premium, given that they affect future cash flows and the components of the discount rate. Political events have only an indirect effect on assets insofar as policy decisions by the government might change future cash flows and inflation or force the central bank to adjust monetary policy, thereby changing the risk-free rate.

Pástor and Veronesi (2013) looked at all kinds of policy uncertainties, not just geopolitical risks, and found that this uncertainty does indeed command a risk premium that is independent of the risk premium from economic factors. In their model, they explained this risk premium with uncertainty aversion. Political risk reflects uncertainty about the future (including a possible but uncertain impact of government policies on the economy), and uncertainty-averse investors want to be compensated for the risk of changing policies.

But whether this policy risk premium is positive or negative, large or small, is not clear. On the one hand, policy mistakes by the government can lead to higher taxes, recessions, or even war—all of which reduce future cash flows and should cause investors to demand a positive risk premium. On the other hand, the government provides a put option to financial markets insofar as it has the means to prop up a weak economy through fiscal and monetary policy measures and avoid, or at least dampen, a recession. Therefore, the policy risk premium is reduced by the value of this implicit government put option.

Unfortunately, the value of this put option declines in a weak economy, just when it might be needed the most. This decline occurs because the government has not only economic goals but also political ones. In a weak economy, a government might be tempted to engage in populist policies that improve voter support but might be damaging to businesses and the overall economy in the long run. Moreover, in weak economic times, a government might be ousted and replaced by a new government that follows more extreme economic policies. Whether these are left-wing or right-wing policies does not really matter; in both cases, the long-term economic impact of populist policies tends to be negative.

Because policy uncertainty is higher in weak economic times, Pástor and Veronesi (2013) predicted that the policy risk premium increases as well. They found empirical evidence in favor of this prediction by looking at the Economic Policy Uncertainty (EPU) indices that were developed by Baker, Bloom, and Davis (2016) and their relationship with different economic indicators. Economic policy uncertainty is higher in a recession or in times of weak economic activity in the United States than in times of strong growth. Pástor and Veronesi also found that heightened policy uncertainty filters through to financial markets by increasing both realized and implied volatility as well as correlations between stocks. What they could not find, however, is statistically significant evidence that equity market returns are higher in the aftermath of heightened policy uncertainty. They identified some statistical evidence in favor of higher equity market returns in the 12 months after a period of heightened policy uncertainty but not in the 3 or 6 months after that.

Measuring Geopolitical Risk

A more recent approach to measuring the impact of geopolitical risks on the fair value of financial assets was undertaken by Caldara and Iacoviello (2019). They constructed a dedicated Geopolitical Risk (GPR) index by looking for words associated with wars, civil wars, and terrorism in 11 newspapers in the United States, Canada, and the United Kingdom since 1985.[1] For historical purposes, they went back to the year 1900 with the help of three newspaper archives.[2] **Exhibit 1** shows the historical GPR index with some major geopolitical events marked. The two world wars clearly stand out in the first half of the 20th century, but other prominent events—such as the Falklands War, the Gulf War of 1990, and the September 11, 2001 (hereafter 9/11), terrorist attacks—also stand out. Because the GPR index is based on a textual analysis of newspapers in North America and the United Kingdom, it is a measure of the public perception of wars in these regions. Regional wars that did not involve US or British troops are thus clearly underrepresented in the index. Still, we have to admit that from the viewpoint of investors, global financial

---

[1]The index is designed in such a way that the average index level for the years 2000 to 2009 is 100 points.
[2]The archives used were those of the *New York Times*, the *Chicago Tribune*, and the *Washington Post*.

Exhibit 1.   Historical Geopolitical Risk Index

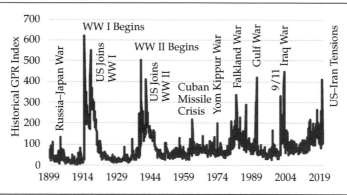

Source: Caldara and Iacoviello (2019).

markets are dominated by geopolitical events involving the United States because it is the largest economy in the world, with the largest stock market, the leading global currency, and one of the largest bond markets. Hence, geopolitical events appear to have the greatest influence on financial markets if they appear on the radar screen of a US audience.

The GPR benchmark index available since 1985 can be used to analyze the impact of geopolitical risks on the economy and on financial markets in general. Caldara and Iacoviello (2019) found that moderate increases in geopolitical risks tend to have a negligible impact, but for a two-standard-deviation spike in the GPR index, they noted that company fixed investments decline by 1.8% over the subsequent 12 months. To put this into perspective, such a two-standard-deviation event corresponds to a spike in the GPR index of 82 points and is roughly what happened when Russia annexed Crimea in 2014 and after the 2005 London bombings. In comparison, the 9/11 terrorist attacks were a six-standard-deviation event and thus had a much larger impact.

In addition to the decline in company fixed investments, Caldara and Iacoviello (2019) found a temporary setback in consumer confidence and a 0.4% decline in employment in the 12 months following a two-standard-deviation spike in the GPR index. Given the impact on consumer sentiment and employment, we should expect that an increase in the GPR index leads to an increase in the risk premium, k, in the fair value equation presented earlier and hence a decline in equity markets and other risky assets. Caldara and Iacoviello (2018) investigated the immediate impact of an increase in the GPR index on stock markets around the globe and found that in the month after a 100-point spike, stock markets typically declined by 1% to 3%.

Exhibit 2.   Impact of Geopolitical Shock on Stock Markets

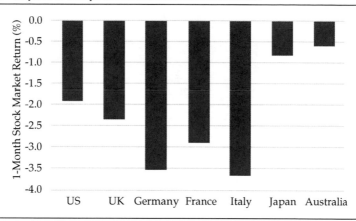

Source: Caldara and Iacoviello (2018).

But, as **Exhibit 2** shows, stock markets reacted differently in different countries. The United States' market was close to the global average. Markets in Europe tended to show bigger declines, while markets in Asia suffered less. This phenomenon might well be another reflection of the fact that the GPR index is based on information from North American and British newspapers and thus focuses more on risks that are prominent in the West. Furthermore, Caldara and Iacoviello (2018) found weak evidence that investment flows reverse after a spike in the GPR index, so that emerging markets and international developed markets suffer outflows while the United States experiences capital inflows. This flight to safety is also corroborated by a small decline in two-year Treasury yields of 20 basis points.

However, in a follow-up version of their 2018 paper, Caldara and Iacoviello (2019) built a value at risk model to simulate the propagation of a geopolitical shock through the economy and markets and found that the impact on stock markets is short-lived and starts to disappear after two quarters. This effect makes sense given that the risk premium, k, is likely to normalize if a risk has been digested by the market and leaves long-lasting impacts on financial markets only if it triggers a persistent change in economic growth (thus changing future cash flows), inflation, or the risk-free rate.

One drawback of the GPR index is that it focuses on only a very narrow set of geopolitical risks—namely, threats or incidents of war and terrorism. It ignores other risks that I would call geopolitical in nature, such as the US–China trade war. **Exhibit 3** compares the GPR index with the Global EPU

Exhibit 3. GPR Index versus Global EPU Index

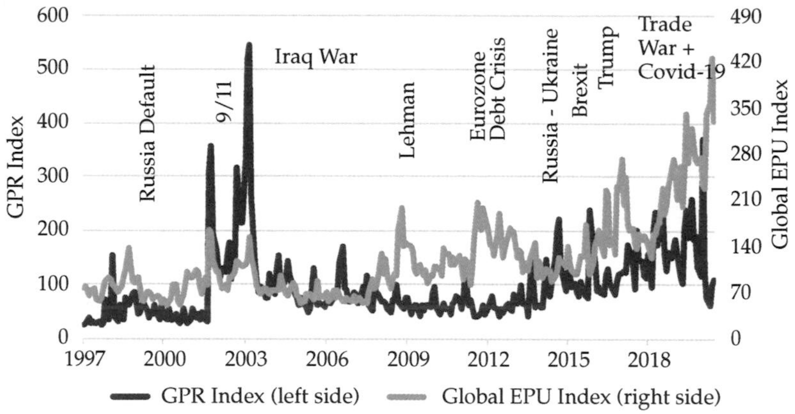

Sources: Caldara and Iacoviello (2019) and Baker et al. (2016).

(GEPU) index, which builds on the country-level EPU indices developed by Baker et al. (2016).

The purpose of EPU indices for different countries and globally is not so much the measurement of geopolitical risks but the measurement of risks to economic policy of all kinds. Thus, in some cases it shows heightened risk whenever these risks were triggered by geopolitical events (e.g., after 9/11 or the Iraq War), but it also shows spikes after events that I would classify as purely economic developments, such as the Global Financial Crisis of 2008–2009 and the eurozone debt crisis of 2011–2012. In recent years, the EPU index for the United States has been extremely high as a result of the US–China trade war. This event is geopolitical in nature, as we will see in Chapter 6, but it is not captured by the GPR index. Hence, while both the GPR and EPU indices are interesting ways to quantify risks, neither of them is a panacea for investors.

Finally, one needs to be aware that stock market risks as measured traditionally by the Cboe Volatility Index (VIX) are not linked to all risks. The VIX and its international cousins are calculated based on one-month, option-implied volatility and are, by definition, short-term in nature. They do not incorporate long-term risks from economic or geopolitical events. For example, the VIX has been relatively calm throughout most of the US–China trade war, with only the occasional small spike, as shown in **Exhibit 4**. In general, however, the VIX more closely resembles the GPR index in recent years than the EPU index. Meanwhile, at the height of the Global Financial Crisis during the collapse of Lehman Brothers and during the Covid-19–related crash

Exhibit 4. Geopolitical Risks versus Stock Market Volatility

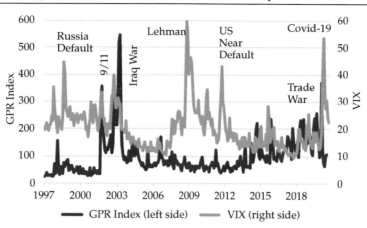

Sources: Caldara and Iacoviello (2019) and Cboe.

in spring 2020, the VIX spiked dramatically. In other words, the VIX is a measure of imminent risks, while both the EPU and GPR indices are measures of broader sources of risk.

Case Study: The Cost of Wars and the Peace Dividend

So far, I have been concerned only with the risk premium, k, in the fair value equation. To see how geopolitical events can influence the other variables, looking at the cost of wars and the so-called peace dividend is worthwhile. Fighting wars can be expensive, even for a large country such as the United States. **Exhibit 5** shows the peak of defense spending, as a percentage of GDP, in some of the major wars the United States has fought throughout its history. The cost of World War II was overwhelming, and the Civil War is well known to have been costly not only in terms of casualties but also in terms of money. In fact, the percentage for the Civil War, shown in Exhibit 5, reflects only the cost to the Union because no reliable estimates are available for the cost to the Confederacy. Given that the Civil War was catastrophic for the Confederacy, though, one can speculate that the true defense cost of the war might have been comparable to that of World War II. But even smaller wars, such as the recent engagements in Iraq and Afghanistan, caused serious strains on the US budget, with total defense expenditures sucking up more than 4% of GDP in some years.

Economic theory states that increased defense spending is good for defense contractors, but that might lead to a crowding out of private consumption

Exhibit 5. Peak Defense Spending during US Wars

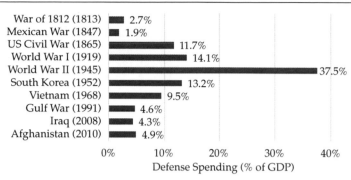

Defense Spending (% of GDP)

Source: Daggett (2010).
Notes: The year of peak defense spending is given in parentheses. The fiscal years do not match calendar years, so in some cases, the peak spending year occurred after the war in question was over. GDP numbers before World War II are retrospective estimates.

and investments by the government because capacity that would have been used for civilian products must now be dedicated to defense. Furthermore, increased defense spending implies bigger deficits and thus higher interest rates and taxes in the future, both of which can lead to a slowdown in private consumption and investments.

Conversely, after the end of the Cold War, the prospect of a peace dividend got traction in investment circles. The military standoff between the United States and the Soviet Union came to an end, and defense budgets were being cut. If defense spending crowds out private investments and consumption, then these cuts should lead to increased private investments. This increase should lead to stronger economic growth because the private sector is much bigger than the government sector, and increased investments in the private sector more than compensate for the losses in government spending. Finally, as defense spending declines, the budget deficit should decline and the cost of debt might decline as well. And because interest rates for the private sector are priced relative to Treasury yields, lower cost of debt for the government should also lead to lower financing costs for the private sector.

Exhibit 6 shows the decline of defense spending throughout the 1990s, before the 9/11 attacks and the engagements in Afghanistan and Iraq triggered a renewed increase in military spending. The decline in defense budgets coincided with declining government deficits in the 1990s, giving some plausibility to the theory of the mechanism behind the peace dividend. However, Exhibit 6 also shows that the federal deficit is much more volatile than the

Exhibit 6.   US Defense Spending and Federal Deficit

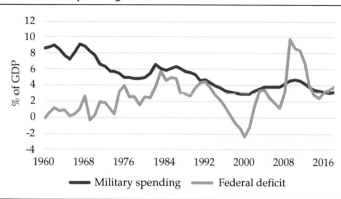

Sources: World Bank and the Federal Reserve Bank of St. Louis.

defense budget and is largely influenced by economic circumstances (e.g., the Great Recession of 2009) and domestic policy measures, such as tax cuts and hikes.

Nevertheless, Mintz and Huang (1990) set out to test the peace dividend empirically. They looked at the relationship between the US defense budget and US economic growth. On the one hand, they checked for a direct negative link between US defense spending and economic growth. If this link were to exist, then the reduction of a geopolitical risk (in this case, the Cold War) would lead to a decline in defense spending and higher economic growth. For investors, that would mean higher expected future cash flows $E[CF_t]$ and thus a rising fair value of risky assets, such as stocks. On the other hand, Mintz and Huang checked for an indirect peace dividend by looking at the relationship between lower defense spending and future private investment, which could be triggered by lower interest rates. Lower interest rates should be reflected in some combination of lower risk-free rate r_f and lower rate of inflation π in the discounted cash flow model presented earlier in the chapter.

Unfortunately, the evidence in favor of the peace dividend is mixed, at best. Mintz and Huang (1990) found no direct effect of reduced defense spending on economic growth and no empirical validation of a crowding out of the private sector. However, their study investigated the years after World War II, when military spending was relatively low. In an all-out war, such as World War II, or a war fought on home soil, such as the Civil War, military spending could become so large that it would crowd out the private sector. As we will see in the next chapter, where a war is fought and how intensive the war is do make a difference for an economy.

Like many authors before and since, Mintz and Huang (1990) also found little evidence of an indirect peace dividend. The problem with identifying an indirect peace dividend is that the signal is subject to a lot of noise, such as the regular economic and credit cycles that have a far stronger impact than the defense budget on interest rates and private investment. The authors did find that with an approximately five-year delay, a statistically significant increase in private investment occurs after a decline in defense spending; however, this effect appeared only after they optimized the lag structure of their regression model, suggesting that the effect is weak or dispersed over time.

A follow-up study by Mintz and Stevenson (1995) involving a sample of 103 countries showed that the peace dividend could be identified in only approximately 10% of the countries in the sample and thus seems unlikely to be a real effect. A comprehensive literature review of the topic by Dunne, Smith, and Willenbockel (2005) showed that the papers that identified a significant peace dividend usually used an economic model that made some flawed assumptions about the efficiency of the defense sector and the private sector. The assumptions resulted in stronger apparent economic growth whenever resources were shifted from the military to the private sector. Hence, the relationship between reduced defense spending and increased private investments is probably small and might even be an artifact of the specification of the economic models used to empirically test it.

Conclusions

This chapter has provided a simple framework for the way geopolitical events can affect the valuation of financial assets. As we have seen here, the impact can be short-term if geopolitical risks lead to increased risk premiums that eventually normalize. Different approaches have been taken in recent years to measure geopolitical risks and economic policy uncertainty. All these approaches create useful proxies for the geopolitical risk premium, but none of them is a panacea. The approaches all use different definitions of *uncertainty* and *risk*, and hence, neither of them has a good correlation with the impact of geopolitical risks on financial markets. But all these approaches do indicate that at least a short-term impact on risky assets is possible.

However, the framework introduced in this chapter also shows that geopolitical events might have a long-term impact on financial markets. If geopolitical events affect future economic growth, expected cash flows of assets can change and introduce a permanent shift in valuations. Similarly, changing economic fortunes triggered by a geopolitical event might shift the discount rate used to calculate the present value of future cash flows and hence affect asset valuations.

Throughout the next three chapters, I will investigate the empirical evidence on both the short- and long-term impacts of geopolitical events on the economy and financial markets.

Bibliography

Baker, S. R., N. Bloom, and S. J. Davis. 2016. "Measuring Economic Policy Uncertainty." *Quarterly Journal of Economics* 131 (4): 1593–636.

Caldara, D., and M. Iacoviello. 2018. "Measuring Geopolitical Risk." International Finance Discussion Paper 1222.

Caldara, D., and M. Iacoviello. 2019. "Measuring Geopolitical Risk." Board of Governors of the Federal Reserve.

Daggett, S. 2010. "Costs of Major U.S. Wars." Congressional Research Service Report for Congress. https://fas.org/sgp/crs/natsec/RS22926.pdf.

Dunne, J. P., R. P. Smith, and D. Willenbockel. 2005. "Models of Military Expenditure and Growth: A Critical Review." *Defence and Peace Economics* 16 (6): 449–61.

Hawking, S. 1988. *A Brief History of Time.* New York: Bantam.

Mintz, A., and C. Huang. 1990. "Defense Expenditures, Economic Growth, and the 'Peace Dividend.'" *American Political Science Review* 84 (4): 1283–93.

Mintz, A., and R. T. Stevenson. 1995. "Defense Expenditures, Economic Growth, and the 'Peace Dividend': A Longitudinal Analysis of 103 Countries." *Journal of Conflict Resolution* 39 (2): 283–305.

Pástor, L., and P. Veronesi. 2013. "Political Uncertainty and Risk Premia." *Journal of Financial Economics* 110 (3): 520–45.

Chapter 2: Armed Conflict and Terrorist Attacks

> War, huh, yeah,
>
> What is it good for?
>
> Absolutely nothing.
>
> —*Norman Whitfield and Barrett Strong, "War"*

Wars and armed conflict in general are a recurring phenomenon in geopolitics. In fact, I would guess that the first thing that comes to readers' minds when they think about the influence of geopolitics on investments is the potential impact of wars and—more recently—terrorist attacks.

The past hundred years have been marked by two world wars that led to two major shifts in the global political and economic power structure. First, the United States emerged victorious in both World War I and World War II. Moreover, both wars were fought outside the mainland United States, and, as a result, the country's infrastructure and economy remained intact. As the United States emerged as both the economic and political superpower after 1945, it was rivaled in the political dimension by only the Soviet Union. In the Western world, the end of World War II marked the beginning of the Pax Americana, an era of relative peace that was policed by the US military. Of course, wars continued to break out around the world, but those conflicts were taking place mostly in small countries in the developing world, where one side was supported by Western countries while the other was supported by communist countries or was fighting for self-determination.

The second major shift triggered by the two world wars was the decline of the British Empire and other colonial powers. Unlike the United States, all European colonial powers were physically devastated by the two world wars, and their infrastructure and economy were destroyed. Whether the countries had been on the winning or losing side of the wars did not matter, though losing countries, such as Germany, suffered heavier losses than victorious countries, such as the United Kingdom. The result for every major European nation was an economy on its knees and an enormous amount of war debt that needed to be paid off.

In the years following World War II, the colonial powers suffered the loss of many of their colonies, and the United Kingdom lost, to the United States, its status as the preeminent economic and political superpower. Until World War II, the world's reserve currency had been the British pound, and commodities were traded in sterling. Similarly, London had been the financial capital of the world, a position it lost to New York City after 1945. The Bretton Woods agreement of 1944 established the US dollar as the world's reserve currency and introduced the World Bank and International Monetary Fund to improve international economic cooperation and prevent the kind of economic warfare and trade conflict that marked the world wars and the Great Depression.

Stock Market Reaction to Wars. The two world wars led to tectonic shifts in the global economy, but many more wars were occurring throughout the 20th century. **Exhibit 1** shows the wars and invasions that the US military has been directly involved in since 1900 together with the S&P 500 Index. The stock market is shown in logarithmic scale, so similar percentage losses and gains lead to similar declines and advances in the chart.

The first thing to notice is that the United States became far more involved in warfare after it took on the role of the world's police force after World War II. The second thing of note is that you would be hard pressed to identify the impact these wars had on the US stock market. For example, you could not identify the Vietnam War years or the War in Afghanistan years

Exhibit 1. US Wars and the Stock Market

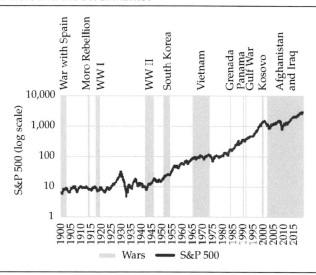

Sources: R. Shiller's website; Correlates of War project (COW); Uppsala Conflict Data Program (UCDP).

in the S&P 500 data if I had not shown them in Exhibit 1. And no common pattern appears in the stock market for every war. Sometimes, the stock market would rally during the war, as was the case with the Korean War, and sometimes, it was mired in an extended sideways movement, as was the case with the Vietnam War. If any pattern comes close to being recognizable, it might be seen in the two world wars, when the stock market first declined strongly before entering an extended rally.

This lack of influence of wars on the US stock market (with the possible exception of the world wars) might not hold, however, for other stock markets. Remember that the US economy and infrastructure were almost unharmed by the wars of the past century, whereas countries in Europe and Asia suffered heavy destruction. Thus, these latter countries' stock markets might have reacted very differently to wars.

To see whether reactions might have been different in war-torn countries, look at the French stock market and the wars France has been involved in during the 20th century, which are shown in **Exhibit 2**.

France was much less involved than the United States in armed conflicts after World War II but in a state of almost constant war during the first half of the 20th century. During that period, the country fought a number of wars against colonial insurrections that eventually led to the independence of many of its colonies. What is probably the most prominent colonial war in which

Exhibit 2. French Wars and the CAC (Cotation Assistée en Continu) Index

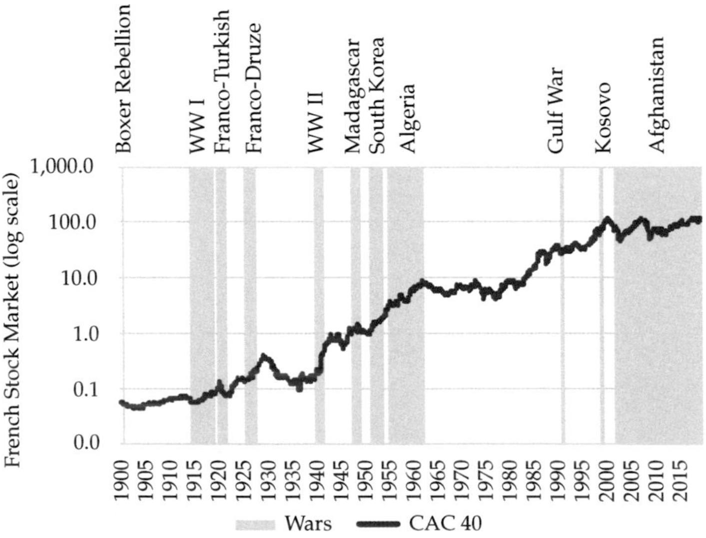

Sources: Global Financial Data; UCDP.

France was involved, the conflict in Vietnam, is not even marked in the chart. That conflict would eventually lead to the involvement of US troops in the country for several years. But just as in the case of the United States, I challenge readers to pinpoint the exact start and end dates of France's participation in the Vietnam conflict from the data in Exhibit 2.[1]

Given the (seemingly) limited impact of wars on the stock market, you might be tempted to dismiss the influence of wars altogether, but if you look at the behavior of the French stock market during the two world wars, you see a remarkable similarity to that of the US stock market. In both world wars, the French stock market first declined and then rallied strongly. Compared with those of the US stock market, however, the gyrations of the French stock market seem to be more pronounced. France was a main theater of war. All the main battlefields on the Western Front during World War I were in France, and although France was occupied by Germany for most of World War II, it was the starting point for the Allied invasion of Germany in 1944. Allied forces had to literally fight their way through the French industrial heartland to reach Germany.

As the reader will see in the remainder of this chapter, these stylized facts about wars—namely, that most wars do not really have a lasting impact on stock markets and that the wars that do have an impact often have a negative impact at the onset of war—are two key findings of the research on wars and their influence on financial markets.

Before I explain the typical investment risks and opportunities emanating from wars, however, a helpful approach will be to zoom in on one particular case study: the US invasion of Iraq in 2003.

Case Study: 2003 Invasion of Iraq

The academic research on the influence of wars on financial markets got a boost with the US invasion of Iraq in 2003. The reason for this boost was twofold.

First, a lot of criticism of the planned US invasion in Iraq arose at the time. Internationally, the US government did not manage to convince even some of its closest allies that Iraq had weapons of mass destruction or was involved in the terrorist attacks of September 11, 2001 (9/11), which started the "war on terror." In a speech at the annual Munich Security Conference in February 2003, German Foreign Minister Joschka Fischer looked directly at US Secretary of Defense Donald Rumsfeld and uttered in English, "Excuse me, I am not convinced"—words that caused some consternation and anger in the US administration and have become part of the political folklore in Germany.

---

[1]Answer: The Vietnam War for France lasted from November 1946 to June 1954, a time frame during which the country also fought a war in Madagascar and participated in the Korean War.

Exhibit 3. Measures of Risk of War in Iraq, 2002

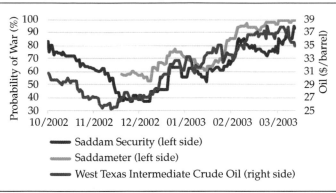

Saddam Security (left side)
Saddameter (left side)
West Texas Intermediate Crude Oil (right side)

Source: Wolfers and Zitzewitz (2006).

Within the United States, the invasion was also heavily criticized. William Nordhaus called wars "the ultimate negative-sum game in which the spoils of the victors are much less than the losses of the vanquished" (Nordhaus 2002). He also criticized the US government for not making any in-depth efforts to estimate the true costs of the war and claimed that the government probably underestimated both its duration and cost. He estimated that the cost to the US economy of an invasion of Iraq could be anywhere between $100 billion and $1.9 trillion. In 2010, the US Congressional Research Service estimated the total costs of the Iraq War to be $784 billion (Daggett 2010).

The second reason the Iraq War became a popular case study for economists is that before the action, for the first time, several measures intended to assess the probability of war were available in real time. Wolfers and Zitzewitz (2006) collected data from the website Tradesports.com that launched futures contracts (so-called Saddam Securities) that paid $100 if Saddam Hussein were to be ousted before a certain date. At the same time, William Saletan of *Slate* gave his assessment of the likelihood of war (the Saddameter) in his daily column.[2]

As **Exhibit 3** shows, the probability of war as determined by the Saddam Securities and the expert assessment of the Saddameter tracked each other reasonably well. The increasing probability of war also was reflected in the rising price of oil at the time. These data allowed researchers to quantify the impact of rising war threats on stock markets. Brune, Hens, Rieger, and Wang (2015) found that an increase in the Saddameter of 1 percentage point

---

[2]William Saletan, "The Saddameter: Are We Going to War? Slate Updates the Odds," *Slate* (November 2002–March 2003), https://slate.com/news-and-politics/saddameter.

led to a decline in the S&P 500 of 1.1 points (given the level of the S&P 500 at the end of 2002, approximately 0.13%).

Safe Assets Gained . . . A more comprehensive analysis of the impact of the run-up to the Iraq War was done by Rigobon and Sack (2005), who looked at the transmission of war threats across asset classes. They concluded that a 25 basis point (bp) decline in the yield of two-year US Treasuries led to an almost equal decline in 10-year US Treasuries, as shown in **Exhibit 4**, indicating that war threats lead to a parallel shift of the yield curve rather than a tilt or shift in convexity. Investors seem to react to rising war threats with a general flight to safety that does not discriminate much between different maturities of Treasuries.

An interesting observation is that inflation expectations declined as the threat of a war in Iraq increased. This response is in contrast to the rise in oil prices that happened simultaneously. Inflation expectations are caught between two competing forces when investors evaluate the effects of war. On the one hand, a war in a major oil-producing country, such as Iraq, is likely to reduce the supply of oil and should thus lead to higher oil prices and higher inflation, at least as long as the oil supply remains disrupted. On the other hand, wars are costly and might have a negative impact on household consumption and investment, leading to lower economic growth. As a result, inflation expectations should decline in anticipation of this economic slowdown.

Evidently, in the case of the war in Iraq, fears about a potential oil supply shock were dominated by fears about an economic slowdown, possibly because other major oil producers, such as Saudi Arabia, were committed at the time to increasing oil production while Iraq went offline.

Exhibit 4. Impact of Rising War Threats on Fixed-Income Markets, Early 2003

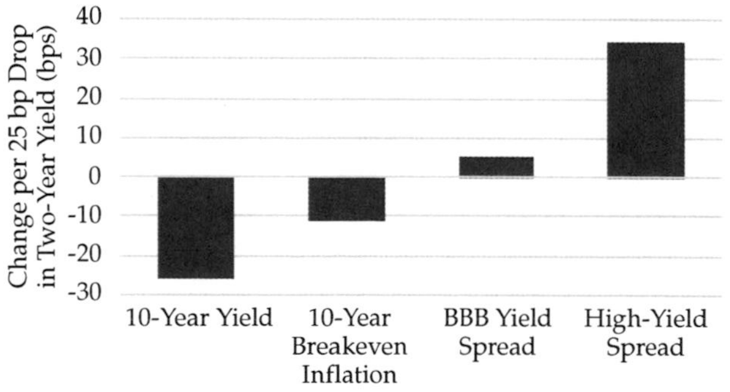

Source: Rigobon and Sack (2005).

The hypothesis that growth concerns dominated in the reaction of fixed-income markets is also reflected in the rising spreads of investment-grade and high-yield bonds over Treasuries. As the threat of war increased, yield spreads widened significantly because investors priced in higher default risks for risky issuers in a slowing economy.

. . . while Risky Assets Lost. The flight to safety triggered by rising war fears in early 2003 was also visible in the returns of the S&P 500, as shown in **Exhibit 5**. Rigobon and Sack (2005) estimated that a 25 bp decline in two-year Treasury yields was commensurate with a 3.85% drop in the S&P 500. Both oil and gold acted as safe havens in this episode, however, and rallied substantially as Treasury yields declined. The effect on the US dollar exchange rate, measured in the Rigobon and Sack study as the broad trade-weighted exchange rate, was minimal.

With the Invasion . . .? Then, something strange happened as war with Iraq became all but inevitable in early March 2003. Stock markets started to rally, and around the time of the invasion on 20 March 2003, the S&P 500 experienced a regime shift, as shown in **Exhibit 6**. Looking back on these events today, we know that the S&P 500 reached its low point for the 2000–03 bear market on 13 March 2003. Apparently, the onset of war triggered a "relief" rally in the stock market that turned out to last until late 2007.

Given these observations, you might conclude that the stylized pattern regarding the impact of war on financial markets is a general flight to safety in the run-up to a major war, with government bonds, gold, and (potentially) oil rallying and with both stocks and risky bonds dropping. With the onset of the war, a relief rally is triggered (in the case of the Iraq War). Many investors continue to believe that this pattern is a common feature of the

Exhibit 5. Impact of Rising War Threats on Risky Assets and the US Dollar, Early 2003

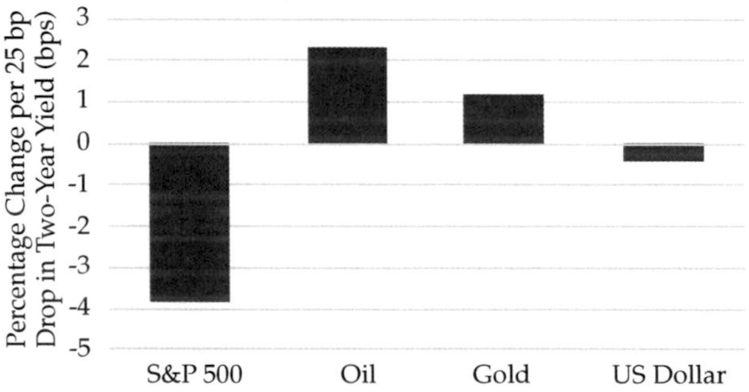

Source: Rigobon and Sack (2005).

Exhibit 6. The S&P 500 at the Onset of the Iraq War

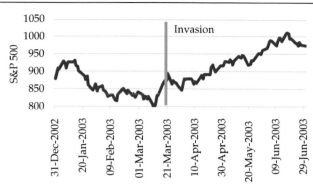

Source: Bloomberg.

influence of wars on markets. The situation calls for almost the inverse of the old Wall Street adage "buy on the rumor, sell on the fact." In the case of wars, the right thing for investors to do appears to be "sell on the rumor, buy on the fact."

With Wars, Anything Can Happen

However, extrapolating from one case study to all wars is dangerous. As Exhibits 1 and 2 make amply clear, there are no universal truths with respect to the impact of wars on financial markets. In fact, the impact of wars on financial markets is so complex that time-series regression methods and other common econometric tools typically indicate no statistically significant effect of war on stocks, currencies, or bonds. As a result, researchers today primarily use "event studies" to identify the impact of wars on markets.

The basic idea of an event study in this case is to compare the behavior of a market just before the onset of a war with the behavior of the same market shortly after. For example, you might calibrate the return of the S&P 500 in the 50 days before the onset of war with the help of a simple capital asset pricing model (the CAPM of Sharpe [1964] and Lintner [1965]) or a Fama–French three-factor model (Fama and French 1993). Then, you could look at the return of the S&P 500 on the day of the event or a number of days after the event (typically, 6 or 11 trading days) to determine the cumulative abnormal return (CAR) of the market relative to what could be expected from the calibration.

The problem with these event studies is that the results depend on the calibration used. A calibration based on the CAPM will give a different result from a calibration based on the Fama–French factor models. And more importantly, because stock markets are dynamic, the length of the calibration window is crucial. A calibration based on the behavior of the stock market in the 50 trading days before the event might give different results from a calibration based on the 10 trading days before the event. Similarly, how long you observe the market after the event might lead to different results, particularly if rallies or corrections are short-lived, lasting only a few trading days, as is often the case.

With these caveats in mind, we can look at the stylized facts of wars and their impact on capital markets that researchers have found over the years. Probably the best starting point for a summary of these facts is the economy itself. Caplan (2002) examined two datasets. The narrow dataset covered 15 industrialized nations from 1881 to 1988, whereas the broader set covered 66 countries (both industrialized and developing countries) from 1950 to 1992. Because the broad dataset covered a shorter time span and a broader range of countries, it often produced results that were less pronounced than those of the narrow dataset. I thus restrict myself here to the results of the narrow dataset, which covered only industrialized countries. The main results of Caplan's study are summarized in **Exhibit 7**.

One of the most important findings of the Caplan (2002) study is that whether a war is fought on foreign or domestic territory matters tremendously. As I pointed out at the beginning of the chapter, the United States benefited from the fact that both world wars were fought mostly in Europe and Asia. The domestic US infrastructure was left intact. Europe and Asia, as well as most of northern Africa, were not so lucky. The domestic economies of these areas suffered significant destruction.

Exhibit 7.   Macroeconomic Impact of Wars

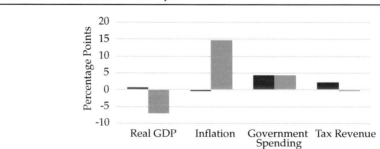

Source: Caplan (2002).

The difference between foreign and domestic wars is particularly pronounced for GDP growth and inflation. Wars fought on foreign territory tend to be mildly positive for economic growth, whereas wars fought on domestic soil quickly destroy the economy. Caplan (2002) found that on average, foreign wars provided a boost of 0.7 percentage points per year to the domestic economy of the belligerent, while domestic wars cost approximately 7.1 percentage points per year.

For a country that is mired in a war on its territory, these costs are severe. The costs are nonlinear and accelerate as the war continues. On average, after three years, the size of the GDP of such a country is expected to have shrunk by one-fifth, and after five years, the size of the GDP is expected to have halved. In other words, three years of domestic war have approximately the same impact on a country's economy as the Great Depression had on that of the United States and approximately two to three times the impact of the Global Financial Crisis of 2008. That most investors react to the onset of wars with a shrug of the shoulders is primarily a result of the fact that industrialized countries have not gone to war for more than seven decades. Wars have been fought exclusively in small countries with GDPs a fraction of the output of the United States. So, on a global scale, the wars of the past decades did not seem to matter. Of course, investors who specialize in emerging and frontier markets have a very different perception. For them, the outbreak of war in one of the countries in which they are invested might have a significant impact on their investments.

Another important difference between foreign wars and domestic wars is the impact they have on inflation. Because countries that fight a war on home soil face rapid destruction of their economies and, at the same time, an exponential growth of debts to finance the war, they are often forced to resort to a rapid expansion of the monetary base. Thus, on average, prices rise by 14.5 percentage points per year for as long as the war continues. Remember the strong rally of the French stock market during the two world wars shown in Exhibit 2? Those rallies were driven mostly by the rapid inflation at the time. Because stocks are real assets, they can protect investors from the inflationary effects of domestic wars.

On a more uplifting note, the inflationary effect of World War I is also responsible for Paris's rise to become the center of the art world. In the 1920s, artists such as Picasso and writers such as Ernest Hemingway and F. Scott Fitzgerald all moved there. Saddled with crippling war debt, France faced extremely high inflation, with annual inflation rates as high as 57% in 1920 and averaging 29% per year between 1917 and 1921. The result was that living in France was extremely cheap as long as you were paid in hard currency, such as the US dollar, which appreciated rapidly. Thus, relatively poor artists from the United States or, in Picasso's case, Spain could afford a lavish lifestyle in France, which created a wave of immigration to Paris throughout the 1920s.

Caplan's (2002) research contains some stylized facts about wars that are virtually identical for foreign and domestic wars. Because wars are expensive, they have to be financed, leading to increased government spending and rising budget deficits. In fact, wars are, economically speaking, little more than large fiscal stimulus packages driven by rapidly rising defense spending and by stable to declining nondefense spending. No wonder GDP growth accelerates when a country engages in a foreign war. Government spending increases while other businesses in the domestic economy continue with business as usual.

The (Mostly) Unpredictable Impact of Wars on Investments

Given the substantial impact wars can have on GDP, government spending, and inflation, a measurable impact likely also occurs on the returns of financial assets. Yet, as I mentioned before, most traditional econometric studies have found few clear signals. Guidolin and La Ferrara (2010) used event studies to investigate 112 conflicts between 1974 and 2004. They looked at both internal conflicts (civil wars) and international conflicts, and they did not differentiate between foreign and domestic wars. **Exhibit 8** shows only the results for the 28 international conflicts they studied.

Guidolin and La Ferrara (2010) examined the behavior of asset prices in the week of the onset of war and calculated the abnormal return relative to a baseline estimated from the 100 weeks of trading before the onset of war. They then calculated what share of events showed abnormal returns in the week of the onset of war that was statistically significantly different from zero with a 5% confidence level.

Exhibit 8. Share of Wars with Significant Impacts on Asset Prices

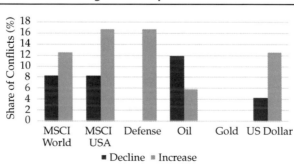

Source: Guidolin and La Ferrara (2010).

Of the 28 international conflicts studied, two showed a statistically significant negative reaction by the MSCI World Index, and three showed a positive reaction. Similarly, in the case of the MSCI US Index, two events triggered a negative stock price reaction and four triggered a positive stock price reaction. So, the majority of the wars (22 or 23 out of 28) did not create a stock market reaction that was significantly different from zero! In other words, most wars simply do not seem to matter for stocks, and those that do sometimes trigger a rally (as in the case of the Iraq War) and sometimes, a correction. I focus on this result in greater depth in the next section.

Guidolin and La Ferrara (2010) found two relatively clear results. First, if a war matters, it seems to be unanimously positive for defense stocks because these companies are the main beneficiaries of the increased government spending. Surprisingly, however, although the US dollar tends to appreciate in reaction to the onset of war, the authors could not find a statistically significant reaction of the gold price for any of the events they studied. This result flies in the face of the common perception of gold as a crisis hedge. More detailed studies have recently shown, however, that gold does act as a crisis hedge, just not in the way many investors think it does. I discuss this phenomenon further when the discussion involves the way investors can hedge the risk of war. First, however, we need to consider why stocks sometimes rally and sometimes drop at the onset of war.

The War Puzzle

The most commonly found research result about the reaction of asset markets to the onset of war is that risky assets, such as stocks, decline, whereas government bonds rally. Omar, Wisniewski, and Nolte (2017) examined international conflicts between 1995 and 2007 and found the CAR of stock markets in the 100 days surrounding the outbreak of war to be negative, on average. For the S&P 500, they found an average decline of 3.4%, which was about equally split between the 50 days before and the 50 days after the outbreak of war. For the MSCI World Index, they found a similar average decline, though this decline was more pronounced after the outbreak of war.

Meanwhile, as **Exhibit 9** shows, the Omar et al. (2017) research revealed that both government bonds and oil can provide a hedge against the risk of war because both asset classes tend to rally in this environment.

This general finding leaves us with a puzzle. Why do stock markets rally in some cases after the outbreak of a war? The puzzle becomes even more confounding if we look at the behavior of the stock market in, for example, the run-up to the Iraq War in 2003. Before the outbreak of war, a higher probability of war led to lower stock prices, but once the probability of war

Exhibit 9. CARs before and after the Outbreak of War

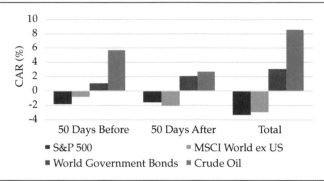

Source: Omar et al. (2017).

jumped from, say, 95% to 100%, stock prices rose. Rational investors should not behave like that. Either war is bad for stocks, in which case the outbreak of war should lead to further stock market declines, or it is good for stocks, in which case stocks should rally as war becomes more likely, even before the actual outbreak of war.

A Matter of Attention—or Lack Thereof. When Brune et al. (2015) investigated this so-called war puzzle, they found that wars that have a prolonged build-up phase tend to provide a relief rally at the onset of war; wars that happen suddenly or come as a surprise to markets lead to stock market corrections. The Iraq War that started in 2003 was a much publicized event discussed both in policy circles and among the general public and investors for months. Thus, the stock market had sufficient time to incorporate all the ups and downs of the political process in the prices of stocks and bonds. In such an environment, the stock market acts like the proverbial "weighing machine"—incorporating the views of millions of investors around the world. A sudden war, in contrast, just like a terrorist attack, does not provide the market with sufficient time to fully assess the impact the event might have on various companies. In these cases, markets react in the short term with a sudden flight to safety, and stock markets correct while government bonds rally.

This insight provides investors with a potential competitive edge. Although most wars do not really matter for global stock markets, some do. But both the media and financial markets are often oblivious to the political developments that can lead to the outbreak of war. Investors who are able to monitor geopolitical risks can often identify "wars that could matter" before other investors. They can then monitor these geopolitical risks and protect their portfolios to some extent against the price shock at the onset of war.

The war puzzle, however, remains a puzzle. Why do stock markets rally after a long-lasting run-up to a well-publicized war? Why does it make a difference if the probability of war is 95% or 100%? Two explanations for the war puzzle are possible—one psychological and one rational.

Explanation 1: The Challenge of Probabilities. The psychological explanation of the war puzzle focuses on our inability to assess probabilities. To understand this approach, assume that in the case of peace, you hold a specific portfolio that contains a lot of stocks but mostly stocks that do well in peacetime. In times of war, however, you would prefer to invest in a war portfolio—one that still invests in stocks but preferably in stocks that do well in times of war, such as defense stocks. Now assume a conflict starts to escalate, and war is becoming increasingly likely. At first, war is relatively unlikely, and investors stick with their peace portfolios, but the more likely war becomes, the more stocks they start to sell out of this portfolio. Because most investors do not invest in the war portfolio at this point, the selling pressure for peace stocks dominates the buying pressure on war stocks, and stock markets decline as war becomes more likely.

At some point, however, the likelihood of war reaches an inflection point when the war portfolio becomes the dominating portfolio. In this instance, investors abandon their peace portfolios altogether and switch into the war portfolio. What happens then is that the selling pressure for peace stocks is suddenly dominated by the buying pressure for war stocks, so stock markets start to rally as the outbreak of war becomes more likely, as shown in **Exhibit 10**.

Where exactly is the tipping point? Nobody knows, and it might well differ from crisis to crisis, but it is rooted in the phenomenon of subjective probabilities (Tversky and Kahneman 1992). Most human beings tend to think that extremely unlikely events are more likely than they truly are and that extremely likely events are less likely than they truly are. Or, as I usually put it,

> Most investors have only three probability settings: It will not happen, it is 50/50, and it will definitely happen.

What this tendency means is that, most of the time, investors will remain in the peace setting until a certain threshold for the probability of war is passed, at which point investors essentially behave as if the chance of war and peace is 50/50. In reaction, they reduce their portfolio holdings in assets that seem at risk. Once war becomes so likely that investors think it must happen, they shift the portfolio again, this time into the war portfolio, and they abandon the peace portfolio.

Exhibit 10.   A Behavioral Explanation of the War Puzzle

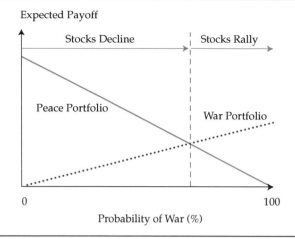

Source: Brune et al. (2015).

Explanation 2: A Rational Shift between Portfolios. The rational explanation for the war puzzle does not require investors to be too stupid to handle probabilities. Instead, all you have to assume is two different portfolios—a peace portfolio and a war portfolio—with different risks and returns. The peace portfolio has a higher expected return, so most of the time, investors remain invested in it. As the probability of war increases, investors start to invest in a mix of the peace portfolio and the war portfolio.

This mix of two portfolios increases risk and reduces return, however, so investors remain reluctant to increase their allocations to the war portfolio and the resulting decline in utility. For a high probability of war (i.e., beyond the tipping point in **Exhibit 11**), the combination of war portfolio and peace portfolio has a lower utility than investing in the war portfolio outright. Thus, once the probability of war increases above that tipping point, investors shift their portfolios altogether into the war portfolio and create a stock market rally.

Hedging War Risks

Which brings us neatly to the question of what such a war portfolio looks like. Given that wars tend to trigger stock market declines, investors need to be able to either construct an all-weather portfolio that has the optimal allocation to stocks and hedging assets (so that in case of war, the portfolio will suffer as little as possible), or investors need to shift from a peace portfolio to a war portfolio as the risk of war increases.

Exhibit 11.   A Rational Explanation of the War Puzzle

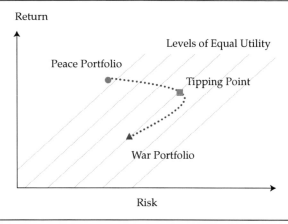

Source: Brune et al. (2015).

Based on their analysis of the behavior of stocks, government bonds, and oil around the outbreak of war, Omar et al. (2017) calculated the optimal hedge portfolio consisting of these asset classes. Exhibit 9 shows that both government bonds and crude oil tend to rally in the six months surrounding the outbreak of a war. On the one hand, the rally in government bonds reflects the flight to safety that takes place as the risk of war increases. The rally in oil, on the other hand, seems likely to be the result of the fact that most wars that have really mattered for financial markets since the end of World War II have been wars fought over the access to such natural resources as oil. And if war breaks out in a major oil-producing region, you must expect a significant spike in oil prices that can hedge the decline in stocks.

Such a hedge seems to be conditional, however, on the supposition that wars are fought over resources. As I show in later chapters, not all wars are fought over access to natural resources, and, as the global economy becomes less and less reliant on fossil fuels, future wars might not be fought over oil but, rather, over access to other resources that are valuable inputs in the modern economy.

Nevertheless, Omar et al. (2017) calculated the optimal hedge portfolios shown in **Exhibit 12**. Of course, no investor should implement these portfolios as they are because the optimal portfolio will depend on the individual circumstances of the investor. But these portfolios at least give us some guidelines on how best to hedge against war risks. And here, the message is simple: Government bonds provide the best hedge against war risks, especially if you are looking for a low-volatility hedge. For portfolios that aim for higher

Exhibit 12. Optimal Portfolio Allocation in the Case of a Sudden Outbreak of War for the Investor Goals of Minimum Portfolio Variance and Maximum Sharpe Ratio

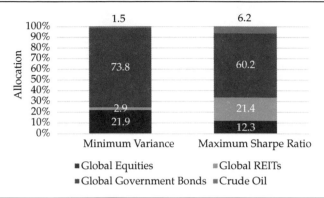

Note: Portfolios calculated for US dollar investors. REIT stands for real estate investment trust.
Source: Omar et al. (2017).

volatility, a small allocation, in the region of 1%–5%, to crude oil can be considered as an additional hedge.

The Curious Case of Gold as a Crisis Hedge

A traditional crisis hedge that so far has not been discussed much is gold. Klement (2014) and Erb and Harvey (2013) argued that gold is not a good crisis hedge, at least not if we are looking at correlations between gold and the Cboe Volatility Index (VIX) or gold and the S&P 500. In a recent study, however, Baur and Smales (2018) used the Geopolitical Risk (GPR) index that we encountered earlier as a way to measure the relationship between the price of gold and rising geopolitical risks. Unlike the VIX and the S&P 500, the GPR index is specifically designed to measure only geopolitical risks; it does not react to financial risks or other triggers of stock market angst.

Even so, Baur and Smales (2018) found no general correlation between the price of gold and the overall GPR index. They did find a significantly positive correlation between the price of gold and the threat of war. The GPR index can be split into two subindices—one measuring the threat of war based on news reports of political actions that might lead to war and one measuring actual acts of war, such as the invasion of one country by another. As **Exhibit 13** shows, both stock markets and cyclical commodities, such as copper, tend to decline when geopolitical risks increase. Gold, however, behaves differently. The price of gold tends to rally by 2% for every 100-point increase in the GPR index, but the price remains virtually unchanged once war breaks out.

Exhibit 13. Effect of a 100-Point Increase in the GPR Index

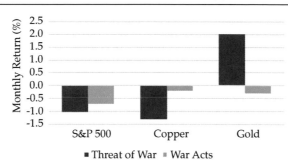

Source: Baur and Smales (2018).

Thus, the research of Baur and Smales (2018) indicates that gold is, indeed, a global safe haven that might protect against the rising risk of war. Gold prices seem to anticipate the risk of war, however, and rally as war becomes more likely. By the time wars break out, gold prices have seemingly incorporated the news already and show little reaction. With gold, it really seems to be a case of "buy on the rumor, sell on the fact."

Terrorism and the Changing Nature of Armed Conflict

So far in this chapter, I have focused on international wars. Historically, how-ever, such interstate wars have been only a small fraction of all the armed conflicts at any time. The UCDP has collected information about all armed conflicts globally since 1946 and categorized them into four major types, as shown in **Exhibit 14**:

- *Interstate conflicts:* The "traditional" wars between two sovereign countries that we have investigated so far.

- *Internal conflicts:* The classic civil wars and insurrections that remain within the boundaries of an individual country. On average, approximately two-thirds of all active conflicts at any time are such internal struggles.

- *Internationalized internal conflicts:* The internal conflicts in which either the government or the insurrection troops receive support from other international forces that actively participate in the armed conflict. The classic examples of this kind of conflict are the war in Iraq and the war in Afghanistan fought by US and allied troops together with gov-ernment troops in the affected country in their struggle against terror organizations.

Exhibit 14. Number of Conflicts Worldwide

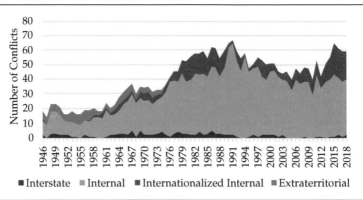

Source: UCDP.

- *Extraterritorial conflicts:* The conflicts between a government and an insurrection or rebel group that take place outside the territory of the government. In essence, these types are the colonial wars for independence in Africa, Asia, and Latin America. The last extraterritorial conflict ended in 1974.

Historically, internationalized internal conflicts have been rare, but they became significantly more common in the 1980s and then again after the 9/11 terrorist attacks. A key trigger for the first wave of internationalized conflicts was the increasingly assertive role that both the United States and the Soviet Union played in the 1960s–1980s. In those roles, they supported governments aligned with them (e.g., the United States in Vietnam and the Soviet Union in Afghanistan). Another important factor for the increasing internationalization of civil wars was the shift in tactics by Islamic rebel and terrorist organizations.

In Islam, as in almost all religions, suicide is forbidden. The holy Qur'an (4:29) states, "And do not kill yourselves [or one another]. Indeed, Allah is to you ever Merciful." Moreover, Thabit Ibn Al-Dahak narrated that the Prophet Mohammed said, "Whosoever kills himself with anything in this world will be tortured with it on the Day of Judgement." Yet beginning in the early 1980s, some militant organizations, such as Hezbollah during the Lebanese Civil War, resorted to suicide bombings as a means of psychological warfare and armed struggle. The tactic has been extremely difficult for government troops and police forces to prevent.

To justify suicide attacks, these extremist groups have redefined and misconstrued the meaning of such crucial terms as "jihad" (Hutchins 2017).

Jihad has a variety of meanings within Islam but is commonly translated in English as "struggle." However, in keeping with Islam as a peaceful religion (the word Islam is rooted in the Arab word "salaam," meaning "peace," and the holy Qur'an uses the word salaam 129 times), the mainstream interpretation of jihad is to follow an internal struggle to fulfill God's will. Yet Islamic extremists have redefined jihad to mean a violent struggle or "holy war" and to circumvent the prohibition of suicide in the holy Qur'an (Esposito 2015), framing the act of suicide bombing as an act of martyrdom. This misconstrued interpretation of jihad is used by extremist organizations to recruit followers and justify their acts of terror.

Exhibit 15 shows that the number of terrorist attacks began to rise significantly in the 1980s and with them rose the fatalities caused by terrorists. Of course, not all these terrorist attacks were performed by Muslim extremists, but the violence spread by Muslim terrorists was the most fateful insofar as it provoked a reaction by the local governments. In the Lebanese Civil War, for example, the local government was eventually forced to allow an intervention by US troops to help stop the violence—a decision that led to even more terrorist attacks by Hezbollah—on both local civilians and US troops. Thus, a vicious cycle was created in which overwhelmed local governments asked for military interventions by allied forces, which, in turn, led to more terrorist attacks and casualties among the international forces, and this escalation provoked, in turn, more intensive intervention by allied forces, and so on.

With the rise of Al Qaeda in the 1990s, terrorist organizations became increasingly well organized and well funded, which has allowed them to bring the struggle to the homeland of what they perceived to be Western invaders. The 1993 World Trade Center bombing might have been unsuccessful, but eight years later, the attacks of 9/11 proved to be the first successful attacks

Exhibit 15.   Number of Terrorist Attacks and Casualties

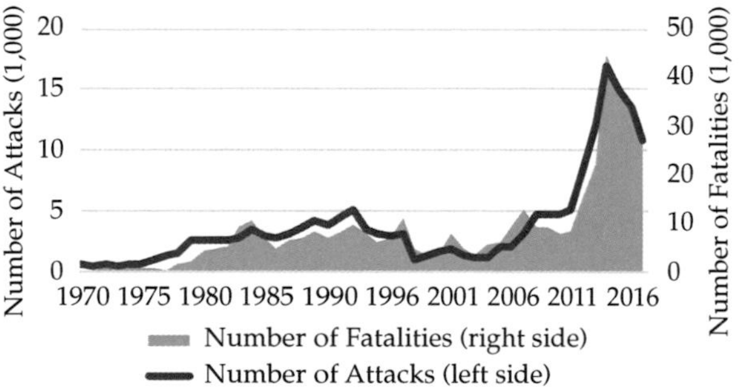

Source: Global Terrorism Database. Retrieved from www.start.umd.edu/gtd.

on the home soil of the United States since the 19th century. As Western forces ramped up the pressure on these next-generation global terrorist organizations, the terrorists intensified their efforts to spread their terror globally. Today, more than 10,000 terrorist attacks are conducted each year, most of them by Al Qaeda, the Islamic State (IS or ISIS), and other terrorist organizations linked to these two organization, including al-Shabaab (associated with Al Qaeda) and Boko Haram (associated with IS).

Of course, global financial markets most of the time have not cared about terrorist attacks because the vast majority of such attacks happen in developing countries—hence, under the radar screens of most investors in the developed world. As a result, academic research on the economic and financial impact of terrorist attacks before 2001 was confined mostly to niche areas covering emerging markets. The watershed moment for the research in this area was the 9/11 terrorist attacks, which have been investigated thoroughly by now and triggered a rich literature on the impact of terrorist attacks on the economy and financial markets. So, to discuss what we have learned about terrorist attacks, I turn to this event.

Case Study: 9/11

If you wanted a terrorist attack to have the maximum impact, you could hardly have done any better than 9/11. At the time of the attacks, the US economy was already slowing down. Job creation was declining, and the unemployment rate was rising. The dot-com bubble had burst a year earlier, and many formerly high-flying investments were in free fall. Then, right in the middle of this softening economy, the terrorist attacks managed to hit the financial capital of the United States, wiping out most of the employees of the largest Treasury dealer in the country (Cantor Fitzgerald) and forcing the NYSE and the New York Mercantile Exchange to close for several days, thus reducing stock and commodity market liquidity dramatically. The total economic costs of the 9/11 attacks are generally estimated to be $50 billion to $100 billion (0.5%–1.0% of US GDP at the time); the lowest estimates come in at approximately $35 billion and the highest estimates at approximately $109 billion (Rose and Blomberg 2010).

At the time, many economists thought the attacks would push a fragile US economy into recession, but in fact, as **Exhibit 16** shows, growth in the United States accelerated from –1.7% in the third quarter (Q3) of 2001 to +1.1% in Q4 (with quarterly changes stated as annualized rates, as is the custom). But although the nation overall did well, the epicenter of the attacks, New York City, suffered a strong decline in economic output. The growth of the Gross City Product (GCP) of New York City was zero in Q4 2001 and

Exhibit 16. Economic Growth around the 9/11 Attacks

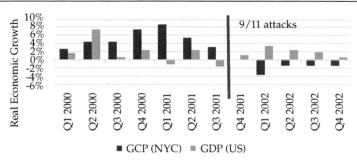

Source: Office of the Comptroller of New York City.

dropped sharply to −3.6% annualized in Q1 2002 as the loss of businesses unfolded.

The biggest impact for the city of New York was the loss of jobs as a result of the destruction of many businesses in downtown Manhattan. Payroll jobs growth fell off a cliff in Q4 2001 because of the terrorist attacks, as shown in **Exhibit 17**, significantly diminishing the city's tax revenues.

What kept the US economy afloat (relatively speaking) was the quick reaction by both the Federal Reserve and the US government (Makinen 2002). Immediately after the attacks, the Federal Reserve issued a crucial statement to reassure markets that the central bank was operating as normal and that the discount window was available to any bank that needed liquidity. This statement immediately calmed down financial markets and prevented a liquidity crunch.

Additionally, the Federal Reserve immediately started to buy Treasuries in the open market, thereby injecting $100 billion in liquidity per day in the

Exhibit 17. Payroll Jobs Growth around the 9/11 Attacks

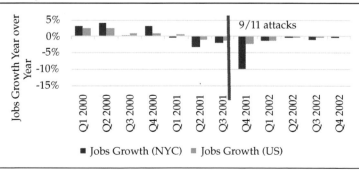

Source: Office of the Comptroller of New York City.

three days following the attacks. On top of that, the Federal Reserve coordinated with central banks in Europe, Canada, and Japan to support the US dollar. In this way, another $90 billion was injected into the currency markets.

Nevertheless, the cash system suffered some disruptions. All flights were grounded across the United States for several days, which meant that some regional banks were at risk of running out of cash because banknotes could not be delivered from the regional branches of the Federal Reserve. Luckily, flights were restored in time to prevent any significant disruptions in cash transactions.

The medium-term effects of the terrorist attacks were mitigated by the Federal Reserve's 0.5 percentage point rate cut on 17 September 2001, the day the NYSE reopened, and again on 2 October 2001. An additional 0.25 point cut was enacted by the end of 2001. Arguably, these rate cuts were motivated not only by the terrorist attacks but also by the slowing economy. Regardless, cutting the federal funds rate from 3.5% in August 2001 to 1.75% at the end of 2001 certainly helped prevent the terrorist attacks from causing more extensive economic damage than they did.

The second pillar of the policy reaction to the 9/11 attacks was a set of US government fiscal stimulus measures designed to prevent household consumption from faltering. At the time, a major concern for policy makers was that consumer confidence would be severely hit by the terrorist attacks, causing households to curb consumption. As I will discuss later, one of the key characteristics of terrorist attacks is to trigger a decline in consumer confidence.

Immediately after the attacks, the federal government authorized $40 billion in emergency funds to help with the relief efforts. In January 2002, the tax cuts of 2001 initiated by President George W. Bush were phased in as planned, which increased the federal budget deficit by an additional $31 billion in 2002. Finally, six months after the terrorist attacks, Congress enacted a stimulus bill that extended unemployment benefits and allowed for accelerated depreciation of business investments. This stimulus bill increased the federal budget deficit by another $50 billion in 2002 (Makinen 2002).

We know today that the fiscal stimulus matched or even exceeded the total economic costs of the terrorist attacks and thus helped overcome their medium- to long-term economic impact. Yet if policy makers had known back then what we know today about the impact of terrorist attacks on consumer sentiment and consumer behavior, the fiscal response would probably have looked different. The fiscal packages were deployed after much delay and were not focused on the regions that were hit the hardest. Much of the impact of the stimulus measures was lost because of this scattershot approach.

The impact of the terrorist attacks was felt in particular by four segments of the US economy—airlines, insurers, agriculture and the food industry, and small businesses:

- *Airlines.* Among the hardest hit industries was the airline business. The industry was already incurring losses in the first half of 2001 as a result of the slowing economy. The grounding of all flights immediately after the attacks and the subsequent reluctance of many people to fly dramatically worsened the financial situation of most US airlines. On 22 September 2001, the federal government granted airlines an aid package of $15 billion, $5 billion of which was paid directly to the airlines to cover the indirect losses emerging from the attacks in New York City and Washington, DC, such as lost passenger revenues because of grounded flights. The remaining $10 billion was made available as government-guaranteed loans. The vast majority of these loans, however, were never issued to the airlines. Despite this aid package, the financial situation of many airlines worsened dramatically. US Airways entered Chapter 11 bankruptcy protection on 11 August 2002, followed by United Airlines on 9 December 2002. The only US airline that remained profitable throughout 2001 and 2002 was Southwest Airlines, though the company suffered a 53% drop in net income in 2002 from the previous year.

- *Insurers.* Until the 9/11 terrorist attacks, most insurance contracts covered damages from terrorist attacks. As a result, insured losses of the event amounted to more than $40 billion. But the main issue for insurers was not so much the direct costs of the attacks but their inability to calculate appropriate insurance premiums in the aftermath. Because of the lack of historical data, insurers and reinsurers could not calculate premiums that would adequately cover the risk and potential damages of a future terrorist attack. Most reinsurance contracts are underwritten on a calendar-year basis, so many insurance companies were unable to reinsure potential losses from terrorist attacks starting in 2002. Reinsurance companies would either deny coverage or ask for premiums that were so high as to be unaffordable. As a result, insurance companies petitioned their state regulators to allow them to drop coverage for terrorist attacks. In most states, insurance contracts now exclude terrorist attacks from coverage if damage exceeds $25 million, if the insured has more than 50 fatalities, or if the attack involves nuclear, biological, or chemical weapons.

- *Agriculture and the food industry.* These businesses were also hit hard by the terrorist attacks because in the aftermath, all ports of entry on the borders to Canada and Mexico were shut down, which endangered perishable food items. Even after the borders reopened, inspections were much tighter than before, leading to longer wait times and higher spoilage. The situation escalated dramatically with the anthrax mail attacks that started in October 2001. These attacks demonstrated how vulnerable the US food system could be to bioterrorism. In reaction to these events, the federal government stepped up its inspection activities. The US Food and Drug Administration hired an additional 400 employees to inspect imported food, and the Animal and Plant Health Inspection Service of the US Department of Agriculture (USDA) hired an additional 350 inspectors and 20 veterinarians to help process imports at the borders. Additionally, the USDA's Food Safety and Inspection Service employees were put on high alert to watch for signs of bioterrorism.

- *Small businesses.* Finally, the hardest hit segment of the economy was small businesses located at or around the centers of attack. The attacks disrupted or destroyed more than 18,000 small businesses, most of them located near the World Trade Center in New York City. Because small businesses tend to have few cash reserves, a significant disruption such as the 9/11 attacks can quickly become life threatening for them. The US Small Business Administration reacted to the terrorist attacks by increasing its staff in New York City and Maryland and by offering emergency loans. Within a year, more than 5,000 loans totaling $435 million were made to businesses in downtown Manhattan and more than 100 loans for a total of $16.6 million had been made to businesses in and around Ronald Reagan Washington National Airport. Nevertheless, loans were made slowly, and the bureaucratic hurdles associated with them meant that many small businesses believed they did not get the assistance they needed.

The Impact of 9/11 on Financial Markets

Despite the shortcomings of some of the fiscal and monetary policy measures taken after the 9/11 attacks, the responses were effective overall, both in preventing a major disruption of the US economy and in avoiding a lasting impact on financial markets. The US dollar did start to weaken in the aftermath of the 9/11 attacks—despite the purchases of central banks around the world. Three days after the attacks, the US dollar was down more than 3% on a trade-weighted basis. Remember, however, that the US economy was already in recession at that time (the National Bureau of Economic Research later determined that the recession had started in March 2001, six months before the attacks) and that the weakness in the US dollar was likely more a reflection of the economic slowdown and the significant rate cuts by the Fed than a general concern about the dollar as a safe haven. In fact, later terrorist attacks around the world all showed that the 9/11 attacks did not make a dent in the perception of the US dollar as the world's reserve currency and of Treasuries as the world's ultimate safe-haven asset.

Because of the (relatively) quick and effective response to the terrorist attacks, stock markets around the globe also quickly recovered their losses. **Exhibit 18** shows the S&P 500 around the time of the 9/11 attacks. The NYSE remained closed for four days following the attacks, but the S&P 500 still dropped 4.8% on the day the exchange opened again. Yet only 19 days were needed for the index to recover all its losses. The DJIA was harder hit than the S&P 500 by the events of 9/11 because of its larger allocation to airlines and the aircraft manufacturer Boeing. The immediate drop of the DJIA was 7.1%, which increased to more than 10% after a week. Nevertheless, after 40 days, the DJIA also had recovered its losses.

An interesting question to ponder is how international markets reacted. Unlike the NYSE, international markets did not close and thus had to digest the news in real time. One would assume that financial markets in countries that are likely to be terrorist targets or that have a high share of exporters that are hit by the disruption in international trade and flights would have suffered big losses and taken a long time to recover. Chen and Siems (2004) showed, however, that reactions of international stock markets to the 9/11 attacks were all over the place, with seemingly no correlation between the size of the local stock market's drop and the structure of the market. They did find a tentative correlation between the structure of the financial services industry in the local market and the drop (i.e., countries with more robust and better developed banking markets suffered less), but the evidence the authors presented

Exhibit 18.   S&P 500 around the 9/11 Attacks

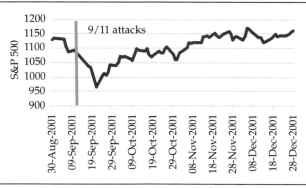

Source: Bloomberg.

is weak. For instance, the United Kingdom has one of the deepest and most liquid banking systems in the world, but both British financial stocks and the Financial Times Stock Exchange (FTSE) 100 Index dropped more than their US counterparts in the aftermath of 9/11 and took longer to recover. Furthermore, keep in mind that the major central banks coordinated their efforts to supply liquidity in the days following the attacks, a fact that further complicates the assessment of the international impact of the 9/11 attacks.

Finally, **Exhibit 19** shows an inexplicable result: On average, markets that suffered more on the day of the attacks recovered their losses more quickly than markets that suffered less. In fact, US stock markets suffered losses that were in line with the global average but were among the first to recover, even though the US economy and US capital markets were the ones hit by the attacks.

To my knowledge, no studies have been undertaken to systematically investigate the international spillover effects of the 9/11 attacks and the relationship of 9/11 to local stock market performance. What has been done in the years since the attacks, however, is a systematic analysis of the impact of terrorist attacks in general.

The Impact of Terrorist Attacks on an Economy

The attacks of 9/11 launched an intense research effort into the economic causes of terrorism, the reaction of governments to terrorism in the form of counterterrorism measures, and the impact of terrorism on society. This research was recently summarized by Gaibulloev and Sandler (2019). The economic consequences of terrorist attacks are only one dimension of the big picture. Although the writings on the economic causes of terrorism and the costs of counterterrorism are particularly important for analysts covering

Exhibit 19. The International Impact of 9/11

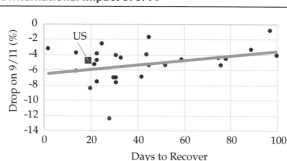

Source: Chen and Siems (2004).

individual stocks in the defense and security sector, those findings are beyond the scope of this book. So, I focus here on the macroeconomic and financial market reactions that are relevant to all investors.

The main result of the studies on the macroeconomic impact of terrorist attacks is that, in general, the impact is small and transitory. Blomberg, Hess, and Orphanides (2004) found that if a country experienced transnational terrorist attacks, the effect on GDP per capita was a statistically significant but small reduction of 0.048% per year. Tavares (2004) found a similarly small growth impact of 0.029%–0.038%, depending on the specification of the economic test. These numbers indicate that terrorist attacks generally are not able to derail an economy, but there are significant exceptions to this generality to keep in mind.

Blomberg et al. (2004) showed that large economies, such as the United States and most Western European countries, are much less affected by terrorist attacks than small economies, which suffer more from terrorist attacks, as do less developed countries. In regional regressions, they found that African countries suffered growth impacts that were approximately ten times worse than those seen by countries in the Organisation for Economic Co-operation and Development and that Asian economies suffered GDP declines that were approximately three times worse.

Unfortunately, as Sandler and Enders (2008) pointed out, no studies have investigated the differential impact of terrorist attacks on developing and developed countries. In the Blomberg et al. (2004) study, the Asian economy sample included both developed Asian economies, such as Japan, and developing economies.

The African countries were all emerging markets, however, so you can infer from the strong negative effect that emerging markets are likely to be most severely hit by terrorist attacks. This effect makes sense intuitively because these developing nations, unlike developed countries, often have a less developed monetary system. Given the example of the need for rapid monetary and fiscal stimulus after the 9/11 attacks, developing countries are at a disadvantage in deploying emergency measures to dampen the macroeconomic effects of terrorist attacks.

Investors should also be aware that terrorist attacks are isolated events in most countries. Some countries, however, such as Israel, have suffered from prolonged and persistent terrorist activities. Eckstein and Tsiddon (2004) looked at the macroeconomic impact of Palestinian terrorist attacks in Israel and estimated that the country's GDP per capita growth per year could be approximately 2.5% higher if all terrorist activities ceased. They also estimated the likely impact of the Second Intifada, which started in September

2000. In the three years that the researchers covered (the Intifada eventually lasted until February 2005), they estimated it had cost the Israeli economy approximately 10% of GDP.

Abadie and Gardeazabal (2003) focused on the Basque Country in Spain, which was under constant threat from the ETA terrorist organization (for *Euskadi Ta Askatasuna*, meaning "Basque Country and Freedom") in the 1980s and 1990s. They found that over a 20-year period, the GDP per capita of the Basque Country was approximately 10% lower than in a counterfactual scenario without terrorism. This finding indicates that prolonged terrorist activity in a small economy can have effects similar to those of a war and reduce GDP by double digits.

As in the case of the 9/11 attacks, several industrial segments are particularly vulnerable to terrorist attacks—in particular, segments that require foreign direct investment and tourism:

- *Foreign direct investments* (FDI). Outside investment in a country tends to be significantly negatively affected by terrorist attacks because foreign investors consider the country riskier than elsewhere. Furthermore, the expected return on investment in a country that suffers regular terrorist attacks is lower than elsewhere. Large businesses in large open economies tend to reallocate their investments from troubled to calmer countries. Although this effect is generally small, it can be 5% of the GDP of the recipient country in the case of a small economy experiencing a significant increase in terrorist activity (Gaibulloev and Sandler 2019). Sandler and Enders (2008) estimated that a single terrorist attack in Spain causes net FDI to drop by approximately $23.8 million. Transnational terrorism in Spain reduced FDI by approximately 13.5% per year. For Greece, they found similar effects. In their estimate, transnational terrorism reduced FDI in Greece by approximately 11.9%. In these cases, local businesses that relied on foreign investments (e.g., industrial companies that are part of global supply chains) could suffer severe declines in revenues and investment activity.

- *Tourism.* The tourism industry can also be hit significantly by terrorist attacks, though (surprisingly) the empirical evidence is mixed. The impact of terrorist attacks is not immediately visible because tourists typically take time to revise their vacation plans, but the effect can be substantial. The biggest decline in tourism manifests itself after two to five quarters. The impact on the tourism industry can also be measured in neighboring countries because tourists tend to avoid the entire region rather than a single country. In reaction to declining bookings, however, both airlines and tourism companies quickly provide rebates for vacations in affected countries so that the negative effect on tourism tends to be short-lived. These rebates might also explain why some countries (in particular, Spain, Greece, and Austria) show significant lasting effects on tourism, whereas others (e.g., France and Denmark) do not.

The Main Victim of Terrorist Attacks: Sentiment

Terrorist attacks are as much a means of causing fear as they are a way to destroy buildings and infrastructure. One of the main aims of terrorists is to shake the confidence and feeling of security of everyday people. In the equation in Chapter 1 for the present value of financial assets, terrorist attacks should increase the risk premium on stocks and bonds and thus reduce their price. Furthermore, a general feeling of uncertainty should keep people from consuming more and thus hurt the economy through that channel.

Drakos and Kallandranis (2015) measured the impact of terrorist attacks in the European Union on macroeconomic sentiment indicators. Looking at 604 terrorist incidents between 1985 and 2009, they found that overall economic sentiment indices declined significantly in the aftermath of a terrorist attack. They found no significant impact of terrorist attacks, however, on manufacturing, service, or construction sentiment indicators. The entire decline in economic sentiment was concentrated in "consumer sentiment." But terrorist attacks are estimated to have reduced consumer sentiment indicators by approximately 1.88 percentage points in the years since the 9/11 attacks—a small effect that, furthermore, does not translate into a significantly negative impact on consumption.

In short, the research on the impact of terrorism on consumer sentiment has shown that the decline in consumer sentiment tends to be transitory and typically does not constitute a significant threat to consumption and economic growth. No wonder that the causality between terrorism and economic growth tends to be stronger in one direction than the other. Low economic growth typically causes an increase in the risk of terrorist activity, but increased terrorist activity does not always causally affect economic growth (Meierrieks and Gries 2013).

Because terrorist attacks affect the risk premium of stocks and bonds but generally do not have lasting macroeconomic effects, the stock market reaction to terrorist attacks also tends to be transitory. **Exhibit 20** shows the time needed for the US stock market (measured by the S&P 500) to recover its losses from certain disruptive events. Since the 1960s, most terrorist attacks in the United States have caused only intraday swings; the stock market recovered its losses within one trading day. The attacks of 9/11 and the Kent State

Exhibit 20. Impact of Terrorist Attacks on US Stocks

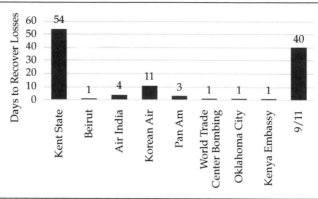

Source: Chen and Siems (2004).

shootings of 1970, both of which happened during a prolonged bear market, took longer for a market recovery. The other outlier was the Korean Air bombing on 30 November 1987, a few weeks after the October 1987 stock market crash.

In essence, we can conclude that in normal times, terrorist attacks cause only small declines in stock markets, and the declines are recovered within a few days. Hence, investors should typically consider terrorist attacks a buying opportunity (cynical as this might sound). The recovery seems to take longer if terrorist attacks hit when investor sentiment is already depressed as the result of a bear market or other factors. Even then, however, the impact is usually digested within a few weeks or months.

The size of the market correction after a terrorist attack also tends to be small. **Exhibit 21** shows the average stock performance in the days after a terrorist attack. For this chart, Karolyi and Martell (2010) did not look at aggregate stock indices but instead at companies directly affected by individual terrorist attacks. They examined a sample of 75 global companies that were directly hit by terrorist attacks; many of them were oil companies, such as Royal Dutch Shell and BP, or international consumer companies, such as Coca-Cola, operating in developing countries—for example, Colombia and Nigeria. The authors found that, on average, the share price of affected companies lost 0.83% on the day of the attack, for a drop in market value of $401 million. But the losses were typically recovered quickly, and within a few weeks, share prices were back to preevent levels.

Analyzing stock market aggregates and indices, Nikkinen and Vähämaa (2010) found that the UK FTSE 100 Index experienced a significant decline in returns of approximately 0.2% on the day of a terrorist event. Unsurprisingly,

Exhibit 21.   Average Stock Behavior 10 Days Before/After Terrorist Attacks

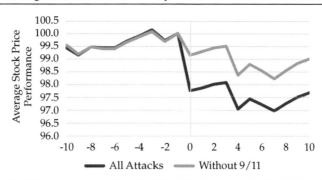

Source: Karolyi and Martell (2010).

the volatility of the FTSE 100 also increased a bit (approximately 0.2 percentage points), and the distribution of returns became more skewed to the downside and more fat tailed. An international study by Chesney, Reshetar, and Karaman (2011) showed a similar sized return impact—on the order of 0.2%–0.4% for global stock markets. US markets tend to suffer less than European markets after terrorist attacks, even if the attacks happen in the United States.

From a sector and industry perspective, the study by Chesney et al. (2011) does not provide any surprises. The industries that tended to be most adversely affected in their sample were airlines, insurance companies, and banks; the defense companies, pharmaceutical companies, and commodity producers tended to rally. Keep in mind, however, that just like wars, most terrorist attacks do not trigger a statistically significant stock market response. For example, in the case of the FTSE All World Index, only 30 out of 77 days with terrorist attacks had a significant negative impact, and of those 30 days, only 15 were considered extreme.

Nevertheless, in some circumstances, terrorist attacks can have a large and persistent impact on stock markets. As discussed, countries that experience frequent and long-lasting terrorist attacks, such as Israel, suffer significant economic damages. Arin, Ciferri, and Spagnolo (2008) found a larger impact of terrorist attacks for Indonesia and Turkey than for the United Kingdom. Eldor and Melnick (2004) looked at the impact of the persistent terrorist attacks in Israel with a special emphasis on the Second Intifada that started in 2000. By comparing the development of the Israeli Tel Aviv 100 Index (by now the Tel Aviv 125 Index), which was affected by the Intifada, with the S&P 500, which was not, they estimated that the terrorist attacks

Exhibit 22. Market Habituation to Terrorist Attacks

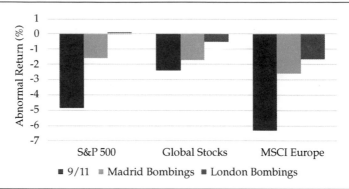

Source: Chesney et al. (2011).

caused the Israeli stock market to be approximately 30% below the level it would have been without terrorism. They also found that Israeli stock markets reacted more to terrorist incidents that caused fatalities than to those that did not and that stock markets did not become accustomed to terrorist attacks; that is, the reaction remained the same even after several attacks.

This last finding is in contrast to a series of studies on stock market reactions to terrorist attacks that show a habituation effect. In essence, investors become accustomed and desensitized to terrorist attacks. For a terrorist attack to have the same stock market impact as a previous one, it needs to be more destructive. Chesney et al. (2011) showed this effect nicely in the series of three major Al Qaeda terrorist attacks in the West. **Exhibit 22** shows that the 9/11 attacks in New York City and Washington, DC, caused US stock markets to decline by almost 5% on the day and caused European markets to drop even more. The Madrid train bombings on 11 March 2004 caused a decline of only 1.5% in the United States and 2.6% in Europe, and these losses were recovered within a week. Finally, the London bombings on 7 July 2005 caused merely an intraday swing in the US markets and a 1.6% decline in European stocks, which was recovered within two days.

Conclusions

Both wars and terrorist attacks tend to have only a transitory impact on financial markets, but clear exceptions test that tendency. The macroeconomic impact of wars tends to be significantly bigger in small economies and developing countries that cannot digest the negative effects of war as easily as large, open economies—such as that of the United States—can. More importantly, wars that are fought on a country's home territory are usually more devastating for the countries involved. As a result, extended wars on home turf are often very negative for stock markets at the onset of the war. As domestic wars progress, however, governments are typically forced to print money to pay for the war effort, causing a significant spike in inflation, which in turn benefits real assets, such as stocks, but destroys the value of the currency.

Foreign wars, in contrast, tend to have only a minor effect on stock markets, one seemingly driven by the increase in defense spending of the participating countries. As a result, foreign wars act like a fiscal stimulus program geared toward the defense industry.

Investors also need to be aware that financial markets react differently to, on the one hand, wars that slowly build up with an extended prewar period and, on the other hand, wars that happen suddenly. The anticipation of a war tends to depress stock markets and leads to a downward shift in government bond yields. Gold and oil prices often rally in anticipation of a geopolitical crisis, such as a war. At the onset of war, these effects are frequently reversed, and a short-term stock market rally occurs while gold prices stall. This reaction is in contrast to the effect of sudden wars, which typically depress stock markets and lead to a classic flight to safety, with government bonds rallying and all kinds of risky assets suffering.

Because terrorist attacks cannot, by definition, be anticipated, stock market reactions to such attacks tend to be initially negative, except for countries that suffer from extended periods of frequent terrorist attacks (e.g., Israel). However, the macroeconomic impact of terrorist attacks is vanishingly small. Thus, stock markets generally recover quickly after terrorist attacks, and the only lasting impact tends to be on the microeconomic level. Some industries, such as the travel and insurance industries, suffer sustained negative effects, while others, such as the defense, pharmaceutical, and commodity-related industries, typically gain.

Bibliography

Abadie, A., and J. Gardeazabal. 2003. "The Economic Costs of Conflict: A Case Study of the Basque Country." *American Economic Review* 93 (1): 113–32.

Arin, K. P., D. Ciferri, and N. Spagnolo. 2008. "The Price of Terror: The Effects of Terrorism on Stock Market Returns and Volatility." *Economics Letters* 101 (3): 164–67.

Baur, D. G., and L. A. Smales. 2018. "Gold and Geopolitical Risk." Available at SSRN: https://ssrn.com/abstract=3109136.

Blomberg, S. B., G. D. Hess, and A. Orphanides. 2004. "The Macroeconomic Consequences of Terrorism." *Journal of Monetary Economics* 51 (5): 1007–32.

Brune, A., T. Hens, M. O. Rieger, and M. Wang. 2015. "The War Puzzle: Contradictory Effects of International Conflicts on Stock Markets." *International Review of Economics* 62 (1): 1–21.

Caplan, B. 2002. "How Does War Shock the Economy?" *Journal of International Money and Finance* 21 (2): 145–62.

Chen, A. H., and T. F. Siems. 2004. "The Effects of Terrorism on Global Capital Markets." *European Journal of Political Economy* 20 (2): 349–66.

Chesney, M., G. Reshetar, and M. Karaman. 2011. "The Impact of Terrorism on Financial Markets: An Empirical Study." *Journal of Banking & Finance* 35 (2): 253–67.

Daggett, S. 2010. *Costs of Major U.S. Wars*. Washington, DC: Congressional Research Service.

Drakos, K., and C. Kallandranis. 2015. "A Note on the Effect of Terrorism on Economic Sentiment." *Defence and Peace Economics* 26 (6): 600–08.

Eckstein, Z., and D. Tsiddon. 2004. "Macroeconomic Consequences of Terror: Theory and the Case of Israel." *Journal of Monetary Economics* 51 (5): 971–1002.

Eldor, R., and R. Melnick. 2004. "Financial Markets and Terrorism." *European Journal of Political Economy* 20 (2): 367–86.

Erb, C. B., and C. R. Harvey. 2013. "The Golden Dilemma." *Financial Analysts Journal* 69 (4): 10–42.

Esposito, J. L. 2015. "Islam and Political Violence." *Religions* 6 (3): 1067–81.

Fama, E., and K. French. 1993. "Common Risk Factors in the Returns on Stocks and Bonds." *Journal of Financial Economics* 33 (1): 3–56.

Gaibulloev, K., and T. Sandler. 2019. "What We Have Learned about Terrorism since 9/11." *Journal of Economic Literature* 57 (2): 275–328.

Guidolin, M., and E. La Ferrara. 2010. "The Economic Effects of Violent Conflict: Evidence from Asset Market Reactions." *Journal of Peace Research* 47 (6): 671–84.

Hutchins, R. 2017. "Islam and Suicide Terrorism: Separating Fact from Fiction." *Counter Terrorist Trends and Analyses* 9 (11): 7–11. www.jstor.org/stable/26351566.

Karolyi, G. A., and R. Martell. 2010. "Terrorism and the Stock Market." *International Review of Applied Financial Issues & Economics* 2 (2): 285–314.

Klement, J. 2014. "Facts and Fantasies about Gold." *Journal of Risk and Control* 1 (1): 1–12.

Lintner, J. 1965. "Security Prices, Risk, and Maximal Gains from Diversification." *Journal of Finance* 20 (4): 587–615.

Makinen, G. 2002. *The Economic Effects of 9/11: A Retrospective Assessment*. Washington, DC: Congressional Research Service.

Meierrieks, D., and T. Gries. 2013. "Causality between Terrorism and Economic Growth." *Journal of Peace Research* 50 (1): 91–104.

Nikkinen, J., and S. Vähämaa. 2010. "Terrorism and Stock Market Sentiment." *Financial Review* 45 (2): 263–75.

Nordhaus, W. D. 2002. "The Economic Consequences of a War with Iraq." NBER Working Paper 9361 (December).

Omar, A. M. A., T. P. Wisniewski, and S. Nolte. 2017. "Diversifying Away the Risk of War and Cross-Border Political Crisis." *Energy Economics* 64: 494–510.

Rigobon, R., and B. Sack. 2005. "The Effects of War Risk on US Financial Markets." *Journal of Banking & Finance* 29 (7): 1769–89.

Rose, A. Z., and S. B. Blomberg. 2010. "Total Economic Consequences of Terrorist Attacks: Insights from 9/11." *Peace Economics, Peace Science and Public Policy* 16 (1): 2–11.

Sandler, T., and W. Enders. 2008. "Economic Consequences of Terrorism in Developed and Developing Countries: An Overview." In *Terrorism, Economic Development, and Political Openness*, vol. 17, edited by Philip Keefer and Norman Loayza, 17–47. Cambridge, UK: Cambridge University Press.

Sharpe, W. F. 1964. "Capital Asset Prices: A Theory of Market Equilibrium under Conditions of Risk." *Journal of Finance* 19 (3): 425–42. www.jstor.org/stable/2977928.

Tavares, J. 2004. "The Open Society Assesses Its Enemies: Shocks, Disasters and Terrorist Attacks." *Journal of Monetary Economics* 51 (5): 1039–70.

Tversky, A., and D. Kahneman. 1992. "Advances in Prospect Theory: Cumulative Representation of Uncertainty." *Journal of Risk and Uncertainty* 5: 297–323.

Wolfers, J., and E. Zitzewitz. 2006. "Prediction Markets in Theory and Practice." NBER Working Paper 12083 (March).

Chapter 3: Access to Resources

In reality, most large wars have contained within them a violent and persistent economic conflict. The War of the Austrian Succession, for example, could be more grittily described as "the war for the coal and iron resources of Silesia." . . . For my great-great-grandfather, the Napoleonic Wars didn't mean charging across the plains of Waterloo but trudging through the pepper vines of Java in order to seize the riches of the Dutch East Indies from Napoleon's ragtag defenders. Even more than sugar and spices, the British were after the amazing tin deposits on the island of Belitung, whose name is still preserved in the title of the world's biggest mining company, BHP Billiton.

—*Ferdinand Mound (2019)*

Are All Conflicts about Resources?

The preceding quote from Ferdinand Mound reflects a common sentiment among historians and the public alike. Politicians may declare that they fight wars to liberate a country or spread democracy, but the true reason behind the armed conflict, many argue, is to gain access to resources.

In the late 18th century, the Industrial Revolution started in England and quickly spread across Europe. The Industrial Revolution is arguably the most important economic event of the last 800 years. Readers may be surprised to learn what is considered the most important economic event before that—the introduction to the Western world of the number zero, to indicate nothingness.[1]

The Industrial Revolution allowed civilizations to escape the "Malthusian trap," which describes the cyclical outbreak of famines as a population grew too large to sustain itself with food and water. Thanks to steam-powered machines, it became possible to mechanize agriculture and mass-produce all kinds of household goods. But to build and run these machines,

---

[1]The number zero has been in widespread use in Mesopotamia since the third century BCE and in India since the fourth century CE but did not reach Europe and the Western world until the 12th century CE, enabling the invention of accounting and other important economic innovations.

the industrialized world needed coal and minerals of all sorts. And soon enough, the domestic supply of these minerals would not suffice to power the factories.

The easiest way to expand access to crucial resources was to invade resource-rich lands around the globe. Thanks to the Industrial Revolution, England and other colonial powers had better guns and could make short shrift of indigenous people wherever they dared to resist. And once an area was colonized, it not only provided access to resources but also featured a large number of potential customers for industrial goods produced in England. In other words, colonization and the Industrial Revolution went hand in hand. The Industrial Revolution created a need for resources, which triggered the colonization of foreign lands. This colonization, in turn, created more growth opportunities for British exports, which, in turn, intensified the need for resources, and so on.

As **Exhibit 1** shows, the GDP per capita of England increased sooner and faster than in such countries as Germany and Sweden, which did not have colonies or acquired their colonies only in the late 1800s. It is doubtful that this early advantage of the British Empire is solely due to the country's head start in the Industrial Revolution. Rather, a combination of geographical expansion and increased mechanization gave the British Empire a growth advantage in the first half of the 19th century. Noncolonial powers took longer to catch up with the growth the British Empire experienced in the first half of the 19th century, but by the onset of the 20th century, this advantage of colonial powers had largely disappeared.

So, who could argue with this view that many international conflicts revolve around access to scarce resources? In the remainder of this chapter,

Exhibit 1. GDP Per Capita Growth after the Industrial Revolution

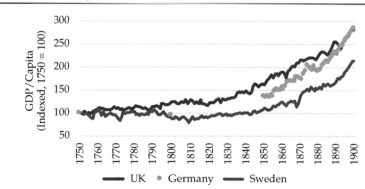

Source: Maddison Project Database, version 2018.

I will briefly review the competing theories on the link between natural resources and geopolitical conflict. After that, I will dive into the most important natural resource of our day: oil. Because oil is the most important commodity in the world, most of the research on geopolitics and resources has focused on the impact of oil supply disruptions on economic growth, inflation, and financial markets. As we will see, oil shocks cannot and should not be ignored by investors.

After the discussion of oil, I will briefly focus on other resources that are of geopolitical importance, ranging from industrial and rare earth metals to the most important renewable resource—water.

Resources and Geopolitics: Two Explanations for Conflict

Many geopolitical conflicts seem to center around resource-rich countries, whether one is considering the US war in Iraq, the Civil War in Libya, or the standoff between the United States and Iran over the Iranian nuclear program, which triggered a renewed US embargo against Iranian oil exports. To explain why resource-rich countries seem to attract conflict so often, political scientists and economists have come up with two competing explanations (Bayramov 2018).

First is the school of thought that *resource abundance* leads to more aggressive behavior and an increased likelihood of conflict. The main impetus for this view comes from the seminal work of Paul Collier and Anke Hoeffler, who claimed that civil war is more likely to happen in countries that are rich in natural resources (Collier and Hoeffler 1998). They argued that in resource-rich countries, unrest may start as disadvantaged segments of the population start to rebel against the government and the powerful elites. Whether this conflict is due to legitimate grievances or simple greed, the idea is that rebel groups form to capture the state's assets and distribute them differently (i.e., typically, to their own advantage). There is certainly a lot of truth in this argument, but the greedy rebel argument is also likely to be an oversimplified one. As Cramer (2002) argued, many factors have to come together to trigger civil strife. Without social inequality or a lack of opportunities in general, an outbreak of civil unrest would be unlikely even in a resource-rich country.

Furthermore, this school of thought does not have an easy time explaining interstate conflict. One argument why resource-rich countries should be more aggressive internationally is the so-called great power theory, which states that resource-rich countries want to expand their influence and have the financial means to do so because of their exports. This line of thought argues that resource-rich countries are more likely to attack neighboring countries if there are substantial additional resources located close to the border. A successful international campaign secures more resources and leads not only to more geopolitical influence but also to higher revenue from the resource extraction that finances these nations.

Another explanation why resource-rich countries may be more aggressive has been put forward by Colgan (2014), who found that revolutionary petro-states are more than three times as likely to start an international conflict than nonrevolutionary non-petrostates. The argument here is that oil-rich countries have the financial means to fight war and that revolutionary leaders are less bound by domestic checks and balances. However, Colgan's claim was largely debunked by Caselli, Morelli, and Rohner (2015), who examined a more comprehensive set of international conflicts and found that petrostates are less likely to initiate interstate conflicts.

In summary, the argument that resource abundance leads to increased geopolitical conflict seems to have merits for civil strife but has significant shortcomings in explaining international conflict. Thus, we must look for other reasons why resource-rich countries remain mired in geopolitical conflict so frequently. And here the resource scarcity school of thought may be able to help.

The *resource scarcity* view of geopolitical conflict takes the opposing view to the resource abundance approach and argues that countries with a scarcity of natural resources try to gain influence over resource-rich countries via political or military means. There are two common explanations why resource-poor countries might try to gain influence over resource-rich lands.

The first line of thought uses the Malthusian trap to come to its conclusions. If a country faces significant shortages of resources, it might endanger the population's living standards or, in modern times, the country's economic growth. As a result, countries want to ensure that they have access to natural resources, either by directly owning them or by installing friendly governments in resource-rich countries. As previously discussed, the colonization of much of the developing world in the 19th century was likely driven by these Malthusian motivations. Moreover, modern oil wars, such as the Iraq War and the ongoing Second Libyan Civil War, where both sides of the civil war are supported by competing foreign countries, are arguably examples of this line of thought.

Today, however, this neo-Malthusian view of the world is considered oversimplified. Nevertheless, advocates of the peak oil theory, which states that we are approaching the all-time peak in oil production and that we will face increasing supply shortages in coming decades, argue along these lines. As I will show later in my discussion of hydraulic fracturing, or fracking, these peak oil theories, which gained some popularity about a decade ago when oil prices were far above \$100 per barrel, have largely been invalidated by the developments of the last decade.[2]

The second line of thought expands the reasons for why a lack of resources may lead to international conflict. Gleditsch and Theisen (2010) claimed that it is not a scarcity of resources *per se* that leads to conflict but inefficient distribution and access to them. Thus, these researchers argued, one can overcome resource-driven conflict in two ways. First, one can ensure easier access to natural resources through trade liberalization and globalization. Second, one can introduce market-driven mechanisms that ensure a more efficient use of resources.

The cap-and-trade policies introduced around the world to limit CO_2 emissions are policy tools derived from this line of argument. The idea is that if there is a market price for a resource, then more expensive resources will be used only for applications that have higher added value or higher productivity, whereas low-productivity or low-value-added applications will be forced to develop alternatives. Finally, part and parcel of this line of thought are so-called cornucopian theories that state that resource scarcity is merely a mirage and that technological progress will enable mankind to circumvent any resource scarcity it may encounter. Of course, human ingenuity is virtually endless, but in order to motivate the search for new technologies, scarce resources must first be priced correctly. Nobody is going to develop a technology to reduce the consumption of a resource that is free.

The empirical evidence seems to agree with many of these resource scarcity arguments, though there is certainly a need to define scarcity more broadly than just the amount of proven reserves of a specific commodity. But by using this resource scarcity theory of geopolitical conflict, we can see how this plays out in real life in the case of the world's most traded and important commodity of all: oil.

Oil, the Ultimate Geopolitical Commodity

Energy security is a top priority for every country in the world. Without energy, economic growth grinds to a halt and the economy starts to shrink rapidly. According to the US Department of Energy's Energy Information Administration (EIA), the United States spent \$1.1 trillion, or 5.8% of GDP, in 2017 on energy. Just 10 years ago in 2010, this portion was much higher, about 8%–9% of GDP, which is about the global average. Thanks to the

---

[2]Marion K. Hubbert proposed the peak-oil theory (that oil production would peak and then decline) in 1956. A peak was observed around 1970, but the subsequent decline was not permanent; moreover, oil discoveries led to the substantial postponement of the expected peak. It still has not been reached.

boom in fracking, as well as increased energy efficiency, the United States has become less dependent on imports and thus spends less today on energy than it used to. Given this high share of energy expenditures, it is no wonder that energy commodities—in particular, oil—have become a major driver of geopolitics in the 20th century.

Securing access to energy at affordable prices has led to the introduction of the Strategic Petroleum Reserve in the United States, strategic reserves of natural gas in the United Kingdom, and other forms of stockpiling in countries that try to ensure the country has sufficient supply to keep the economy going in case of a major supply outage. And it is behind the push of politicians around the world to allow oil exploration in offshore fields and hard-to-access fields in the Arctic and the Antarctic. Finally, witnessing the energy revolution triggered by fracking technologies in the United States, other countries are also promoting fracking as a way to increase energy safety. That these efforts to access oil in ecologically vulnerable areas lead to political backlash and diplomatic strains is visible in many countries today.

Energy markets have been liberalized since the 1970s when futures on energy commodities began trading on international commodity exchanges. With this liberalization of the price of oil and other energy commodities came massive fluctuations in the price. Looking at the last 20 years, the price of a barrel of West Texas Intermediate (WTI) crude oil on the New York Mercantile Exchange rose from a low of around $17.50 per barrel in 1999 to a high of about $145 per barrel in the summer of 2008—a 728% increase in less than 10 years. It has since fallen almost as dramatically; as of this writing (August 2020), it is around $40. The annualized volatility of crude oil is 33%, much higher than the roughly 20% annualized volatility of most stock markets. And because oil is so important for the global economy yet so volatile, it should not be a surprise that oil price shocks can have a significant influence on the global economy and financial markets.

Not All Oil Shocks Are Alike. As Kilian (2009) so aptly put it, "Not all oil shocks are alike." The economy reacts differently to demand shocks than it does to supply shocks. Kilian differentiated between three different types of oil price shocks, a classification system that has become standard and is important for investors to remember:

- *Supply shocks* are driven by unanticipated changes in the production of oil. Supply shocks can be negative, such as when Saudi Arabia had to shut down its Abqaiq oil processing plant after a drone attack in 2019, leading to a 5% decline of global output overnight. As Kilian (2009) showed, such supply disruptions generally are short term in nature, and although they do lead to a spike in oil prices, they rarely have a lasting impact on the economy or financial markets.

- However, the fear of lasting supply disruptions can lead to *oil-specific demand shocks* if oil importers start to stockpile crude oil in anticipation of a longer outage. For example, if the Abqaiq outage had led to a general concern that Saudi outages could not be recovered quickly, oil consumers might have started to stockpile oil and drastically increased the global demand for this commodity. Similarly, the expectation of a prolonged war in an oil-exporting country or an open-ended restriction of production (e.g., the OPEC embargoes of the 1970s) can trigger such a demand shock. These oil-specific demand shocks are the biggest danger for the global economy because study after study has shown that they lead to spikes in oil prices, drops in stock markets, and a decline in economic growth. Worse still, such oil-specific demand shocks can last a long time and thus can cause significant damage to the global economy and financial markets.

- Finally, Kilian (2009) showed that the most common shocks are *aggregate demand shocks* that are triggered by a general increase or decline in demand for crude oil. These aggregate demand shocks are essentially a reflection of the global business cycle and will thus not be discussed in detail in this chapter. It suffices to say that aggregate demand shocks, if in an upward direction, are the best kind of shocks since they lead to higher oil prices but also to rising stock markets because investors understand that the higher oil prices are a reflection of strong economic growth.

In this chapter, I will focus only on supply shocks and oil-specific demand shocks, since these shocks can be and often are triggered by geopolitical events. In the end, the nature of the event that triggered the shock will determine the reaction of investors.

If the event is a brief disruption of supply, investors will increase the risk premium they use to discount future cash flows of an asset, but there will be little impact on the expected long-term inflation rate (since the shock is expected to be transitory) or expected cash flows. As a result, the prices of risky assets tend to decline sharply in reaction to such a supply shock but then recover as investors realize the spike in oil prices is going to be short-lived. In essence, such a supply shock leads to a stock market reaction that is similar to a terrorist attack, something I discussed in the last chapter.

If the disruption in supply leads to precautionary demand for crude oil, the shock will be longer lasting and the impact on asset prices will be more fundamental. In a first step, the risk premium for risky assets will increase, leading to a sharp sell-off in those assets and a flight to safety. In a second step, inflation expectations are likely to rise because the lasting nature of the demand shock means that oil prices remain high for longer; thus, inflation should increase at least in the next one to three years. This situation, in turn, means that expected cash flows will be discounted with even higher nominal rates and the present value of assets will decline.

However, not all risky assets will necessarily suffer a lasting decline in prices, as I will show. As the oil-specific demand shock is unfolding, investors will also adjust the expected future cash flows of their assets. While net consumers of oil and other energy commodities will likely see their future cash flows decline, net oil-producing industries will experience an increase in future cash flows that may compensate for the increase in discount rates. Thus, these assets may either decline or increase in price depending on which factor dominates.

Things get even more complicated if the high price of oil lasts long enough to trigger a reaction by central banks. If the inflation shock caused by the spike in oil prices is no longer deemed transitory, central banks are inclined to hike interest rates, thus increasing the real risk-free rate of return (and thus the discount rate) and influencing the expected future cash flows of businesses. The net effect of such a central bank reaction to fight inflation is usually a decline in the aggregate stock market, though again, some industries (e.g., insurance) may benefit from it.

How big the adjustments to expected cash flows, inflation, and so on will be depends on the size of the oil spike, which, in turn, depends on the size of the disruption of the balance in supply and demand. A group of economists has investigated the link between disruptions in the supply and demand for crude oil and the price of oil. The results all tend to fall in the same range. Aastveit, Bjørnland, and Thorsrud (2015) estimated that a 1% decline in oil supply leads to a 5%–10% increase in the price of oil. Similarly, Caldara, Cavallo, and Iacoviello (2019) showed with their model that a supply shock of 0.75% creates a 6% increase in the price of oil. For the rest of this chapter, I will use the assumption that a disruption of supply of 1%–2% will trigger a 10% spike in oil prices, and I will investigate how such a 10% spike in oil prices propagates through the economy and financial markets.

Oil Price Shocks and Economic Growth. The impact of oil prices on economic growth has been the subject of intensive research. Oladosu, Leiby, Bowman, Uría-Martínez, and Johnson (2018) found 149 papers published since 2000 that examined the oil price elasticity of GDP in net oil-importing countries. Out of this vast sample, they focused on the results of

19 international studies. **Exhibit 2** shows the results of a 10% increase in the price of oil on developed market economies. The table shows the worst-case model outcome (i.e., the biggest decline in GDP found in the literature), the best-case model outcome (i.e., the smallest decline or biggest increase in GDP), and the average and median of all models. Furthermore, the table differentiates between short-term impact on GDP (defined as up to one year), medium-term impact (defined as one to three years), and long-term impact (defined as more than three years).

Exhibit 2 shows that a 10% oil price shock leads to a decline in GDP growth of 0.2–0.3 percentage points, on average, in the short term. The eurozone economy seems to be somewhat sheltered from the negative effects of the price shock and experiences, on average, smaller declines in GDP growth. This result has been found in many studies and can also be seen in the case of China, which seems to be more sheltered from oil price shocks than other economies, as shown in **Exhibit 3**. The most common explanation of this observation is that oil price shocks lead to stronger growth in oil-exporting countries and thus to more demand in them. Countries with

Exhibit 2.   Impact of a 10% Oil Price Shock on GDP: Developed Markets

Country	Horizon	Worst Case	Average	Median	Best Case
US	ST	−1.24	−0.19	−0.08	0.16
	MT	−1.32	−0.36	−0.32	0.17
	LT	−0.40	−0.25	−0.36	0.00
UK	ST	−1.66	−0.31	−0.14	0.04
	MT	−1.74	−0.28	−0.08	0.02
	LT	−0.13	−0.08	−0.12	0.00
Eurozone	ST	−1.55	−0.14	−0.10	0.14
	MT	−1.62	−0.19	−0.13	0.05
	LT	−0.28	0.01	−0.05	0.03
Japan	ST	−1.54	−0.28	−0.03	0.24
	MT	−0.78	−0.18	−0.01	0.21
	LT	−0.68	−0.45	−0.67	−0.01
Australia	ST	−1.19	−0.34	−0.20	0.22
	MT	−1.31	−0.67	−0.67	0.00

Note: ST is short-term impact (up to one year), MT is medium-term impact (one to three years), and LT is long-term impact (more than three years).
Source: Oladosu et al. (2018).

Exhibit 3. Impact of a 10% Oil Price Shock on GDP: Developing Markets

Country	Horizon	Worst Case	Average	Median	Best Case
China	ST	−0.96	−0.15	0.09	0.24
	MT	−0.30	0.03	0.15	0.21
	LT	−0.26	−0.25	−0.25	−0.01
India	ST	−0.46	−0.30	−0.35	−0.09
	MT	−0.08	−0.07	−0.07	−0.05
Northern Africa	ST	−0.11	−0.07	−0.07	−0.03
Sub-Saharan Africa	ST	−0.30	−0.08	−0.06	0.00

Note: ST is short-term impact (up to one year), MT is medium-term impact (one to three years), and LT is long-term impact (more than three years).
Source: Oladosu et al. (2018).

a large export-oriented economy, such as China and Germany, benefit from this increase in demand and thus experience a boost in exports that partially offsets the decline in domestic demand triggered by the higher oil prices.

Another important observation in Exhibit 2 is that oil price shocks take a while to fully unfold. In most countries, the medium-term impact of an oil price shock is worse than the short-term impact. The timing of when the oil price shock has the biggest impact on an economy depends on structural factors, such as labor market rigidities, share of consumption in the economy, and share of energy prices in the overall consumption basket. For most countries, however, the peak of the oil price shocks tends to be felt four to eight quarters after the shock (that is, in the second year after the price spike). The numbers should also make investors aware that in the vast majority of cases, an oil price shock will not lead to a slowdown in GDP growth that is large enough to trigger a recession. However, an economy that is already teetering on the brink of recession or that is slowing down rapidly can be pushed into recession by an unexpected oil price shock.

Exhibit 3 shows the same data as Exhibit 2 for a selection of developing countries. The lesson learned from this table and from the research on the impact of oil price shocks on GDP is that most developing countries suffer a decline in GDP growth similar to that of developed countries if they are net importers of oil. I have already mentioned the special case of China as a major global exporter. Another exception is African countries, which barely react to an increase in oil prices. This is simply a reflection of the fact that most African countries are so underdeveloped that they do not depend much on oil imports. This lower oil intensity of their economies means that they withstand an oil price shock better than other developing countries.

Structural Differences of Economies Determine the Different Reactions to Oil Shocks. How much an oil price shock will affect an economy depends on the structure of the economy. These structural differences between countries determine not only the vulnerability of an economy to significant oil-specific demand shocks but also its reaction to smaller changes in oil prices. After all, a 10% increase in oil prices does not happen every day. Most of the time, oil prices are (relatively) well behaved and react to smaller disruptions in the balance between supply and demand, such as unplanned refinery outages or surprising strength in investment demand. Furthermore, seemingly unrelated effects can trigger stock market and commodity volatility. After Hurricane Katrina hit New Orleans in 2005, for example, the supply of gasoline and other distillates in the United States was severely disrupted because of the large number of refineries and shipping facilities in that region, triggering spikes in gasoline prices that were not observed in other countries. Thus, while global oil supply remained unchanged, regional weather effects created shocks to the US economy.

Kang, Ratti, and Vespignani (2017) set out to measure how the interaction between stock markets and commodity markets influenced the variability of industrial production over time. **Exhibit 4** shows that in the long run, about 11.9% of the variation in industrial production in the United States is driven by variation in oil prices. This number is a little higher than in France and Japan and substantially more than in Germany and the United Kingdom.

In the case of Germany, the export-oriented economy provides an internal buffer to domestic demand when oil prices fluctuate. In the United Kingdom

Exhibit 4. Share of Volatility in Industrial Production Explained by Oil: Developed Countries

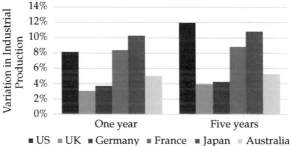

Source: Kang et al. (2017).

and other commodity-exporting countries, such as Australia, a similar effect arises from the substantial share of output generated by commodity-related businesses located in these countries. If oil prices rise, domestic demand for industrial goods declines but output from energy and mining companies increases, thus providing a natural hedge against the negative effects of oil price volatility. The economies of the United States, France, and Japan are far more dependent on domestic demand than commodity exporters are and thus experience a larger influence of commodity volatility on their economic activity over time.

Exhibit 5 shows the results of Kang et al.'s (2017) analysis for two high-income (i.e., developed) countries, the United States and South Korea, and four middle-income (i.e., developing) countries, Brazil, Russia, India, and China. Again, commodity exporters, such as Russia and Brazil, tend to have a lower sensitivity to commodity volatility than the United States, although the effect is mild compared with China. The reason for this rather small effect is that Russia and Brazil are so dependent on their commodity exports that these economies are unbalanced in the other extreme. Rising oil prices lead to a significant increase in national income and thus domestic demand, triggering a sharp increase in industrial production. The lack of diversification in the economy leads to a bigger impact of commodity volatility but with the opposite sign relative to commodity importers, such as South Korea or India.

Oil Price Shocks and Consumption. The main transmission mechanism of oil price shocks to domestic demand is, however, not via industrial production but via consumer demand. Kilian (2008) traced the effects of higher oil prices through the US economy.

Exhibit 5. Share of Volatility in Industrial Production Explained by Oil: United States, Brazil, Russia, India, China, and South Korea

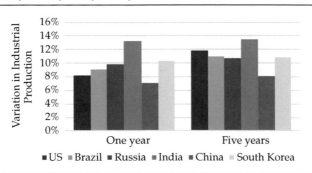

The important thing to note here is that consumer demand only indirectly depends on the price of crude oil. Private consumers do not buy barrels of crude oil and refine them in their basement. Instead, they go to the gas station and fill up their cars, they use heating oil and gas to heat their homes, and they feel the pinch of higher energy prices whenever they go to the supermarket and pay more for groceries because of higher costs for packaging and transportation. Thus, consumption reacts to the price of distillates, not crude oil.

Most of the time, the correlation between crude oil and distillates, such as gasoline and heating oil, is high, but as Hurricane Katrina showed, in some circumstances the two can decouple. New Orleans and southern Louisiana, the region directly hit by Katrina, are the location of a large fraction of the total refining capacity in the United States. When the hurricane hit, these refineries had to go offline for a long time, creating a shortage in gasoline and other distillates that could be felt throughout the country in the weeks after the hurricane.

Weather phenomena are not geopolitical events (although in the age of climate change, they might become just that), but imagine that instead of a hurricane, either a terrorist attack or an armed conflict destroys the refining capacity of a country. Such shocks in the energy infrastructure can lead to supply shocks or oil-specific demand shocks in a country or region.

The case of Ukraine should be a warning for every investor. Ukraine relies heavily on natural gas exports from Russia, and Russia is not afraid to use these exports as a geopolitical tool.

- In 2005, the Russian state-owned energy giant Gazprom demanded higher prices for natural gas deliveries to Ukraine. A new price of $160 per 1,000 cubic meters was agreed on, but in return, Ukraine asked that the price increases be introduced gradually and that it be able to charge higher transit fees for Russian gas flowing through its pipelines to Western Europe. After the two countries failed to resolve the dispute, Gazprom stopped delivering natural gas to Ukraine on 1 January 2006, in the middle of winter. Only three days later, Ukraine settled the dispute and agreed to pay $230 per 1,000 cubic meters for the next six months to obtain Gazprom's gas that was mixed with cheaper gas from central Asia. The effective cost for Ukraine was then $95 per 1,000 cubic meters.

- In 2009, Ukraine and Gazprom wanted to renew their agreement, but Gazprom refused to negotiate until Ukraine had paid its debt for previous deliveries: $2.4 billion. Ukraine partially paid the debt by year-end 2008, but the discussions about an extension of the gas contract broke down again. On 1 January 2009, Gazprom stopped the delivery of 90 million cubic meters of natural gas per day to the Ukraine. On 2 January 2009, Hungary, Romania, Poland, and Bulgaria all reported that their gas pressure had dropped as well, and the UK government was prepared to tap into its strategic gas reserves since pipeline pressure from the continent had dropped. On 7 January 2009, all Russian gas exports through Ukrainian pipelines ceased and were redirected to Europe through other pipelines. Nevertheless, gas pressure in European pipelines dropped even more. On 18 January 2009, Ukraine and Russia finally managed to settle the dispute. Ukraine agreed to leave its transit fees for natural gas unchanged and pay Western European prices for natural gas from Russia (less a 20% rebate for 2009).

Ostensibly, these gas disputes between Russia and Ukraine were about the price of gas delivered to Ukraine, but the political dimension was hard to overlook. Russian president Vladimir Putin was strictly opposed to the Eastern expansion of NATO that led to Hungary, Poland, and other former Warsaw Pact countries becoming members of the Western military alliance. Ukraine oriented itself more and more toward the West, with the aim to eventually become a NATO member. The gas disputes were often seen as a warning shot by Putin to "reconsider" these plans.

The gas disputes showed that access to energy can become a geopolitical tool. Thus, it is instructive to look at the results of Kilian (2008) on the effect that oil price spikes have on household consumption. Unfortunately, there is a significant gap in the economic literature in estimating these effects for countries other than the United States, so we have to make do with US estimates.

Exhibit 6 shows the estimated reduction in consumer demand in the United States given a 10% increase in retail energy prices (note the difference

Exhibit 6. Impact of a 10% Increase in Retail Energy Prices on US Consumption

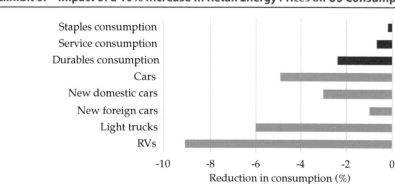

between crude oil and retail energy prices). In his study, Kilian (2008) showed that the reaction of US consumption to changes in energy prices is far less pronounced today than in the 1970s and 1980s. Thus, in Exhibit 6, I show only the results for the time period 1988–2006.

As can be expected, the consumption of food and other staples is hardly affected by rising energy prices. A 10% increase in retail energy prices leads to a mere 0.2% decline in staples consumption and 0.7% in service consumption. The main impact is felt in the consumption of durable goods, which drops by about 2.4%, on average. However, here the decline in consumption is extremely focused on cars. When gasoline becomes more expensive, consumers either postpone the purchase of a new car or buy smaller, more economical cars instead of SUVs and other light trucks. This phenomenon can be seen in the data. Consumer spending on cars and car parts declines by 4.9%, spending on new domestic vehicles declines by 3%, and sales of new imported cars decline by just 1%. The reason for this discrepancy is presumably that US car manufacturers build, on average, a higher share of SUVs and other big cars, whereas imported cars tend to be smaller. The strong decline in sales of light trucks (SUVs, vans, and pickup trucks) shows that manufacturers of these cars suffer more than manufacturers of cars that use less gasoline.

Interestingly, the type of vehicle that is most sensitive to increases in gas prices is recreational vehicles (RVs), which gives rise to the RV indicator. Most people need a car to get to work or go shopping, but not many people need an RV. Thus, RV sales are the first to decline before a recession and the last to recover afterward. This highly cyclical demand for RVs in the United States not only affects the stocks of RV manufacturers but also can be used as a remarkably reliable recession indicator.

Oil Price Shocks and Inflation. Oil price spikes have a significant impact on the expected inflation rate in a country. If energy prices directly make up 4.4% of the Consumer Price Index (CPI) basket, as was the case for the United States in September 2019, then a 10% increase in retail energy prices will lead to a 0.44% increase in headline inflation. Of course, the impact of energy prices goes beyond these first-round effects and filters through to rents and prices of all kinds of goods and services. But in a first estimate, the impact of higher energy prices on inflation is easy to calculate for any country.

Most of the time, central banks will ignore oil price increases due to supply shocks, knowing full well that such price shocks are transitory in nature. Unlike in the 1970s, when central banks in the United States and Western Europe reacted to the oil crisis by hiking interest rates to curb inflation, monetary policy today has evolved to a stance where such transitory shocks do not create a monetary policy reaction. Instead, central banks let these supply shocks work their way through the system and expect inflation rates to settle down after 12–18 months. Of course, the main challenge for central bankers then is to differentiate between transitory shocks and persistent shocks that are triggered by precautionary increases in oil-specific demand. Doing so is part of what makes monetary policy decisions so hard. In real life, it is simply very difficult to decide whether an energy price shock is going to be transitory or persistent.

On top of that, not all central banks are equally concerned about energy price spikes and their impact on inflation. **Exhibit 7** shows the share of variation in inflation that is driven by oil price volatility. In the United States, about a quarter of the volatility in inflation is driven by energy price fluctuations, whereas in Europe, this share is typically around only 10%–15%. In Japan, it is even lower. The main driver behind this smaller influence of energy prices on inflation is simply the lower energy dependency of countries in Europe compared with the United States.

Exhibit 8 shows a similar picture for middle-income countries. The share of variation in inflation explained by energy price volatility is much lower outside the United States. It is no wonder US politicians are much more obsessed with energy security than politicians in Europe or Asia! The US economy is simply more vulnerable to energy price shocks than other countries.

Why Have Oil Shocks Become Less Impactful to the US Economy? One consistent finding in studies of the impact of oil price shocks on the economy is that both demand and supply shocks have a much smaller impact on most developed economies today than in the 1970s and 1980s. Blanchard and Gali (2007) investigated the drivers behind these changes for the United States, the United Kingdom, France, Germany, Italy, and Japan.

Exhibit 7. Share of Volatility in Inflation Explained by Oil: Developed Countries

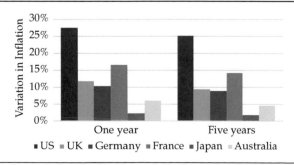

Source: Kang et al. (2017).

Exhibit 8.   Share of Volatility in Inflation Explained by Oil: United States, Brazil, Russia, India, China, and South Korea

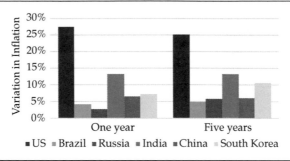

Source: Kang et al. (2017).

Their analysis covered two historical periods: 1970–1983 and 1984–2005. The break date was chosen because it roughly corresponds to the end of the high inflation era of the 1970s and early 1980s and the beginning of the so-called Great Moderation of relatively benign swings in the business cycle, inflation, and monetary policy.

Blanchard and Gali (2007) showed that three effects were responsible for the declining impact of oil price shocks on the economy:

- Most developed economies reacted to the oil price shocks of the 1970s by introducing energy-saving measures in households and cars. Over time, these measures have reduced the energy dependency of these economies. The energy intensity of the US economy roughly halved between 1980 and 2010. In Europe, the energy intensity of the economy declined by about one-third over the same time period but from a much lower starting point, so European countries typically have an energy intensity that is less than half that of the United States.

- Labor markets have become more flexible since the 1980s. Oil price shocks may lead to higher inflation, but these inflationary shocks no longer automatically lead to increased wages. Furthermore, businesses have an increased flexibility to react to higher commodity prices with cost reductions through layoffs.

- Finally, central banks have become smarter in managing inflationary shocks triggered by higher oil prices. In the 1970s, many central banks reacted to the oil crises with higher interest rates to curb inflation. Today, central banks will likely ignore such transitory inflation shocks and react only once an oil price shock filters through to core inflation.

Although these three factors can explain the declining sensitivity of developed economies to oil price shocks from the 1970s to the early 2000s, the US economy has gone through an even more dramatic transformation over the last decade. Driven by a new technology, the geopolitics of oil is changing rapidly.

Fracking: A Geopolitical Game Changer

Until about 2008, crude oil production in the United States was in steady decline. Conventional oil fields in Texas and Alaska were quickly being depleted, and offshore fields were either inaccessible or not productive enough to make up for the decline in onshore production. But with the advent of hydraulic fracturing (i.e., fracking) techniques, US oil production started to increase rapidly. Horizontal drilling techniques and fracking allowed US energy companies to access vast reservoirs of shale oil and shale gas all over the mainland United States. The US production of crude oil rose so fast that by 2015, the United States became a net exporter of oil and oil derivatives, and in 2018, it overtook both Russia and Saudi Arabia to become the world's largest oil producer, as shown in **Exhibit 9**.

The impact of this fracking boom on the US economy is huge. During the early 2000s, an oil price shock would have led to an economic slowdown that would have depressed private investment by up to 6% over three years. With the onset of the fracking boom, however, investment in the energy industry started to increase whenever oil prices rose, which led to a reduction in the negative response of investment to oil price shocks. By 2015, the relationship between oil price shocks and investment in the United States had completely reversed. Today, a 1% oil price shock leads to an estimated *increase* in investment of 5% after three years (Bjørnland and Zhulanova 2019).

Exhibit 9.   US Oil Production

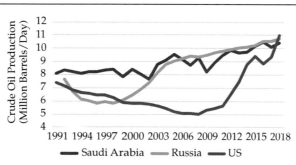

Source: US Department of Energy's EIA.

Increased investment means higher income for private households. The research of Bjørnland and Zhulanova (2019) showed that in the early 2000s, personal income *declined* by up to 1.5% in reaction to a 1% oil price increase, but today, personal income in the United States *increases* by 1%. This increase is mostly driven by better job prospects and higher wages in the energy industry and is not equally distributed across the United States. The states that tend to benefit the most from oil price shocks are North Dakota, South Dakota, and Texas, where the biggest shale oil basins are located.

Higher income also means that higher retail energy prices no longer lead to a sharp decline in consumption. Consumption still declines a bit in reaction to higher oil prices, but compared with the early 2000s, the decline in consumption is now only about a quarter as large. In short, the fracking boom has made the US economy much more robust with regard to oil price shocks.

The US fracking boom can be felt around the globe. As Kilian (2017) reported, the most important source for oil imports into the United States used to be Saudi Arabia. With the rise of domestic oil production, crude oil imports from Arab OPEC countries dropped from 20% of US oil use in 2008 to less than 10% in 2015. Saudi Arabia, as the biggest producer in the region, suffered the brunt of this decline, with US imports from Saudi Arabia declining from 12% of US oil use to 6%. But other regions were also hard hit. Oil exports from West Africa to the United States almost completely disappeared between 2008 and 2015.

Until late 2015, the United States had an export ban for crude oil, except for limited amounts that could be exported to Canada, but unlimited amounts of refined products could be exported everywhere. Between 2008 and 2015, the export of refined products from the United States increased from 2 million barrels per day to 4.5 million barrels per day. In comparison, in the seven years from 2001 to 2008, exports rose from 1.25 million barrels per day to 2 million barrels per day. This increase, of course, put pressure on oil prices outside the United States. Kilian (2017) estimated that between late 2012 and mid-2015, the price of a barrel of Brent crude oil was about $10 lower because of increased US oil exports. However, oil prices found a new equilibrium after declining by about 50% in 2014 and 2015. Today, prices for Brent crude oil are no longer depressed because of US exports.

The rapid decline in oil prices, which was driven more by a slowdown in global aggregate demand than by the US shale boom, meant that traditional oil exporters, especially Saudi Arabia, faced significant losses of revenue. Normally, OPEC would have been able to counteract the decline in oil prices through production cuts, but with the United States importing less and less oil from OPEC countries, Saudi Arabia and other countries were forced to keep production high to generate necessary revenues for their economy. Nevertheless, starting in 2014, Saudi Arabia suffered a decline in its net foreign assets of about $150 billion, which continues to this day, as shown in **Exhibit 10**.

The loss of oil revenues has had significant consequences for the Saudi Arabian government. Faced with lower revenues, the government could either reduce government spending or raise revenues through other sources. A reduction of government spending is politically very risky since almost all Saudis depend on the generous social services and heavily subsidized energy offered by the government. Reducing government expenditures could easily trigger civil unrest in Saudi Arabia.

Thus, since 2014, the country has increasingly tried to raise funds from alternative sources. In 2014, the debt-to-GDP ratio of Saudi Arabia was a mere 1.6%. By the end of 2018, the ratio had risen to 19.0%, mostly because Saudi Arabia's budget deficit reached 15% in 2015 and 12% in 2016. However, the budget deficit remains very high, at around 5% per year, and is expected to increase as global demand for oil declines in reaction to slower global growth in the coming years. At the current rate, Saudi Arabia's debt-to-GDP ratio could hit 100% by 2040.

Thus, it is no wonder that Saudi Arabia is starting to sell its crown jewels. The IPO of Saudi Aramco is an attempt to raise desperately needed funds from international investors and at the same time transfer some of the risk to these investors. This situation, in turn, makes Saudi Arabia increasingly vulnerable to geopolitical tensions. The attacks against the Saudi Aramco facilities in Abqaiq in 2019, as well as attacks against Saudi pipelines in the same

Exhibit 10. Saudi Arabian Net Foreign Assets

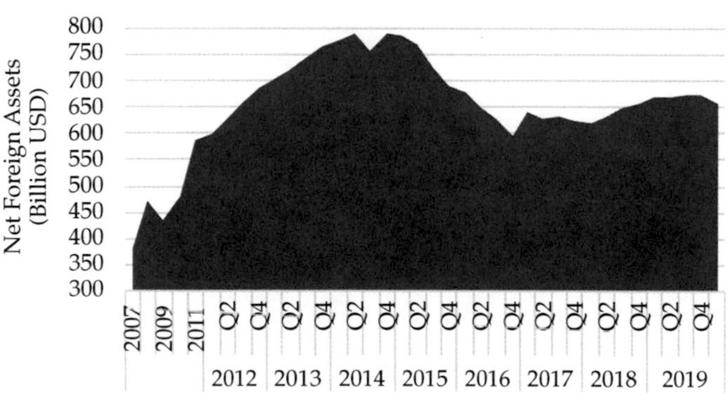

Source: Saudi Arabian Monetary Authority (SAMA).

year, showed that Saudi oil infrastructure is vulnerable to armed attacks from Iran and other adversaries. As the fiscal situation of Saudi Arabia becomes more precarious, we should expect such vulnerabilities to be exploited more frequently, making supply disruptions in Saudi Arabia more likely in the future. And this is not good news, as I will show next.

Saudi Arabia Is Special

Every nation believes it is special, but when it comes to oil, Saudi Arabia truly is special. The country may no longer be the biggest oil producer in the world and no longer have the world's largest proven reserves (that distinction now belongs to Venezuela), but Saudi Arabia remains the country with the most spare capacity to produce additional oil should it be needed. This fact means that if a country reduces its oil production for geopolitical or other reasons, Saudi Arabia, together with its fellow OPEC members, can compensate for this production shortfall. Because Saudi Arabia is the largest oil producer in the Middle East, it typically has to shoulder most of the burden. Similarly, if Saudi Arabia is unwilling or unable to increase oil production in the face of a demand shock, other OPEC members and Russia typically do not expand their production either. Therefore, Saudi Arabia has the geopolitical clout to trigger an oil crisis if it so wishes.

A study by two economists from the University of Cambridge, Mohaddes and Pesaran (2016), used historical production outages of 27 oil-exporting countries to build a model of the likely global impact of supply shocks in various countries. The contrast between Saudi Arabia and the other countries could not be more striking. **Exhibit 11** shows the impact of a one standard deviation decline in oil production in Saudi Arabia and Iran on GDP growth around the world. For Saudi Arabia, such a decline would mean that its oil

Exhibit 11. Impact of a Supply Shock in Saudi Arabia vs. Iran: GDP Growth

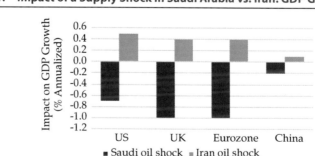

Source: Mohaddes and Pesaran (2016).

production would decline by about 11%, which implies a decrease in global oil supply of about 1%.

A supply outage in Saudi Arabia has the opposite impact on the global economy of a supply outage in Iran. If Iran cannot sell oil in the global market anymore (e.g., because of the Western sanctions against the country), Saudi Arabia and other OPEC countries can easily substitute their own production for Iranian oil. In fact, to calm down global oil importers, OPEC typically overcompensates for a supply shock by one of its smaller members by producing more oil after the supply shock than before. Doing so creates a positive oil supply shock that boosts the global economy. For most of Europe and the United States, this boost in growth accounts for an estimated 0.4% of GDP, whereas for China, it results in a smaller acceleration, about 0.1%.

In contrast, if supply from Saudi Arabia declines, the other OPEC countries do not have enough spare capacity to make up for the lost output. Hence, a decline in Saudi oil production filters through to global markets, and the resulting shock to GDP growth is substantial. Mohaddes and Pesaran (2016) estimated it to be about 1% of GDP (annualized) for the United Kingdom and the eurozone for the duration of the Saudi output disruption. The US economy is a bit more resilient because it can tap into its strategic petroleum reserve and thus buffer some of the negative impact. Even in this case, however, US GDP growth is expected to decline by an annualized 0.7%.

The transmission mechanism through which the economy is boosted or slowed is shown in **Exhibit 12**. In reaction to a supply shock in Iran, oil prices drop as other suppliers overcompensate for the loss of supply. Thanks to this supply boost, stocks rally slightly as well, but the effect is minimal. A supply shock in Saudi Arabia, in contrast, leads to a more than 20% spike in oil prices and an approximate 10% drop in global stock markets. Both oil and

Exhibit 12. Impact of a Supply Shock in Saudi Arabia vs. Iran: Stock Markets and Oil Price

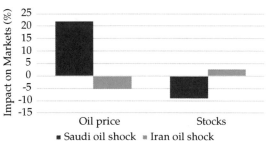

Source: Mohaddes and Pesaran (2016).

stock markets in this instance reflect the dramatic economic impact a Saudi supply shock has. At the same time, higher oil prices and lower stock markets reinforce a Saudi oil shock because the decline in stock markets affects economic sentiment and may create a reluctance of private households and businesses to invest.

How this played out in real time could be observed during the first episode of Iranian oil embargoes from 2012 to 2016. The United Nations, the United States, and the EU had issued a variety of sanctions against Iran that effectively cut the country off from the international financial markets. These sanctions were designed to force the Iranian government to stop its nuclear enrichment program and start negotiations for a permanent solution. In early 2012, the United States and the EU introduced embargoes on Iranian oil exports that led to a decline of Iranian oil production by about a quarter in 2012.

That this supply shock did not lead to a spike in oil prices was due to the other OPEC member states, led by Saudi Arabia, expanding their production. Between 2011 and 2015, Saudi oil production increased by 710,000 barrels per day—replacing almost the entire amount of Iranian oil production decline of 760,000 barrels per day, as shown in **Exhibit 13**. But other OPEC countries expanded their production as well. Iraqi oil output grew by 1.24 million barrels per day, creating a significant increase in global oil supply that kept oil prices in check and boosted global economic growth.

Oil Shocks and the Stock Market

We have seen that oil-specific demand shocks can be quite detrimental to economic growth. They can lead to a substantial decline in GDP growth and

Exhibit 13. Saudi Oil Production during Iran Sanctions

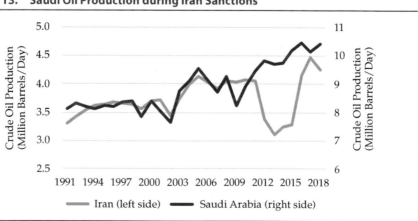

Source: US Department of Energy's EIA.

consumer demand for cars and other durable goods if the reduction in supply or the unexpected increase in precautionary demand cannot be compensated for by Saudi Arabia and other major oil producers. This is not only the case when there are supply disruptions in Saudi Arabia; it can also happen when there is already significant aggregate demand from a booming world economy. In such a boom scenario, we should expect oil-specific demand shocks to have a bigger effect because it is less likely that OPEC countries and other producers will have sufficient spare capacity. In contrast, during an economic slowdown, there typically is sufficient spare capacity to offset additional demand or a supply disruption. Nevertheless, oil-specific demand shocks and short-term supply shocks do lead to slower economic growth and higher inflation most of the time.

For stock markets, this means that the present value of stocks may decline as expected inflation rates and risk premiums increase while expected cash flows decline—at least for most businesses. As I discussed earlier, however, the reactions of expected cash flows to changing oil prices are not homogenous. Oil-producing businesses and businesses that produce other commodities that benefit from higher oil prices will experience an increase in expected cash flows, whereas oil consumers may experience decreasing cash flows. This means that at an aggregate level (be it a sector or country level), it is not necessarily clear how stock markets will react to oil price shocks.

A lot of work has gone into the exploration of the connection between oil prices and stock markets, especially since 2008, when oil prices surpassed $100 per barrel for the first time and subsequently declined dramatically again to near $30 per barrel. Smyth and Narayan (2018) produced a comprehensive literature review of all the work that has been done over the last decade. Here, I want to focus on the results that are most important for investors.

The type of oil shock determines the stock market reaction. In most countries, the dominant effect of an oil price shock is a decline in stock markets, but these effects tend to be small—especially for large, well-diversified stock markets, such as the US and global stock market indices. Furthermore, the impact of oil price shocks depends significantly on the type of shock. Supply shocks tend to have a small and transitory effect not only on the economy but also on stock markets, whereas oil-specific demand shocks and aggregate demand shocks have much larger and longer-lasting effects. Aggregate demand shocks lead not only to higher oil prices but also to higher returns for stocks since, in this case, the demand shock is triggered by stronger economic growth. Oil-specific demand shocks, in contrast, tend to have a negative effect on stock markets, since these demand shocks typically reflect precautionary demand in reaction to geopolitical events or expected supply shortages that last a long time (Kilian and Park 2009).

Wang, Wu, and Yang (2013) investigated a set of nine oil-importing countries and seven oil-exporting countries. They found that in reaction to a supply shock, the stock markets tended to have only a short-lived, transitory response, but the effect differed by type of market. In oil-exporting countries, the response tended to be positive, whereas in oil-importing countries, it tended to be negative.

Oil-specific demand shocks and precautionary oil demand, in contrast, lead to negative effects in the stock markets of oil-importing countries. Notably, though, Wang et al. (2013) found smaller effects for the United States than did Kilian and Park (2009) but bigger effects for China than in previous studies. Wang et al.'s data, covering 1999–2011, showed that an oil-specific demand shock creates a roughly 6% decline in Chinese stocks over 12 months but only an approximate 1%–2% decline in US and UK stocks. Investors should also be aware that oil-importing countries tend to react to oil-specific demand shocks with some delay. Most of the decline in stock markets happens about 6–12 months after the shock as the impact on the economy unfolds.

Oil-exporting countries benefit from such oil-specific demand shocks because the higher oil price leads to a net increase in national income, driven by oil exports. The reaction of stock markets in such countries is quite a bit faster than that for oil-importing countries, with stock markets peaking three to six months after the initial shock. The rally in stock markets is particularly pronounced in Canada, Norway, Saudi Arabia, and Russia but is not statistically significant in Mexico, Kuwait, and Venezuela. Wang et al. (2013) argued that this finding results from Canada, Norway, Saudi Arabia, and Russia having not only a large oil sector but also a well-developed oil services and engineering sector that benefits from higher demand for oil exploration and engineering works in response to higher oil prices.

A number of studies have looked at stock market reactions to oil price shocks in the short run. Gogineni (2010) examined the abnormal market return for more than 80 industries in the US stock market on the day of an oil price jump. Arouri and Nguyen (2010) investigated the weekly abnormal return of European sectors in the week of an oil price shock; **Exhibit 14** shows their results, which are in agreement with the more granular results of Gogineni. As expected, sectors that are net oil consumers—such as health care, automobiles, and food and beverages—had a negative stock market reaction to an oil price shock, whereas the energy sector had a significantly positive reaction. Basic materials had the second largest positive reaction. The slightly positive reaction

Exhibit 14. Expected Return of Stock Markets Conditional on Extreme Oil Price Movements

Sector/Industry	Expected Weekly Return
Oil and gas	2.06%
Basic materials	0.32%
Financials	0.29%
Consumer services	0.23%
Industrials	0.16%
Utilities	0.08%
Telecom	−0.26%
Automobiles	−0.31%
Household goods	−0.35%
Technology	−0.43%
Food and beverages	−0.49%
Health care	−0.75%

Note: Expected returns are stock market returns for a jump in oil prices in the 5th percentile of the distribution.
Source: Arouri and Nguyen (2010).

of financials to oil price shocks can be traced back to the change in expected inflation and thus the increase in interest rates that goes along with it.

However, Gogineni (2010) also noted that the reaction of stock markets to oil price shocks is nonlinear in the short run. Small daily changes in oil prices tend to trigger small positive stock market reactions, whereas large daily changes in oil prices and changes in times of elevated war risks for the United States trigger stock market declines.

Bittlingmayer (2005) also found a more pronounced negative stock market reaction in those periods when the United States was expected to go to war in an oil-producing country. Since neither Gogineni (2010) nor Bittlingmayer differentiated between types of oil price shocks in their studies, we can only speculate that increased war risk, such as that during the run-up to the Iraq War, leads to additional precautionary demand for oil that drives this adverse stock market reaction.

The nonlinear reaction of stock markets to oil price shocks has been at the center of interest in recent years. Reboredo and Ugolini (2016) used a copula approach to investigate spillovers from oil markets to stock markets and found that more extreme oil price shocks lead to outsized stock market reactions. **Exhibit 15** shows the weekly stock market reaction to the 5% most

Exhibit 15. Returns of Stock Markets Conditional on Extreme Oil Price Movements: Developed Markets

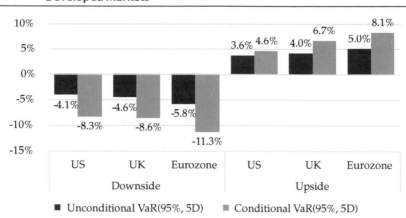

Notes: Returns are average returns for an oil price movement at the 5th and 95th percentiles of the distribution over 5 trading days (5D). VaR = Value at Risk = the expected change in share prices from the oil shock.
Source: Reboredo and Ugolini (2016).

extreme oil price moves in developed markets. The dark bars show the unconditional upside and downside risks of these stock markets, and the light bars show the upside and downside risks given an oil price shock that is in the top 5% or bottom 5% of the historical distribution.

The figure shows that stock markets react much more sensitively to bad news than to good news. For example, the lower end of the weekly downside risk for the US stock market is −4.1%, on average. But in times of adverse oil price shocks, this downside risk more than doubles to −8.3%. In reaction to positive oil price shocks, the upside risk increases only from 3.6% to 4.6%.

The same pattern can be seen in the stock market reaction of Brazil, Russia, India, and China, shown in **Exhibit 16**. Again, adverse oil price movements create a bigger spillover and larger drawdown risks than positive oil price shocks do.

Oil Shocks and Currencies

Stock markets are not the only financial markets that have a significant reaction to oil price shocks. Interest rates have only a small, mostly insignificant reaction to oil price shocks, but currencies do react to swings in oil prices. Paul Krugman (1983) was probably the first economist to investigate the link between oil prices and exchange rates, but nothing much happened in this field after his study until the study of Radhamés Lizardo and André Mollick

Exhibit 16.   Returns of Stock Markets Conditional on Extreme Oil Price Movements: Developing Countries

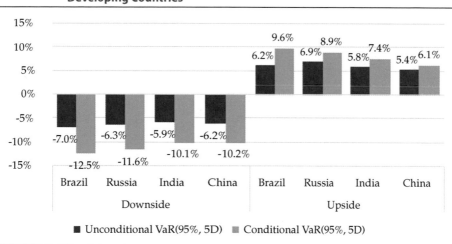

Notes: Returns are average returns for an oil price movement at the 5th and 95th percentiles of the distribution over 5 trading days (5D). VaR = Value at Risk = the expected change in share prices from the oil shock.

Source: Reboredo and Ugolini (2016).

was published in 2010. They investigated the behavior of US dollar exchange rates against the currencies of both oil-exporting and oil-importing economies from the 1970s to 2008. **Exhibit 17** shows that the US dollar depreciates against most currencies in reaction to a 10% increase in the real oil price, with the biggest decline, 4.1%, against the Swedish krona. Only the Japanese yen weakens against the US dollar in reaction to an oil price shock.

However, the study of Lizardo and Mollick did not differentiate between types of oil shocks, a shortcoming that was addressed by Basher, Haug, and Sadorsky (2016). They found that exchange rates hardly move in reaction to short-term supply shocks. However, oil demand shocks lead to a significant appreciation of the currencies of oil-exporting countries versus the US dollar and most oil-importing countries' currencies. They also found that the appreciation of oil-exporting countries' currencies was stronger in regimes with higher currency volatility, indicating that oil demand shocks have a bigger impact on exchange rates if markets are already under stress for one reason or another.

The relationship between the US dollar and the currencies of oil-importing countries is more complex, however, and depends largely on the nature of the demand shock and the relative competitive position of each economy in reaction to these demand shocks. In times of high currency market volatility,

Exhibit 17. Estimated Impact of a 10% Increase in Real Oil Price on US Dollar Exchange Rates

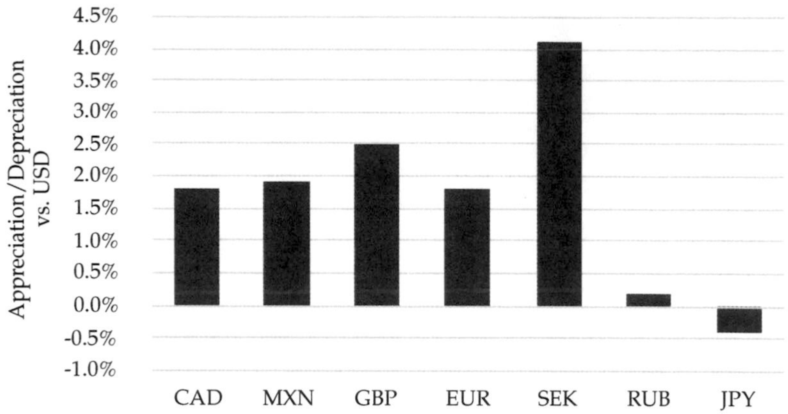

Source: Lizardo and Mollick (2010).

the Japanese yen and the Indian rupee tend to depreciate against the US dollar, and they tend to appreciate against the US dollar in times of low currency market volatility. The South Korean won, in contrast, showed little movement against the US dollar in these calmer periods.

Supply Shocks in Metals

So far, this chapter has focused on oil price shocks, but there are obviously other important commodities used in the global economy. I have focused so much on oil because the total consumption of other nonrenewable commodities, such as metals, is much lower than the consumption of oil and energy commodities. As I discussed previously, the annual consumption of energy commodities in the United States amounts to roughly $1.1 trillion, or 5.8% of GDP. The US Geological Survey reported that US consumption of iron and steel in 2018 was a mere $135 billion (0.7% of GDP); the numbers for copper and aluminum were $11.1 billion (0.06% of GDP) and $11.3 billion (0.06% of GDP), respectively. In other words, a price shock in steel, copper, or any other industrial metal will not have a material influence on the economy of the United States or its stock market.

That is not to say that for some major commodity producers, a price shock in some metals cannot have a significant economic impact that will reverberate through the local stock markets. Chile, for example, is the world's largest copper producer and is responsible for about 27% of global copper production. The mining sector accounts for 10% of Chile's GDP, and copper exports make up 50% of all of Chile's exports. Similarly, the mining sector accounts for about 10% of the GDP of Peru and about 60% of the country's exports.

Bigger commodity exporters, such as Australia, also have a large mining sector. The mining sector accounts for 9% of Australian GDP. But the difference between Australia and such countries as Chile is that the mining sector itself is much more diversified. **Exhibit 18** shows that iron ore and coal are the two biggest exports of the Australian economy, each amounting to about 14.5% of total exports. Thus, a price shock in any one mineral hurts the Australian economy much less than a price shock in copper hurts Chile's or Peru's economy.

Nevertheless, both copper and tin prices have a rich history of market manipulation and collusion that lead to significant price shocks. This is possible in these markets because, unlike the market for iron ore, aluminum, and other minerals, the copper and tin markets are characterized by oligopolistic structures and dominated by a handful of producers.

- Rausser and Stuermer (2014) recounted the major episodes of collusion and price manipulation in the copper market since 1850, shown in

Exhibit 18.   Australian Exports, 2017

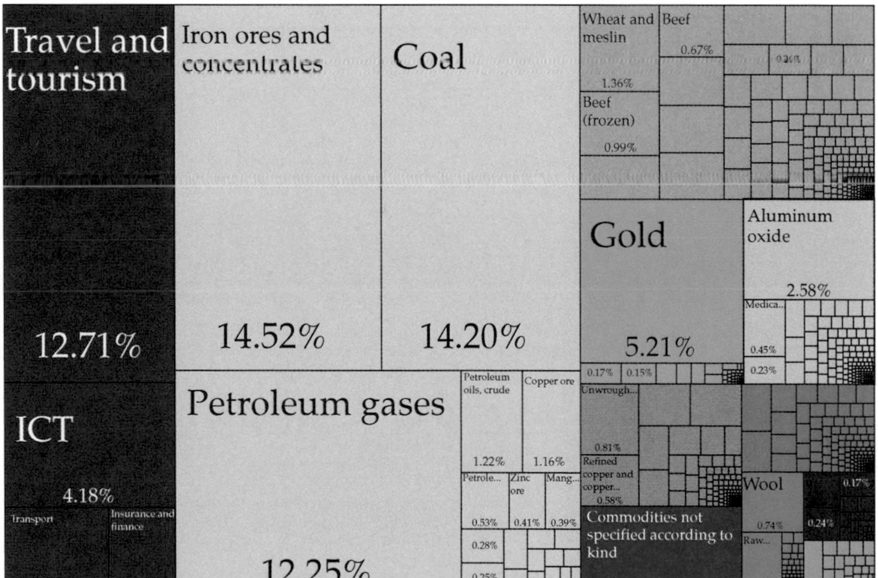

Source: Atlas of Economic Complexity, using raw trade data on goods derived from the UN Commodity Trade Statistics Database (UN Comtrade) and trade data on services from the IMF Direction of Trade Statistics (DOTS).

Exhibit 19: From 1852 to 1860, the Second Copper Trade Association, which controlled at least 70% of British smelter production and 32%–39% of global production, introduced production quotas and fixed prices. By 1856, the real price of copper had risen 46% from the lows of 1851.

- In October 1887, US producers, together with Rio Tinto and two South African producers, formed the Sécretan Copper Syndicate, which bought 160,000 metric tons of copper, financed by French banks and investors. By 1888, the price of copper had risen 56%. The syndicate eventually collapsed when the main financing bank, Comptoir d'Escompte, could no longer finance the stockpiling activities of the syndicate and was forced into bankruptcy.

- In 1899, the Amalgamated Copper Company in the United States, which controlled about 20% of global copper production, together with international partners, started to restrict output and eventually reduced output by 25 million pounds in 1901. Copper prices jumped 35% between 1898 and 1901, before the company decided to no longer limit production.

- From 1918 to 1923, the Copper Export Association controlled 89% of US copper production, the equivalent of 69% of global production. The association started stockpiling copper in 1921 and influenced prices until its dissolution in 1923, which resulted from defections and international competition. From 1921 to 1923, copper prices rose 49%.

Exhibit 19. Real Price of Copper and Tin in 2018 Dollars

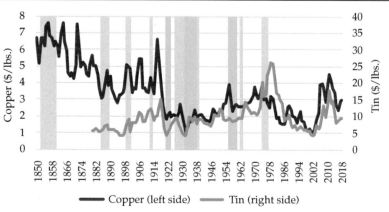

Note: Episodes of copper collusion marked in grey; episodes of tin collusion in yellow.
Sources: US Geological Survey; Jordà, Schularick, and Taylor (2017); Rausser and Stuermer (2014); Stuermer (2018).

- During the Great Depression, Copper Export Inc., which controlled between 65% and 95% of global copper production, sought to stabilize prices through price controls and output restrictions. The cartel managed to reverse the initial slump in copper prices and stabilize them at levels around pre-1930 averages.

- From 1974 to 1978, the Intergovernmental Council of Copper Exporting Countries, similar to OPEC but for copper, which controlled about 37% of global mine production, introduced production and export quotas that led to a 17% increase in copper prices in 1975.

Similarly, Stuermer (2018) recounted three major episodes of price manipulation in tin markets that led to significant price shocks:

- In 1921, the governments of the Malay States and the Dutch East Indies established the Bandoeng Pool, which controlled 50% of global tin production. The cartel withheld about 15% of global production and sold it gradually as prices for tin rose 50% between 1921 and 1923. The pool dissolved once its stockpiles were exhausted in 1924.

- During the Great Depression, the International Tin Agreement introduced output restrictions that led to a 142% jump in tin prices between 1932 and 1934. The agreement was finally dissolved in the run-up to World War II.

- Between 1956 and 1960, the major tin producers outside the United States formed a new International Tin Agreement to control exports and prices, which did not lead to massive price spikes but eventually created an oversupply of tin when the agreement was abandoned in 1960.

This history of price and production controls by international cartels shows that, especially in copper and tin, price shocks are a potential threat for investors, as depicted in Exhibit 19. Cartels have formed throughout history when producers were afraid of potential oversupply from new mines or a decline in aggregate demand. With the rise of globalization, however, these cartels have become less common and less effective.

Rare Earth Metals Are Not a Geopolitical Threat

In recent years, the demand for rare earth metals has increased substantially because these metals are used in the production of batteries, IT hardware, and other high-tech products. Investors are worried about the potential use of rare earth metals as a geopolitical weapon by China. In 2018, China was responsible for 70% of the global rare earth metal supply, with Australia a distant second at 11% of global production. The United States has to import all the rare earth metals it needs at the moment, though several US mines are ramping up production, which will reduce the import dependency of the United States. Nevertheless, China can theoretically control the global market price of rare earth metals because of its dominant position.

However, China has little incentive to drive prices for rare earth metals higher since these metals are used in applications that create demand for Chinese intermediate products. In a world of global supply chains, reducing the US output of products that require rare earth metals would eventually create a backlash in the demand for Chinese products, so export or production controls by China would be counterproductive. Additionally, the impact of production restrictions for rare earth metals on the US economy would be very small indeed. The total imports of rare earth metals into the United States amounts to a paltry $160 million. Except for some specialized manufacturers, nobody in the United States would even notice a reduction in rare earth metal exports by China. **Exhibit 20** shows price fluctuations of two rare earth metals, scandium and yttrium.

Water as a Source of Geopolitical Conflict?

Another commodity that is sometimes connected to geopolitical risks and geopolitical tensions is water. Water scarcity could theoretically lead to internal and external conflict. With climate change creating increased water supply stress, particularly in sub-Saharan Africa and the Middle East, some argue that water scarcity could even lead to water wars. However, the empirical evidence for geopolitical conflict over water is weak or nonexistent.

Exhibit 20. Real Price of Rare Earth Metals in 2018 Dollars, 1959–2019

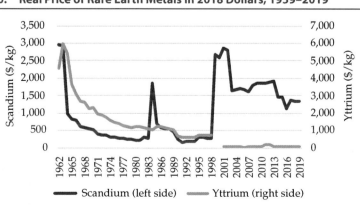

Sources: US Geological Survey and Jordà et al. (2017).

Brochmann (2012) found that conflicts over water are most commonly resolved by cooperation.

One prominent example of such water cooperation is the International Boundary and Water Commission, or the *Comisión Internacional de Limites y Aguas,* which was set up between the United States and Mexico in 1889 to determine the boundary between the two countries along the Rio Grande and other parts of the border. Over time, the mission of the commission expanded, and today it also includes the determination of water usage rights along the Rio Grande and the Colorado River.

Another example showing that differences over water resources are unlikely to lead to conflict is the Mekong River Commission, an intergovernmental organization that manages water rights along the Mekong River in Cambodia, Laos, Vietnam, and Thailand. With origins going back to 1957, the organization was able to facilitate cooperation between its members even during the Vietnam War in the 1960s and 1970s. Koubi, Spilker, Böhmelt, and Bernauer (2014) concluded that trade relations and cross-border payments between neighboring countries act as a check on escalating conflicts over water. If conflicts arise, they remain at the political level and do not escalate into armed conflict.

Of course, just because no evidence exists of intense geopolitical conflict over water in the past does not mean we can rule out a potential water war in the future. However, the resolution of water scarcity issues between countries that are otherwise, shall we say, not the best of friends, such as Israel and its neighbors, indicates that armed conflict over access to water seems a very remote possibility at the moment.

Conclusion

In this chapter, I reviewed the empirical evidence on how conflict over natural resources can affect the global economy and financial markets. The commodity that has by far the biggest impact on the global economy is oil. A 1% decline in oil supply typically leads to an increase in oil prices of 10%. Similarly, a 1% increase in demand leads to an oil price increase of the same magnitude.

How the economy and financial markets react to such oil price shocks depends on the source of the shock. Aggregate demand shocks are driven by rising economic growth and thus lead not only to higher oil prices but also to stronger economic growth and higher stock market returns. Supply shocks and oil-specific demand shocks (e.g., through precautionary demand for oil in anticipation of lasting supply shortages), in contrast, lead to a slowdown in economic growth and a decline in stock market returns.

The impact of rising oil prices on the global economy is declining but remains significant. For oil-exporting countries, higher oil prices mean higher growth, whereas oil-importing countries experience declines in growth typically on the order of 0.3% of GDP in response to a sustained 10% increase in oil prices. However, oil-specific demand shocks seem to have less of an effect on export-oriented countries, such as Germany and China, which benefit from increased demand from oil-exporting countries, dampening some of the negative effects of higher oil prices on domestic consumption.

The United States is a special case, having shifted from an oil-importing country to an oil-exporting country over the last decade. The fracking boom has had significant geopolitical ramifications not only for the United States, which now has an economy that is much more robust in the face of oil price shocks than in the past, but also for traditional oil importers. Most important, Saudi Arabia is facing significantly lower oil revenues than in the past, leading to a quickly deteriorating fiscal position and an increased vulnerability of the country to international conflicts. This situation is particularly concerning since Saudi Arabia is the country with the most spare capacity in the world; supply disruptions in Saudi Arabia cannot be compensated by other oil producers. Thus, oil price shocks originating in Saudi Arabia are more consequential than oil price shocks originating in other countries.

Once oil prices spike, both stock markets and currency markets show significant reactions. In stock markets, the overall market reaction is muted, but energy-related sectors and markets in oil-exporting countries experience a significant boost, whereas markets in oil-importing countries and stocks of businesses that depend on oil as a major input factor (e.g., food and health care companies) suffer. Oil price shocks also tend to lead to an appreciation of oil currencies against the US dollar, whereas the reaction of non-oil currencies against the US dollar is mixed and depends on the individual circumstances of each oil shock.

Finally, in this chapter I discussed the potential for price shocks in markets for metals to influence the global economy and financial markets. I showed that demand for metals tends to be such a small part of the global economy that spikes in metal prices do not have a significant effect on major economies. However, some countries that depend heavily on the export of one specific metal, such as Chile and Peru, can have strong reactions to price shocks in these metals.

This argument also extends to a range of metals that have been much discussed in recent years: rare earth metals. China possesses a near monopoly on rare earth metal production, but imports of rare earth metals to the United States are so miniscule that a price shock in these metals would have no impact on the US economy overall. Nevertheless, shares of companies in IT and other high-tech areas that rely on rare earth metals might suffer transitory price declines in reaction to higher rare earth metal prices.

Bibliography

Aastveit, K. A., H. C. Bjørnland, and L. A. Thorsrud. 2015. "What Drives Oil Prices? Emerging versus Developed Economies." *Journal of Applied Econometrics* 30 (7): 1013–28.

Arouri, M. E. H., and D. K. Nguyen. 2010. "Oil Prices, Stock Markets and Portfolio Investment: Evidence from Sector Analysis in Europe over the Last Decade." *Energy Policy* 38 (8): 4528–39.

Basher, S. A., A. A. Haug, and P. Sadorsky. 2016. "The Impact of Oil Shocks on Exchange Rates: A Markov-Switching Approach." *Energy Economics* 54: 11–23.

Bayramov, A. 2018. "Review: Dubious Nexus between Natural Resources and Conflict." *Journal of Eurasian Studies* 9 (1): 72–81.

Bittlingmayer, G. 2005. "Oil and Stocks: Is It War Risk?" Working paper, University of Kansas.

Bjørnland, H. C., and J. Zhulanova. 2019. "The Shale Oil Boom and the US Economy: Spillovers and Time-Varying Effects." CAMA Working Paper 59/2019 (13 August). Available at https://ssrn.com/abstract=3436499.

Blanchard, O. J., and J. Gali. 2007. "The Macroeconomic Effects of Oil Shocks: Why Are the 2000s So Different from the 1970s?" NBER Working Paper 13368 (September).

Brochmann, M. 2012. "Signing River Treaties—Does It Improve River Cooperation?" *International Interactions* 38 (2): 141–63.

Caldara, D., M. Cavallo, and M. Iacoviello. 2019. "Oil Price Elasticities and Oil Price Fluctuations." *Journal of Monetary Economics* 103: 1–20.

Caselli, F. M., M. Morelli, and D. Rohner. 2015. "The Geography of Interstate Resource Wars." *Quarterly Journal of Economics* 130 (1): 267–315.

Colgan, J. 2014. "Oil Domestic Politics and International Conflict." *Energy Research & Social Science* 1 (March): 198–205.

Collier, P., and A. Hoeffler. 1998. "On Economic Causes of Civil War." *Oxford Economic Papers* 50 (4): 563–73.

Cramer, C. 2002. "Homo Economicus Goes to War: Methodological Individualism, Rational Choice, and the Political Economy of War." *World Development* 30 (11): 1845–64.

Gleditsch, N., and O. Theisen. 2010. "Resources, the Environment, and Conflict." In *The Routledge Handbook of Security Studies*, edited by C. Myriam and B. Thierry, 221–31. New York: Routledge.

Gogineni, S. 2010. "Oil and the Stock Market: An Industry Level Analysis." *Financial Review* 45 (4): 995–1010.

Inklaar, R., H. de Jong, J. Bolt, and J. van Zanden. 2018. "Rebasing 'Maddison': New Income Comparisons and the Shape of Long-Run Economic Development." Maddison Project Working Paper 10 (January).

Jordà, O., M. Schularick, and A. M. Taylor. 2017. "Macrofinancial History and the New Business Cycle Facts." *NBER Macroeconomics Annual* 31 (2016): 213–63.

Kang, W., R. A. Ratti, and J. Vespignani. 2017. "Global Commodity Prices and Global Stock Volatility Shocks: Effects across Countries." CAMA Working Paper 36/2017 (5 May). Available at https://ssrn.com/abstract=2963431.

Kilian, L. 2008. "The Economic Effects of Energy Price Shocks." *Journal of Economic Literature* 46 (4): 871–909.

Kilian, L. 2009. "Not All Oil Shocks Are Alike: Disentangling Demand and Supply Shocks in the Crude Oil Market." *American Economic Review* 99 (3): 1053–69.

Kilian, L. 2017. "The Impact of the Fracking Boom on Arab Oil Producers." *Energy Journal* 38 (6): 137–60.

Kilian, L., and C. Park. 2009. "The Impact of Oil Price Shocks on the US Stock Market." *International Economic Review* 50 (4): 1267–87.

Koubi, V., G. Spilker, T. Böhmelt, and T. Bernauer. 2014. "Do Natural Resources Matter for Interstate and Intrastate Armed Conflict?" *Journal of Peace Research* 51 (2): 227–43.

Krugman, P. 1983. "Oil and the Dollar." In *Economic Interdependence and Flexible Exchange Rates*, edited by J. S. Bhandari and B. H. Putnam, 179–90. Cambridge, MA: MIT Press.

Lizardo, R. A., and A. V. Mollick. 2010. "Oil Price Fluctuations and US Dollar Exchange Rates." *Energy Economics* 32 (2): 399–408.

Mohaddes, K., and M. H. Pesaran. 2016. "Country-Specific Oil Supply Shocks and the Global Economy: A Counterfactual Analysis." *Energy Economics* 59 (September): 382–99.

Mound, F. 2019. "Why We Go to War." *London Review of Books* 41 (11): 11–14.

Oladosu, G. A., P. N. Leiby, D. C. Bowman, R. Uría-Martínez, and M. M. Johnson. 2018. "Impacts of Oil Price Shocks on the United States Economy: A Meta-Analysis of the Oil Price Elasticity of GDP for Net Oil-Importing Economies." *Energy Policy* 115 (April): 523–44.

Rausser, G., and M. Stuermer. 2014. "Collusion in the Copper Commodity Market: A Long-Run Perspective." Working paper (December).

Reboredo, J. C., and A. Ugolini. 2016. "Quantile Dependence of Oil Price Movements and Stock Returns." *Energy Economics* 54 (February): 33–49.

Smyth, R., and P. K. Narayan. 2018. "What Do We Know about Oil Prices and Stock Returns?" *International Review of Financial Analysis* 57 (May): 148–56.

Stuermer, M. 2018. "150 Years of Boom and Bust: What Drives Mineral Commodity Prices?" *Macroeconomic Dynamics* 22 (3): 702–17.

Wang, Y., C. Wu, and L. Yang. 2013. "Oil Price Shocks and Stock Market Activities: Evidence from Oil-Importing and Oil-Exporting Countries." *Journal of Comparative Economics* 41 (4): 1220–39.

Chapter 4: International Economic Cooperation

> "Capitalism" is a dirty word for many intellectuals, but there are a number of studies showing that open economies and free trade are negatively correlated with genocide and war.
>
> —*Steven Pinker*

Chapters 2 and 3 dealt with geopolitical risks that could lead to significant setbacks in the world economy and financial markets. From wars to terror attacks to commodity price shocks, we have looked at the three horsemen of the geopolitical apocalypse. To lift our readers up from the depths of their depression, I focus in this chapter on the geopolitical events and developments that lead to increased growth and are beneficial for the global economy and financial markets. I will examine the international institutions, often criticized, that promote economic cooperation and liberalization. Then, I will consider the benefits and drawbacks of globalization and free trade and discuss economic diplomacy as a means to attract foreign investment.

Building a New World Order

In order to follow the coming discussions, you need to understand the origin of today's economic world order and why it was set up the way it was. This journey takes us to a warship in the Atlantic Ocean, a small town in New Hampshire in the United States, and the capital of Uruguay.

Atlantic Charter. In August 1941, World War II was in full swing. Nazi Germany occupied most of Europe and had recently launched its surprise attack on the Soviet Union. In a month's time, Adolph Hitler, Chancellor of the German Reich, would set in motion his march on Moscow. Nazi Germany seemed unstoppable and destined to win the war in Europe. The United States had not yet entered the war; the attack on Pearl Harbor was still four months away.

It was in this environment that the British battleship HMS Prince of Wales and the US heavy cruiser USS Augusta met in Placentia Bay, Newfoundland, Canada. The two ships had some prominent passengers aboard: One carried Winston Churchill, the Prime Minister of Britain;

the other carried Franklin Delano Roosevelt, the President of the United States. And what did they discuss? How to structure the world once they won the war.

The result of these meetings was the Atlantic Charter, published in December 1941. It formally confirmed that the United States would help the United Kingdom during the war, and it focused on eight principal points to guide the reconstruction after the war ended. Four of these points dealt with military and territorial issues, but four were decidedly economic in nature (O'Sullivan 2008):

- Trade barriers were to be lowered.

- There was to be global economic cooperation and advancement of social welfare.

- The participants would work for a world free of want and fear.

- The participants would work for freedom of the seas.

Bretton Woods. The principles of the Atlantic Charter became the guidelines that the participants of the meetings in Bretton Woods, New Hampshire, would use to create the new economic world order in 1944. During the Bretton Woods negotiations—which were led by some of the world's brightest economic minds, including John Maynard Keynes—it was clear that the mistakes made in the aftermath of World War I and the Great Depression needed to be avoided to prevent another global war.

The famous chronicler of the Great Depression, Charles Kindleberger, showed how four different economic disasters combined to turn the stock market crash of 1929 into the worst economic decline in modern history and provide fertile ground for populists of all sides (see Kindleberger 2013):

- First came the global economic depression, triggered by a stock market collapse that led to a severe decline in investments and consumption.

- Then, politicians reacted to this depression with increasingly protective measures and, through tariffs and quotas, closed their markets to international trade. This process triggered a collapse of global trade that reinforced the depression.

- The depression led to a run on cash and other safe assets, but because most countries were on the gold standard, their central banks could stem the outflow of gold from their vaults only by dramatically *increasing* interest rates. This move worsened the economic depression and led to an even bigger run on specie. Eventually, the global monetary system collapsed and many countries had to suspend the gold standard, creating severe inflation.

- Finally, the collapse of the global monetary system made it impossible for central banks to act as lenders of last resort, so lending activity came to a standstill.

This historical background clarifies why the current economic world order is set up the way it is. At Bretton Woods, it became clear that the United States would have to be the world's economic leader and that the US dollar had to replace the British pound as the world's reserve currency. These realities were simply a reflection of the fact that the United States not only had the biggest economy in the world (and had for several decades by that time), but it also was the only country in the world with an intact physical and financial infrastructure. Unlike the other belligerents of World War II, the United States was not suffering from crippling war debt and thus had sufficient funds to pay for the reconstruction effort.

Hence, the Bretton Woods agreement created a monetary system that set fixed exchange rates of other currencies versus the US dollar. Although the exchange rates were designed to be fixed, a periodic adjustment would be possible if economic imbalances increased. The dollar itself would still be backed by gold, thus providing an indirect gold standard for the global currency markets. The price of an ounce of gold was fixed in US dollars at $35.

The Bretton Woods system of currencies remained in place until 15 August 1971, when the United States had to abandon the convertibility of the dollar into gold. Since then, practically all currencies in the world have been fiat currencies, backed only by the faith and credit of the issuing governments and their ability to tax their citizens. Furthermore, the system of fixed exchange rates has been gradually abolished in favor of floating exchange rates, which automatically serve as a corrective mechanism when economic imbalances increase between countries.

The two major economic institutions that came out of the Bretton Woods agreement and remain prominent today are the International Bank for Reconstruction and Development (now called the World Bank) and the International Monetary Fund (IMF). The World Bank was originally tasked with providing financing for the reconstruction of Europe after the war, but it soon became clear that its funds were insufficient. The United States thus shouldered the cost of reconstruction in Europe directly through the Marshall Plan while the World Bank focused then, and does so to this day, on developmental aid and financial aid to build infrastructure (both physical and financial) in developing countries.

The IMF was intended to provide loans to countries in distress and act as lender of last resort, and it continues to do so. It is an organization owned by its member states. In 1945, the IMF started with 29 member states, but as of 2019, it had 189 members. Members have to pay fees (so-called quotas) that are proportional to the size of the country's economy and the importance of its currency in the global financial system. Quotas also determine voting rights in the IMF. As of late 2019, the 14th review of the quota system is still in force, but a 15th review will be concluded soon and implemented in coming years. Under the 14th review, the United States has the biggest quota, 17.4%, and total voting rights of 16.5%. China has a quota of just 6.4% and only 6.1% of voting rights.

Overall, the quotas are typically criticized as being biased in favor of the advanced economies, with developed countries, together, having a quota of 57.6%. Developing economies in Asia have a quota of only 16.0%, Africa of 4.4%, and Latin America of 7.9% (IMF 2014). Furthermore, some changes in the IMF require a supermajority of 85% of votes, which effectively grants the United States a veto right. This dominance by the developed countries contributed to the establishment in 2016 of the Asian Infrastructure Investment Bank (AIIB), an institution that we will review in chapter 6 when we examine the increasing economic competition between the United States and China.

World Trade Organization. I describe the work of the IMF and the criticism of it in the next section, but first, I want to quickly review the third global institution that shapes the global economy today—the World Trade Organization (WTO). The Bretton Woods agreement did not create an institution to promote free trade. Originally, the plans were to create the International Trade Organization, but these plans quickly faltered in the face of domestic policy pressures in various countries. Instead, on 30 October 1947, 23 countries signed the General Agreement on Tariffs and Trade (GATT), which sought to reduce 45,000 tariffs affecting about one-fifth of global trade.

With the GATT not being a formal institution (rather, an international treaty), trade agreements progressed under it in consecutive rounds of negotiations. Originally, the GATT rounds ignored the contentious issues of tariffs on agriculture and textiles as well as services, but as globalization progressed, the need for a wider trade agreement became evident. In 1986, the trade negotiations in Montevideo, the capital of Uruguay, began. This Uruguay Round eventually led to the creation of the WTO on 1 January 1995.

The WTO is based on two principles—national treatment and nondiscrimination. *National treatment* means that all foreign goods must be treated the same way as domestic goods in each country. *Nondiscrimination* is embodied by the principle of most-favored-nation (MFN), which states that all members of the WTO must treat each other as they do their most favored trading partner. This principle ensures that a country cannot favor one trading partner over others or favor some goods and services over others. In practice, the WTO is criticized for allowing multiple violations of these basic principles, and we will look at this criticism in more detail when I discuss the impact of global trade and free trade agreements.

Unlike the World Bank and the IMF, the WTO has judicial powers over trade disputes. Member countries can file suits at the WTO for perceived violations of trade agreements and WTO standards. Moreover, the WTO can allow retaliatory tariffs if it finds existing practices to be in violation of its rules. For example, on 2 October 2019, the WTO ruled that the government subsidies given to Airbus by various European countries violated its rules, so it allowed the United States to impose $7.5 billion in retaliatory tariffs. On 18 October 2019, the United States imposed those tariffs on European imports ranging from a 10% tariff on aircraft to a 25% tariff on Scotch whisky, French and Italian cheeses, and hundreds of other agricultural products.

The IMF: Benefits and Criticism

In all likelihood, the IMF is the most prominent and the most powerful global economic institution today. The IMF has unfailingly provided loans to governments in distress throughout most of the postwar period. Until the 1990s, however, IMF intervention was always needed in response to failed *domestic* policies. Thus, loans provided by the IMF come with requirements for political and market reform, a prerogative known as "IMF conditionality."

This IMF conditionality is what has made the IMF probably the world's most hated organization. The requirements in order for the IMF to provide loans can range from simple adjustments, such as the devaluation of a currency, to structural changes, such as a liberalization of local labor markets or improved governance to fight corruption. These interventions in domestic policies frequently create resentment against the IMF and draw criticism.

For example, in 1997, the "Four Asian Tigers" (the high-growth economies of Hong Kong SAR, Singapore, South Korea, and Taiwan) ran out of foreign currency reserves after the US dollar started to strengthen against their domestic currencies. Back then, many Asian countries controlled their exchange rates versus the US dollar in narrow bands. In the years before the Asian debt crisis of 1997, the US dollar tended to steadily depreciate against those currencies. This development attracted foreign investments from the United States into these Asian countries and motivated local banks to lend in dollars. When the dollar reversed course, the Asian central banks needed to sell dollars to stabilize their currencies against the greenback. Unfortunately, they quickly ran out of foreign reserves, and the local banks fell into distress as nonperforming loans soared.

The resulting crisis in 1997 may be called the first modern financial crisis caused by the private sector rather than governments. The IMF had to support a range of Asian countries from South Korea to Indonesia with a total of $115 billion in loans. In return, the IMF demanded reforms in the local financial sectors. These reforms were widely criticized as counterproductive and based on a Western template that did not fit local economic circumstances (Bayne 2017). In response to this IMF intervention, most Asian countries started to accumulate vast foreign currency reserves to avoid calling on the fund again.

In the 21st century, it became apparent that in a globalized world, the IMF does not have sufficient funds to fight a major crisis. The Global Financial Crisis of 2008 (GFC) led to financing needs that dwarfed the means of the fund. Even though the fund's reserves have now been increased to $1 trillion, they are insufficient if a major developed economy gets into trouble. Even the small developed economy of Greece could be saved only by a joint effort of the IMF, the European Commission, and the European Central Bank. Never mind the concerted efforts of these three institutions to save Greece in 2011 and 2012, the imposed austerity measures were so severe that Greece suffered a deep depression that led to rioting in the streets, a near-default of the country, and its exit from the eurozone.

Are the structural reforms imposed by the IMF really as harmful as its critics claim? Based on a comprehensive dataset of emerging economies, the IMF recently investigated the impact of structural reforms in six areas (IMF 2019). **Exhibit 1** shows the average impact a liberalization of the domestic financial system and the local product market have on GDP growth.

A liberalization of the domestic banking and financial system, like the one introduced in Egypt in 1992, opens the local market to international banks and lenders. These lenders are often global or regional banks based in developed markets, and critics claim that these lenders exploit local businesses and households by getting them into unsustainable debt.

Several studies have found, however, that the impact of a liberalization of the domestic financial market is uniformly positive (as shown in Exhibit 1) because these external lenders are often more sophisticated and can provide loans at lower prices and with less administrative burden than local lenders. The result is a more efficient allocation of capital than in the past that stimulates investment and employment and boosts growth. After six years, the GDP shown in Exhibit 1 is, on average, 2 percentage points (pps) higher than without financial liberalization.

Exhibit 1.   Effect of Domestic Structural Reforms on GDP Growth

A. Liberalization of Domestic Finance

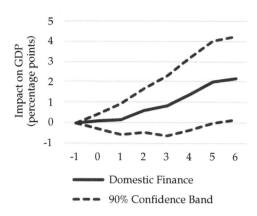

B. Liberalization of Domestic Utilities (or Telecoms)

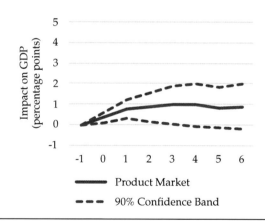

Source: IMF (2019).

A liberalization of local product markets is typically done in the form of the deregulation of the electricity or telecommunications markets, such as the one implemented in Latvia in 2001. This liberalization of crucial infrastructure leads, as Exhibit 1 shows, to lower prices and, typically, an increase in productivity and investments. Again, the impact of such reforms is positive for growth. After three years, the impact on GDP is an increase by 1 percentage point, although the effect lessens after that.

Other structural reforms that the IMF typically implements, if needed, are reforms of external debt financing and international trade. As the recent increase in trade tensions between the United States and other countries has shown, trade liberalization is often perceived as a threat to domestic workers (read: voters) who might work in uncompetitive industries that are bound to decline if foreign competitors are allowed to enter the market.

Exhibit 2 shows that a liberalization of external finance—for example, lifting capital controls or restrictions on foreign direct investment (FDI)—boosts GDP by about 1.25 pps after six years. The main pathway for this growth benefit is through increased labor productivity as modern production methods are implemented by foreign investors.

Exhibit 2. Effect of External Structural Reforms on GDP Growth

A. Liberalization of External Finance

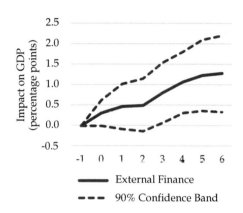

B. Liberalization of International Trade

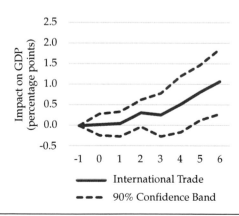

Source: IMF (2019).

Trade liberalization through the reduction of tariffs and import quotas also leads to a significant increase in labor productivity and a boost for GDP of about 1 percentage point after six years (IMF 2019).

The effects of the liberalization of external finances and of international trade have been tested time and again on a large number of countries. Almost unanimously, the consensus is that these two measures lead to stronger economic growth (see Furceri, Loungani, and Ostry 2019 for financial liberalization; see Ahn, Dabla-Norris, Duval, Hu, and Njie 2019 for a recent discussion of the benefits of international trade).

However, the impact of the structural reforms discussed here develops slowly. As Exhibits 1 and 2 show, the impact on economic growth starts to materialize only about three to six years after the reforms have been made. In the short term, the adjustment process, if not managed carefully, can be sudden and painful. If such structural reforms are implemented in an election year, the incumbent government tends to lose, on average, about 3% of the vote share, reducing its reelection probability by about 17 pps. Reforms enacted in an off-election year, however, have little to no impact on an election outcome.

Similarly, if the reforms are enacted when the local economy is already in distress, the incumbent government faces a reduction of about 6% of its vote share during the next election and almost certainly the loss of power (IMF 2019). The rule for politicians is clear: Once elected, the government should enact structural reforms quickly and decisively, in the hope that by the time the next election comes along, the positive effects have kicked in.

The substantial political risks of structural reforms are also a main reason local politicians criticize IMF structural reforms imposed on them and why local news outlets are quick to side with these politicians. Structural reforms, especially when imposed by an outside bureaucracy such as the IMF, provide fodder for populist political messages. Yet, the empirical evidence shows that a country that enacts the four structural reforms discussed in this section—liberalization of domestic finance, liberalization of domestic utilities (telecoms), liberalization of external finance, and liberalization of international trade—can boost its GDP by 5.3 pps after six years. Together with structural reforms in governance (e.g., reduction of corruption) and a liberalization of the labor market, the GDP boost can reach 7 pps after six years, or more than 1 pp of additional growth per year (IMF 2019).

Free Trade and the WTO

The IMF is typically called upon only in times of crisis, but the WTO influences the global economy on a daily basis. In its prior incarnation as GATT, it was already remarkably successful in reducing barriers to international trade over time. The push for a reduction in international trade barriers accelerated in the 1990s with the Uruguay Round and the formation of the WTO. **Exhibit 3** shows that the average tariff on imported goods declined from 8.6% in 1994, the year before the WTO was formed, to 2.6% in 2017. In the United States, average tariffs have declined from 3.8% to 1.7% and in the European Union from 6.3% to 1.8%. The decline in tariff barriers was even more pronounced in emerging markets. China had an average import tariff on goods of 32% in 1991. With the membership of China in the WTO in 2001, tariffs decreased rapidly and are now at 3.8%, on average, as shown in **Exhibit 4**.

The WTO, however, is concerned not only with tariffs; many other trade barriers may have been implemented. For example, import quotas on specific

Exhibit 3.   Average Tariffs on All Imported Goods: Developed Countries, 1988–2017

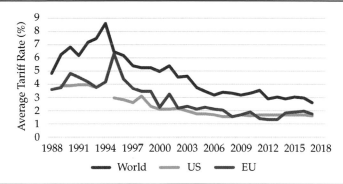

Source: World Bank.

Exhibit 4.   Average Tariffs on All Imported Goods: BRIC Countries, 1988–2017

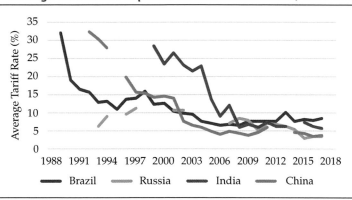

Note: "BRIC" stands for Brazil, Russia, India, and China.
Source: World Bank.

97

goods or from specific countries and such barriers as administrative hurdles and domestic regulations (e.g., for environmental protection or to comply with health and safety standards) increase the costs of trade. In fact, these nontariff trade barriers are often hard to address because to prove that these measures are illegal barriers to trade is difficult.

A classic example of nontariff trade barriers is some of the barriers on agricultural products. A free trade agreement between the United States and the European Union remains elusive because the European Union wants to prevent meat that comes from animals fed growth hormones—a common practice in the United States and in many global meat-producing countries, such as Brazil and Argentina—from entering the EU market. European Union producers are not allowed to feed their animals growth hormones. The European Union argues that hormone-fed meat is a health risk, and it is thus prohibited across the entire EU market. Meanwhile, international suppliers argue that no scientific consensus supports the idea that hormone-fed meat poses a health risk.

Free Trade Agreements. Ironically, while the WTO normally is adamant about reducing trade barriers, it allows trade barriers to rise in one area—namely, free trade agreements (FTAs). An FTA between two or more countries reduces trade barriers between the members of the FTA at the cost of nonmembers. For example, while countries within the European Union can trade goods and services freely without any tariffs, goods imported from outside the European Union are subject to (sometimes substantial) tariffs. This practice is in contradiction to the most-favored-nation rules of the WTO, but the WTO has taken the stance that it allows FTAs as long as the increase in trade between member states outweighs the reduction in trade with outsiders. Another reason the WTO is in favor of FTAs is simply that these pacts can act as a laboratory to experiment with new ideas and rules that can later be adopted on a global level.

Because FTAs are quick to negotiate and allow for solutions that are tailored to the various objectives of trade partners, they have become the most prevalent means of reducing trade barriers around the globe. Every FTA needs to be approved by the WTO, and each WTO member state must notify the WTO if it enters into a new FTA. In 1995, the founding year of the WTO, 49 FTAs were in force with 57 participants. In 2019, 302 FTAs were in force with 481 participants, as shown in **Exhibit 5**.

This massive growth of FTAs around the world has led to some confusion about the differences among them. In Europe, in particular, many countries are part of several FTAs with various levels of integration:

Exhibit 5.   Number of Free Trade Agreements, 1950–2020

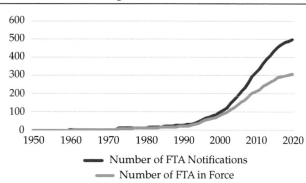

Source: World Trade Organization.

- *Partial trade agreements* allow free trade between two or more nations in specific goods or services but not in others.

- If the partial trade agreement is expanded to most or all goods and services, it becomes a classic *free trade agreement*. In Europe, the European Free Trade Association (EFTA) is one such example. The EFTA includes not only the members of the European Union but also Norway, Iceland, Switzerland, and Liechtenstein.

- If the free trade agreement is expanded to include a common external tariff for imported goods, it becomes a *customs union*. In Europe, the European Union is in a customs union with Turkey that allows most goods and services (with the exception of agricultural products, services, and public procurements) to move freely within the customs union and ensures a common tariff on imports.

- A *common market* consists of a customs union plus the free movement of capital and labor within it. The European Union, with its four freedoms (free movement of goods, services, capital, and people) is a classic example of such a common market.

- Finally, if the members of the common market also introduce a common currency and harmonized economic policies, we get to an *economic union*. In Europe, the members of the eurozone are part of an economic union.

If integration increases even further, we quickly enter the realm where states become part of a federal union, or a political union of states, with an overarching legal setup. The United States, Germany, and Switzerland are classic examples of such federal nations. Thus, a business in Germany is simultaneously the member of a federal republic (Germany), an economic union (the eurozone), a common market (the European Union), a customs union (European Union and Turkey), and several free trade zones (e.g., EFTA, European Union–Japan, European Union–Canada). Depending on its business area, it might also be a member of several partial free trade zones.

Each of these agreements has its own rules and regulations, although in the case of Europe, they tend to be harmonized. If you think this situation is confusing, think of the people who had to disentangle this complex network of trade agreements after the United Kingdom decided to leave the European Union.

Global Trade Growth. Despite this increasing complexity, global trade has grown dramatically since the end of World War II, as shown in **Exhibit 6**. As explained at the beginning of this chapter, the aim of the new world order of the Bretton Woods institutions and GATT was to avoid the mistakes made during the Great Depression. In reaction to the economic downturn that started in 1929, the United States tried to protect its economy with the infamous Smoot–Hawley Tariff Act of 1930. This law dramatically increased import tariffs on all kinds of goods and led to retaliation by US trade partners. The effect was that between 1929 and 1939, the onset of World War II, trade as a share of GDP almost halved—from 5% to 3.3% in the United States and from 10.8% to 5.8% globally. This decline in global trade led to a breakdown of global demand and turned a regular depression, which should have been short-lived, into the biggest economic decline since the Industrial Revolution.

Exhibit 6.   Global Trade as Share of GDP, 1834–2014

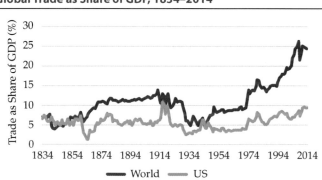

Source: CEPII (Centre d'Études Prospectives et d'Informations) database.

That this has not happened since and, instead, world trade as a share of global GDP had increased to 24% by 2014 is a major accomplishment of GATT and the WTO. These institutions have created tremendous prosperity around the world, especially in developing economies that opened themselves up to global trade.

Exhibit 7 shows trade as a share of national GDP for the BRIC countries (Brazil, Russia, India, and China), the fastest growing emerging economies. With the fall of the Soviet Union, Russia opened itself up to international trade (mostly of oil and gas), which helped that country overcome the giant slump in its economy after the breakdown of communism. Arguably the biggest success story of all the BRIC group is China. With Deng Xiaoping's strategy to gradually open the economy to the world, the country managed not only to increase economic growth dramatically but also to lift a large part of the population out of poverty. The World Bank has estimated that between 1981 and 2015, China managed to lift more than 850 million people out of extreme poverty (defined as living on less than $1.90 in 2011 prices per day) and reduced its extreme poverty rate from 88% to 0.7%. That achievement is astonishing. In fact, free trade has been *the* most effective tool to lift people out of poverty globally. In the 1960s, more than half the world's population lived in extreme poverty (a total of more than 2 billion people). By 2015, fewer than 1 in 10 people around the world, or about 734 million people, remained in extreme poverty.

With more people coming out of poverty, such countries as China can rely less on international trade to run their economy and can focus more on domestic consumption. For example, trade as a share of Chinese GDP has declined from a high of 43% in 2007 to 22% in 2014 simply because the

Exhibit 7. Trade as Share of GDP in BRIC Countries, 1944–2014

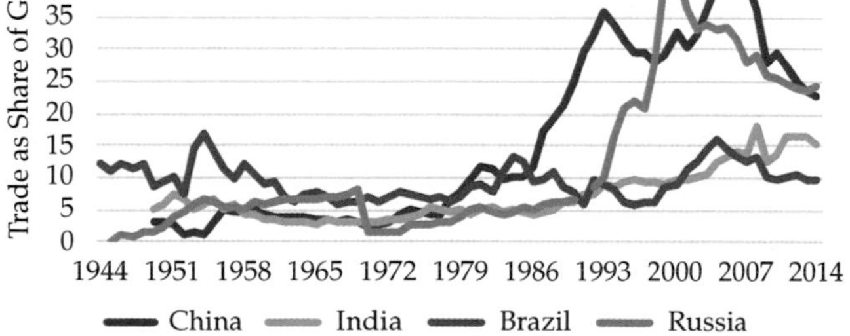

Source: CEPII database.

Chinese are now wealthy enough to form a massive domestic consumer base that allows Chinese companies to produce goods and services for the home market.

But *how* does free trade lead to a decline in poverty? The mechanisms through which free trade affects the economy have been widely studied, and three major pathways have been identified:

- Helpman and Krugman (1985) emphasized that free trade opens an economy up to international competition. This process has some negative effects at first because it lowers the profit margins of domestic businesses. In reaction to these lower profit margins, however, businesses are forced to innovate or look for economies of scale in order to lower their costs. The result is higher productivity of domestic businesses and stronger economic growth.

- Aghion, Bloom, Blundell, Griffith, and Howitt (2005) showed that trade liberalization leads to the import of new technologies and innovations, confirming the thesis that in an open economy, businesses have to innovate or die.

- Finally, trade liberalization broadens the variety of input goods for domestic producers and makes them available at lower prices, so they can produce better products at lower prices themselves (Ahn et al. 2019).

Ahn et al. (2019) showed that trade liberalization leads to a significant increase in productivity. They also showed that the increase in productivity depends on the type of business, how much of its inputs are sourced internationally, and whether the business is owned domestically or by a foreign company. In general, foreign-owned businesses are quicker to benefit from trade liberalization, which indicates that trade liberalization and FDI may mutually reinforce themselves to boost growth.

On average, Ahn et al. (2019) found that if input tariffs drop by 0.5% globally—about the amount witnessed between 1997 and 2007—productivity is boosted by about 1 pp per year. And because a 1 pp increase in productivity filters through to a 1 pp increase in GDP growth, even a small reduction in tariffs can lead to significant growth. Of course, the effect has been larger for developing economies because they could lower tariff barriers much more than industrial countries could during the 1990s and early 2000s, and their resulting growth boost was even bigger. No wonder emerging markets accounted for the majority of global growth during the great push for free trade in the 1990s and 2000s, as shown in **Exhibit 8**.

Exhibit 8. Share of Global GDP Growth, 1980–2020

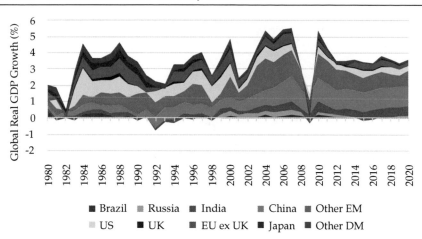

Note: EM stands for emerging market; DM stands for developed market.
Source: IMF.

Is More to Be Gained from Further Trade Liberalization? Although emerging markets were the main beneficiaries of the trade liberalization during the last few decades, developed economies still have something to gain from continued liberalization. Ahn et al. (2019) estimated that abolishing existing tariff barriers could substantially boost the productivity of every advanced economy. **Exhibit 9** shows that the estimated productivity gains from further trade liberalization range from 0.2 pp in Japan to more than 1 pp in the Netherlands.

Two developed countries not shown in Exhibit 9 have even more to gain from further trade liberalization: South Korea could expect productivity growth above 4 pps and Ireland above 7 pps. These two countries stand to benefit so much more than those in Exhibit 9 from trade liberalization because of the structure of their economies. South Korea has higher tariffs than most developed countries and thus has more to gain from further trade liberalization. Meanwhile, Ireland could benefit from reduced tariffs on crucial inputs to its pharmaceutical and chemicals industries.

Although no studies are available about the impact of trade liberalization on stock market returns, we can perform a back-of-the-envelope calculation of its impact. The average potential productivity boost in the developed countries shown in Exhibit 9 is 0.5 pp. The implication is that GDP growth could be boosted by 0.5 pp if trade were completely liberalized. Note that this effect would not be a one-time hit but, rather, an increase in productivity and

Exhibit 9. Potential Gains in Productivity through Complete Trade Liberalization

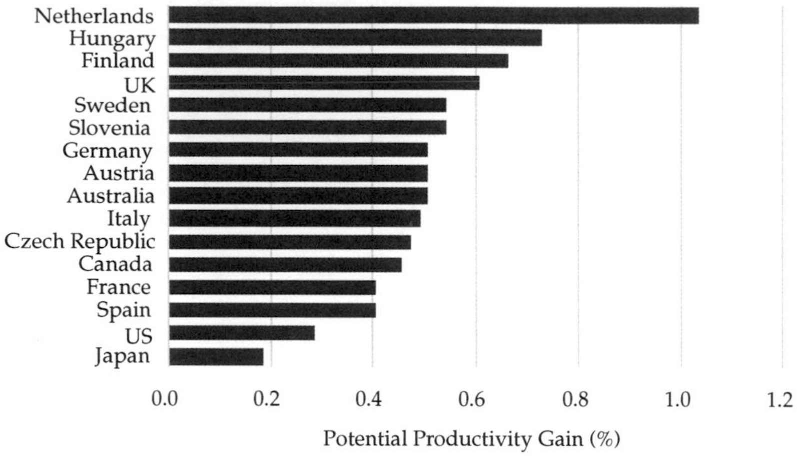

Source: Ahn et al. (2019).

GDP growth every year into eternity. Productivity growth would be permanently lifted by 0.5 pp because the removal of trade barriers would lead to increased flexibility for businesses to enter new markets with their products and services and would motivate businesses to move their production to countries and areas with lower productivity and lower wage costs. By investing in the low-productivity countries, companies can raise productivity in those countries. Meanwhile, businesses in the low-productivity countries can more easily acquire technologically advanced goods that increase their productivity. This pattern is the beneficial spiral of globalization in action: Globalization allows poor countries to increase their productivity and their wealth; businesses in rich countries can reduce costs by relying on global supply chains that allow cost reductions and sourcing of the best inputs from all over the world. This result, in turn, allows businesses in rich countries to keep research and development (R&D) expenses at constant levels or even increase them and focus on their comparative strengths, which then leads to productivity gains in the rich countries. The entire path of potential growth can be lifted by further trade liberalization.

Because global sales tend to grow in line with nominal GDP in the long run, a 0.5 pp increase in GDP growth would lead to a 0.5 pp boost to sales growth. Because globalization increases competition, we have to assume that profit margins will decline somewhat, but a reasonable assumption would still be that 0.5 pp higher sales growth could lead to about 0.25 pp–0.5 pp higher earnings growth. If valuations remain constant, such a boost to earnings growth should lead to a boost in equity market returns of 0.25 pp–0.5 pp per year. In terms of the discounted cash flow model that guides the discussions in this book, trade liberalization directly increases future cash flows of a company and thus increases the present value of such assets as stocks.

Criticism of Free Trade Agreements

Despite the benefits of free trade, criticism of recent practices in FTAs and the lack of benefits for developed economies is increasing. I discuss the impact of trade liberalization and globalization on inequality later in this chapter, but certain other developments may have reduced the beneficial impact of FTAs over time.

The original GATT rounds covered only trade in goods and ignored trade in services or questions about intellectual property (IP) simply because these issues were not relevant at the time. Today, we live in a knowledge and service economy. Thus, FTAs have become more complex; they cover trade in services and protection of IP as well as trade in goods. This increased complexity means that FTAs are increasingly targeted by corporations and lobbyists to ensure a beneficial outcome for special-interest groups—potentially at the cost of other groups.

Rodrik (2018) described three main areas of such rent-seeking behavior. First, trade-related aspects of IP rights (TRIPS) were first tackled in the Uruguay Round of trade negotiations and the inception of the WTO. Since then, the United States and other developed countries have pushed for stricter and more comprehensive TRIPS because IP is a more substantial part of their economies than in developing countries. Furthermore, developed countries typically have better legal expertise in these subjects than do developing countries and a more sophisticated legal system to enforce IP rights. Therefore, including TRIPS in an FTA effectively shifts costs onto developing countries and creates an additional benefit to advanced economies.

Furthermore, because the legal system in developing countries is often less sophisticated and the risk of expropriation of assets by the local government is higher, the advanced economies increasingly demand investor–state dispute settlements (ISDS) to be included in any agreement. These ISDS install local arbitration courts that are outside the country's regular legal system, so local governments can be sued by foreign investors and foreign investors only. These arbitration courts undermine the local legal system and allow a foreign investor to sue local governments for a virtually unlimited number of actions and inactions that may have led to a loss of profits for the foreign investor (Johnson, Sachs, and Sachs 2015). And to make things worse, no appeal of the rulings of these arbitration courts is possible. Arbitration courts

105

may make sense when politically unstable developing countries are involved in the FTA, but why would, for example, the United States insist on such arbitration courts in its proposed FTA with the European Union?

Additionally, modern FTAs increasingly include the requirement not only for free movement of goods and services but also for the free movement of capital. Although this freedom is a good idea in normal times, it can become a huge problem in a crisis when foreign investors might want to withdraw their capital as fast as possible. A "run on the country" can significantly worsen a financial crisis in an emerging market and may even be in conflict with demands by the IMF, which increasingly is in favor of imposing temporary capital controls in a crisis country to avoid the flight of capital.

Finally, the newest studies of the impact of FTAs on developed markets show that all this rent-seeking behavior by industries in developed countries may reduce the benefits of trade not only for developing countries but also for developed countries. Caliendo and Parro (2015) and Hakobyan and McLaren (2016) investigated the benefits of the old North American Free Trade Agreement (NAFTA)—not the new United States–Mexico–Canada Agreement (USMCA)—for the United States in terms of both growth and income distribution. These studies found that the overall welfare benefit for the United States was a mere 0.08 pp, half of which came through more beneficial terms of trade for the United States (i.e., at the cost of other trade partners, mostly Mexico). Although some US workers benefited from NAFTA, others suffered a significant drop in wages and employment. Blue collar workers without a high school degree in industries that were heavily affected by NAFTA (e.g., car manufacturing) suffered a decline in income of 17% relative to workers in industries that were unaffected by NAFTA. That these distributional effects can have a significant impact on the economy and markets through the political channel became clear with the 2016 election of Donald Trump as President of the United States, whose campaign focused on these disenfranchised US workers.

Economic Diplomacy as a Means to Foster Growth

The failures of FTAs in providing universal benefits have been an impetus for the revival of economic diplomacy since the GFC. "Economic diplomacy" is a rather elusive subject without a clear definition; if you read 10 papers on economic diplomacy, you will be left with at least 11 definitions of what it is and what it is not. My favorite definition was given by the Spanish Ministry of Foreign Affairs (2011) as "the use of the political influence held by states to promote their economic interests in international markets." I will stick with this definition in this discussion.

As Bayne and Woolcock (2017) described, economic diplomacy was historically criticized as government intervention in free markets that could cause substantial market failures. With the recognition of market failures through modern FTAs, however, and the opening up of former communist countries and China, where governments remain major players in the economy, economic diplomacy has experienced a revival. After all, if a Western business wants to enter into a joint venture with a Chinese or Russian state-owned enterprise, the Western business leaders must be able to deal with local government officials. The help of ambassadors, trade representatives, and other government representatives from the home country of the Western business is indispensable in these negotiations. Today, economic diplomacy involves not only private businesses, diplomats, and members of the State Department but also members of other government departments—from trade to energy to agriculture. In some cases, the government may even enlist the help of specialized nongovernmental organizations.

The studies of economic diplomacy show that it can be highly effective in boosting exports and attracting FDI. Moons and van Bergeijk (2016) reviewed the empirical evidence on the effectiveness of economic diplomacy and found a substantial positive effect of most economic diplomacy measures. The only exceptions seemed to be state visits, where no economic benefit could be measured.

Investment promotion agencies, which are government-sponsored entities that try to attract FDI, have proven effective. Studies have shown that a 10% increase in the budget for such agencies on average leads to a 7.5% increase in FDI flows (Moons and van Bergeijk 2016). Similarly, export promotion agencies are highly effective in boosting exports. A 10% increase in the budget of export promotion agencies leads to an average 0.6%–1.0% increase in exports, which may not sound like much, but look at it this way: For every $1 spent on export promotion, local exporters earn an additional $40 in revenues.

Finally, economic diplomacy has the advantage that it can be targeted to a specific country. Studies have shown that opening an additional embassy in a country leads to a 6%–10% increase in exports to that country. This boost in exports is driven by the personal relationships built by diplomats with foreign businesses; hence, consulates, which have smaller staffs and typically no local trade representative, have less impact than embassies. Honorary consulates have no impact on exports because they typically do not have the resources to foster trade and business relationships (Moons and van Bergeijk 2016).

Furthermore, the evidence indicates that opening embassies and intensifying diplomatic relationships have an effect on trade and exports between developed and developing countries and between developing countries.

These efforts do not seem to have an effect on the trade relationships between two developed countries, however, which intuitively makes sense because most developed countries already have close business and diplomatic relationships with each other.

International Tax Competition

Although economic diplomacy can provide substantial benefits for exports and trade, other aspects of geo-economics may produce negative effects. Is international tax competition (i.e., the lowering of corporate income taxes to attract foreign businesses) the "dark side" of geo-economics? The idea is that one country unilaterally lowers corporate tax rates to attract investments from neighboring countries. In a world of fully mobile capital with many small economies and no dominating economic power, such a "beggar-thy-neighbor" policy would lead to retaliation by other countries, which would lower their tax rates. This tit-for-tat would create a race to the bottom, where corporate tax rates would reach zero and then remain there forever (Devereux and Loretz 2013).

A quick look at the corporate tax rates in various countries, however, as shown in **Exhibit 10**, indicates that this race to the bottom does not really happen. Yes, corporate tax rates have declined since the 1980s, but they are still not at zero. Hoyt (1991) showed that this race to the bottom stops the moment one assumes that capital is not fully mobile and recognizes that the world has both large and small economies. According to this line of thought, each country has a certain amount of market power in setting taxes because businesses cannot simply pack up their factories and move to another country and/or they need facilities in their own country to gain access to its customers.

Exhibit 10. Top Corporate Income Tax Rates, 1981–2019

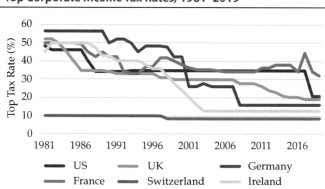

Source: OECD.

This market power allows countries to set corporate tax rates above zero. When competing with smaller economies, however, the small countries typically have less market power and thus will end up with a lower tax rate than larger countries (Wilson 1991).

Forslid (2005) showed that in a world where capital has become increasingly mobile, corporations tend to agglomerate around a common center (e.g., Silicon Valley for information technology, the City of London for European banking, Luxembourg and Ireland for other financial services). Countries can attract such global centers with the help of tax incentives, but a tipping point comes beyond which further agglomeration does not provide additional benefits and additional tax incentives fail to attract additional businesses. Once this tipping point is reached, further liberalization of trade and capital flows leads to dispersion because businesses can now cheaply build local business hubs. In this environment, the benefits of being closer to end customers outweigh the attraction of additional tax incentives.

That international tax competition leads to lower taxes is clearly visible in Exhibit 10. Also evident is that large economies (e.g., the United States, the United Kingdom, and Germany) have market power in setting their taxes and thus end up, on average, with a higher corporate tax rate than smaller countries. The ideal strategy for small open economies is to lower their tax rates as much as possible to attract as many businesses as possible and boost domestic growth.

Switzerland has had a top marginal corporate tax rate below 10% for several decades and is an example of how a low-tax strategy can lead to significant benefits for a country. Singapore is another example of how such a low-tax strategy can work. And Ireland is an example of the transformational power of lower corporate taxes. Historically, Ireland had corporate tax rates that were similar to its European neighbors, but in the late 1990s and early 2000s, the country drastically reduced its top corporate tax rate to 12.5%. This action attracted many businesses from across Europe and fueled Ireland's economic boom (and its housing market bubble) in the early 2000s.

Would the Irish strategy work for every country? Economic studies are ambivalent regarding the impact of international tax competition on economic growth. Covering the years 1970 to 1997, Lee and Gordon (2005) showed that a 10 percentage point decline in the top marginal corporate tax rate can boost economic growth by 1 pp–2 pps. Shevlin, Shivakumar, and Urcan (2019) calculated the effective tax rate paid in each country and used this effective tax rate to show that a 10 percentage point decline in the effective tax rate can increase GDP growth by 0.75 pp and employment by 0.25 pp.

Plenty of studies show no positive effect, however, of tax reductions on economic growth and, to the best of my knowledge, no study has looked at the impact of international tax competition directly on growth. All the studies have focused on tax reductions in isolation rather than in an international context.

In summary, international tax competition is clearly a legitimate activity, but the evidence that this strategy helps boost growth in the long run is effectively restricted to small open economies, such as Switzerland and Singapore.

Globalization—A Multifaceted Development

So far, this chapter has focused on the liberalization of trade and to a lesser extent on the liberalization of the movement of capital. But both free trade and free movement of capital are part of the much broader trend toward globalization. Gygli, Haelg, Potrafke, and Sturm (2019) recently revised the KOF Globalisation Index, which measures the extent of globalization for 203 countries and territories based on 43 variables in three dimensions. The *political dimension* measures globalization for each country on the basis of such indicators as international treaties signed, number of embassies, and participation in UN peacekeeping missions. *Social globalization* for each country is measured by looking at the number of tourists and foreign students, internet access, and press freedom—also, the number of IKEA stores and McDonald's restaurants. Finally, the third dimension of the KOF Globalisation Index is *economic globalization*, which is measured by international trade in goods and services, FDI, tariffs, and taxes.

Exhibit 11 shows the level of economic globalization as measured by the KOF Globalisation Index for high-income, middle-income, and

Exhibit 11.   KOF Index: Level of Economic Globalization, 1986–2016

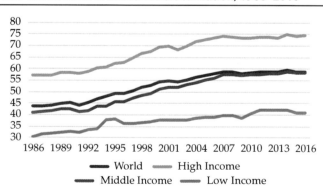

Source: Gygli et al. (2019).

low-income countries. The high-income countries have always been more globalized than lower income countries; it is the middle-income countries that have made more progress in globalization since the 1980s and are thus more likely to have reaped the benefits of increased globalization.

Gygli et al. (2019) also differentiated between *de facto* globalization and *de jure* globalization. De facto globalization is measured by actual international transactions (e.g., the actual trade in goods and services and the actual FDI and portfolio investments). De jure globalization is measured by the legal framework that fosters globalization.

Gygli et al. (2019) showed that it is not the actual trade and capital flows that drive globalization and economic growth but, rather, the country's regulatory framework. The critical factor in fostering growth in a country is the ease with which international trade and international investments can be conducted there. Actual trade flows are a reaction to this regulatory framework.

These authors thus emphasized that investors need to look at the development of de jure globalization in each of the three dimensions to assess the potential for future growth in each country. The sad news is that globalization in both trade and financial flows has stalled since the GFC, as shown in **Exhibit 12**. Financial globalization has even declined somewhat since the GFC. The stalled negotiations for the Transatlantic Trade and Investment Partnership (TTIP) FTA between the European Union and the United States, the renegotiated USMCA trade agreement, and the stalled Doha Round of the WTO for global trade negotiations are all examples of the lack of progress over the last decade. The proximate causes of this stalled progress most likely include increased skepticism by the public and politicians about the benefits of globalization, which is shown by more and more countries

Exhibit 12. KOF Index: Level of Economic (de jure) Globalization, 1986–2016

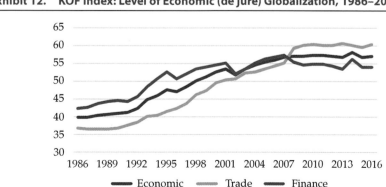

Source: Gygli et al. (2019).

111

electing populist and nationalist leaders, such as Donald Trump in the United States, Narendra Modi in India, and Jair Bolsonaro in Brazil.

These leaders were elected on platforms to protect their domestic economies from unwanted global competition and have acted on those promises with efforts to roll back the globalization process of the past several decades. Exhibit 12 shows that these efforts have so far not led to a major decline in globalization, but note that the data end in 2016 and hence do not include the US–China trade war, for example, or the announcement that the United States will not become a member of the Trans-Pacific Partnership (TPP).

For the time being, globalization seems to be taking a break. Countries remain largely locked into their existing international structures. With the efforts of some political leaders around the globe to unwind the integration of the global economy, however, certain countries and regions are arguably more at risk than others. A simple comparison of share of national GDP in international trade, as shown in **Exhibit 13**, provides guidance as to which countries have the most to lose. The East European countries are the most exposed to international trade. The vast majority of their trade, however, is with other member states of the European Union, and so far, little evidence shows that the European Union will unwind its commitment to free trade. After all, free trade is a big part of its raison d'être. In contrast to the East European countries, both South Korea and Germany are extreme export-oriented economies, with large trade flows going to the United States and China. Hence, as

Exhibit 13. Trade as a Share of GDP, 2014

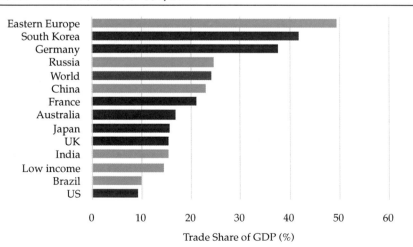

Note: Dark blue indicates developed markets; light blue indicates emerging markets.
Source: CEPII database.

the US–China trade war has already proven, a decline in demand from China and/or the United States can quickly jeopardize economic growth in these exporting countries. In comparison, the United States, thanks in no small part to its large domestic market, is much more isolated from international trade flows.

Globalization and Growth

The impact of globalization on economic growth has been studied intensively. Potrafke (2015) reviewed more than 100 studies based on the KOF Globalisation Index alone and found statistically significant effects of globalization on GDP growth. Gygli et al. (2019) tested the impact of changes in each of the three dimensions of the KOF Globalisation Index on GDP growth. As **Exhibit 14** shows, they found that a 10-point increase in the KOF Globalisation Index led, on average, to a 1.6 pp increase in GDP growth per year in the respective country.

Exhibit 14 shows that of the three dimensions of the KOF Globalisation Index, the most effective driver of growth has been social globalization. A 10-point increase in the social dimension of the index for a country led to a 1.7 percentage point increase in GDP growth; the impact of a 10-point increase in the political and economic dimensions was only about half that amount.

This result makes sense if we remember that social globalization is measured as the free movement of people, information, and culture. Thus, social globalization measures the flow of knowledge and inventions from one country to another. And because our modern economy is driven mostly by innovation and new technologies, the ability to attract the best people and gain

Exhibit 14. Growth Impact of a 10-Point Increase in the KOF Globalisation Index

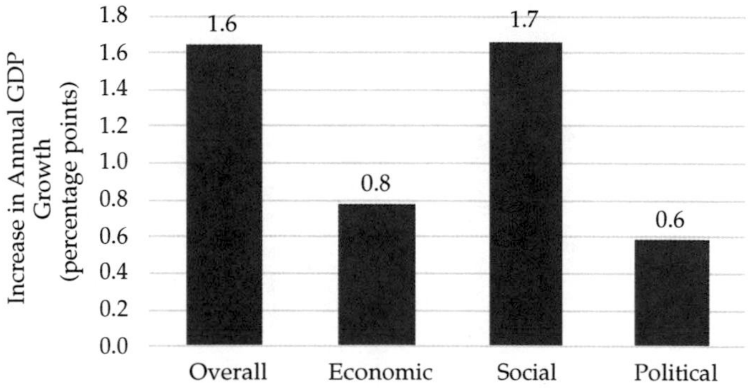

Source: Gygli et al. (2019).

access to the best ideas should be particularly good for economic growth. That the sum of social, economic, and political globalization was more than the effect of globalization overall is a reflection of interactions between variables that somewhat reduce the total impact of globalization on growth.

Even so, we should not ignore the beneficial impact of economic globalization. **Exhibit 15** shows the impact on annual GDP growth of a 10-point increase in the economic dimension of the KOF Globalisation Index as well as its trade and finance subindices. A 10-point increase in economic globalization led, on average, to a 0.8 percentage point increase in GDP per year; a 10-point increase in trade globalization led to a boost of economic growth of 0.5 pps.

Conversely, a decline of the globalization index by 10 points would probably have a substantial negative effect on economic growth. A 10-point decline in the economic globalization index in the United States would be like time travel back to the early 1990s before NAFTA was put in place. Such a reversion of previous progress would likely lead to a decline in US growth of about 0.8 pp per year (again, it would not be a one-time effect but a shift in the potential growth path in the future). In the case of the United Kingdom, its exit from the European Union without a deal would put the country's trade relations back to where they were before it joined the common market in the early 1970s. This effect would imply a decline in economic globalization of about 20 points and a large decline in economic growth potential.

Exhibit 15. Growth Impact of a 10-Point Increase in the KOF Globalisation Index: Economic Components

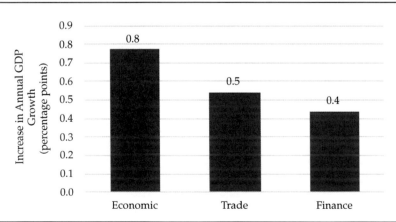

Source: Gygli et al. (2019).

Globalization and Inequality

Globalization can create enormous benefits for people around the world through higher economic growth and increased wealth generation. But the most important reason protectionist policies have become fashionable again in recent years and the reason globalization, at least in the economic dimension, has stalled is that globalization does not benefit all people equally.

From our introductory macroeconomics classes at university, we know from Ricardian trade theory that two countries that trade with each other are better off than if they did not trade with each other. The Heckscher–Ohlin theorem of international trade states, however, that two countries with different factor endowments (factors being capital, labor, and natural resources) will specialize in those goods and services where they have a relative comparative advantage in factor utilization. If, for example, Country A has a lot of capital and not a lot of labor, but Country B has a lot of labor but not a lot of capital, then the cost of capital will be lower in Country A than in Country B and the cost of labor will be lower in country B than in Country A. Hence, Country A will specialize in the production of goods that require a lot of capital but not a lot of labor (e.g., software) while Country B specializes in the production of goods that require a lot of labor but not a lot of capital (e.g., agricultural products). The losers in this world will be the workers in labor-intensive sectors in Country A and the workers in capital-intensive sectors in Country B.

Which is exactly what has happened in an increasingly globalized world. Emerging economies do not have a lot of capital, but they do have a lot of cheap labor. Developed countries have high labor costs but an abundance of capital. Hence, labor-intensive production has been outsourced by developed countries to countries such as China, India, and Mexico, and developed countries have specialized in the production of high-tech goods that require a lot of R&D and capital.

The losers in this game have been the blue-collar workers in labor-intensive industries in developed countries; the winners have been the owners of capital in developed countries. On a global scale, therefore, income inequality within both the developed and the emerging countries has increased, whereas income inequality on a global scale has declined.

Exhibit 16 shows the changing share of total income captured by the top 10% income earners across the globe, in some developed countries, and in some developing countries. The income share of the top 10% in the United States, the European Union, and Japan has increased gradually since the 1980s because the lower skilled workforce, which does not own capital,

Exhibit 16. Share of Total Household Income Captured by Top 10%, 1980–2015

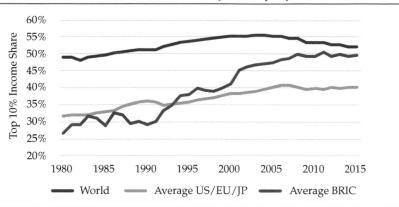

Source: World Inequality Database.

experienced a decline relative to the higher skilled and better paid employees, who not only have better paid jobs but also have capital to save and invest.

The trend toward inequality has been even more pronounced in developing countries, such as the BRICs—although the effect overall has been one of a rising tide that has lifted both the working class and the middle class. Still, unlike the working class in these countries, the members of the emerging middle class have not only earned higher incomes as a result of globalization but also have been increasingly able to invest their savings internationally, where it will earn higher rates of return.

Thus, the income of the middle class in developing countries has grown even faster than the income of the working class. This catch-up effect of the developing world is visible in the World line in Exhibit 16. As income rose faster in the developing world than in advanced economies around the turn of the century, the share of global income captured by the top 10% started to decline, indicating declining inequality between countries and increasing inequality within countries.

The Elephant in the Room. Probably the most famous depiction of these trends is the *elephant graph* of Lakner and Milanovic (2016), shown in **Exhibit 17**. Christoph Lakner and Branko Milanovic collected household income data from surveys in 162 countries and territories between 1988 and 2008, 72 of which had the full data from 1988 to 2008 while another 90 countries' data started in 1993. They transformed national income data into US dollars by using estimates of purchasing power parity (PPP) exchange rates for the year 2005. Then, they divided the global income distribution

Exhibit 17. The Original Elephant Graph: Real Income Growth by Global Income Percentile, 1988–2008

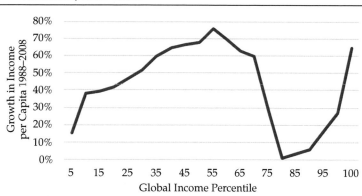

Source: Lakner and Milanovic (2016).

into 20 equal parts and tracked the growth in income in real terms for each percentile.[1]

Exhibit 17 shows the authors' original results. It is called the "elephant graph" because it outlines the shape of an elephant, with the poorest people in the world benefiting from modest income growth (the back of the elephant) and the people in the middle of the global income distribution experiencing far greater growth (the head of the elephant). The people in the 75th to 85th percentile of the global income distribution, on the other hand, seemed to experience almost no real income growth. And, although these people are generally well off in the global context, they tend to be the people in the bottom 20%–30% of the population in developed countries. In other words, these people are the blue-collar workers in labor-intensive industries in the United States and Western Europe who have been displaced by the rising middle class in China, India, and other emerging markets. As we move toward the highest incomes, we again see a dramatic increase in income growth (the trunk of the elephant).

The elephant graph achieved what few economic ideas ever do: It became a global megastar. Critics of globalization and rising inequality have pointed to this graph as evidence that globalization does not work and that the main beneficiaries of globalization are the global elites and the 1%. After all, in developed countries, those groups are the ones who seem to have disproportionately gained from globalization.

---

[1]Technically speaking, the groups are ventiles because the researchers divided global income distribution into 20 equal parts, but the word "ventiles" confuses absolutely everyone.

Critics ignore the fact that if you were in the 10th–70th percentile of the global income distribution—six-tenths of the world's population—you might be very happy.

Examining the Elephant. Remember that Lakner and Milanovic (2016) had data spanning only the time period 1988–2008 for 72 out of 162 countries. Some countries—the former Soviet Republics and the countries of Eastern Europe—opened up in the early 1990s and thus were not included in the original set of household surveys. In their original study, Lakner and Milanovic used data from 63 countries in 1988 and 115 countries in 2008, which is a statistical no-no because it compares two inconsistent samples with each other on the same metric.

Homi Kharas and Brini Seidel from the Brookings Institution looked at the data of Lakner and Milanovic (2016) more carefully and made several adjustments (see Kharas and Seidel 2018). First, they used a consistent sample of countries. The same 72 countries that were available in 1988 were also used in 2008. Second, they used updated PPP-adjusted currency exchange rates that were not available when Lakner and Milanovic made their study. And instead of using 2005 data, Kharas and Seidel used 2011 exchange rates—that is, exchange rates that reflected the dramatic shifts triggered by the GFC.

The result of these revisions is shown in **Exhibit 18**, together with the original elephant chart. Kharas and Seidel (2018) went one step further and looked at the larger sample of countries with household surveys starting in 1993 and tracked them until 2013. The resulting elephant graph from this 1993–2013 sample looks qualitatively similar to the revised elephant graph shown in Exhibit 18.

Exhibit 18. The Revised Elephant Graph

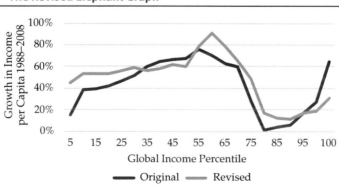

Sources: Lakner and Milanovic (2016); Kharas and Seidel (2018).

What we learn from this closer look at the elephant graph—other than that it matters tremendously to read the original research instead of just quoting a chart a journalist copied into an article—is the following:

- Just as the original elephant graph showed, the main beneficiaries of globalization have been the global middle class and, to a lesser extent, the poorest people.

- But the original elephant graph probably underestimated the gains made by the poorest people in the world. The poorest people in the world may have seen their incomes rise 10 pps more in real terms than originally estimated.

- The working class in the developed countries (i.e., the people in the 75th–85th percentile globally) were the ones who benefited the least from globalization, although the original elephant graph probably underestimated their income gains slightly. Nevertheless, an issue really exists in this regard that needs to be addressed by politicians.

- The global elite benefited much less from globalization than originally thought. The income gains of the top 1% of the global population were just about half of what the original elephant graph suggested. Nevertheless, clearly a strong disparity shows up between the top 1% and the working class in developed countries.

The elephant graph and the impact of globalization on inequality have become a major focus of both political scientists and economists in recent years. Twenty years ago, economists were predominantly concerned with the *average effect* of policy measures on a society. As the old saying goes: "An economist is a person who lies with his head in the oven and feet in the freezer and says that, on average, he feels fine." This benign neglect of the distributional impact of policy measures has allowed inequality to rise to a level where a political backlash has gained traction, one that may influence the future economic world order.

Toward a New World Order?

Rising inequality in both developed and developing nations is one reason the current world order that was established after World War II under US leadership is under strain. Other factors include the pullback of democracy in several countries around the world and the rise of nationalist leaders who are skeptical of the neoliberal economic model and the value of international trade. Until the GFC, the economic foundations of the existing world order had not been questioned because they created rising incomes—if not for all, at least for most people.

Since the GFC, economic growth has stagnated or been lackluster at best, so the tide has stopped lifting all boats. Now, the weaknesses of the existing system have become visible, and populist politicians across the globe are exploiting this rising skepticism with the old remedies of more socialist and/or more nationalist and isolationist agendas. These populist politicians emphasize agendas that put their own national interests above those of other nations. If enacted, such policies could undermine the gains of decades of trade liberalization and economic globalization.

To be fair, as we have seen in this chapter, the main beneficiaries of the existing world order have been a core group of liberal democracies in the West, most of which are located in North America and Western Europe. The United States, for example, has benefited tremendously from the current world order. The RAND Corporation estimates that, thanks to the existing world order, US GDP growth was boosted by about 2 pps per year for a number of years and about 300,000 jobs were created in the United States alone (Mazarr 2018).

Furthermore, economic prosperity and stability have meant that no major global wars have occurred for more than seven decades. And since the end of the Cold War, no country has challenged the military hegemony of the United States, which has potentially saved the country hundreds of billions in defense spending. What is the cost of all those benefits? According to the RAND Corporation, the direct costs of maintaining the current economic world order for the United States have been on the order of $15 billion per year (Mazarr 2018). It's been a bargain.

For countries outside the core of liberal (Western-style) democracies, however, the experience has been mixed. I have discussed the various ways in which FTAs are increasingly shifting against developing countries and in favor of businesses in developed countries. Add to that the fact that both China and Russia have become increasingly assertive on the global political stage, and you get a third reason the current world order is under stress. As **Exhibit 19** shows, the economic center of the world is moving away from the developed countries in the West and toward emerging markets in the East and southern hemisphere. By 2050, the United States is projected to be the only developed country of the seven largest economies in the world. Of course, by then, some of the now-developing countries may be considered developed, but that change is not guaranteed.

As their economic importance increases, emerging markets want to play a more important role in international institutions and challenge the existing rules. In the case of China and Russia, even some fundamental shared

Exhibit 19. **The Ten Biggest Economies of 2018 and Projected for 2050 (based on PPP exchange rates)**

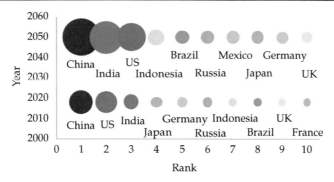

Notes: The size of the bubble indicates PPP-adjusted GDP in US dollars. Developed countries are marked in green, and emerging markets in blue.
Sources: World Bank and PwC (2017).

values—such as liberal democracy and individual freedom—are being questioned.

The relative economic decline of the United States and other developed countries will probably lead to a relative decline in their importance in the future international world order. The existing world order will have to adapt and become more multipolar than it has been.

And therein lies the dilemma for the United States. How can international institutions—the IMF, the WTO, the World Bank—become more flexible and provide more opportunities for countries like China, India, and Brazil to take on leadership roles? In what activities would the United States want to retain a leadership role? Most likely, the United States will have to prioritize and retain leadership in areas that are of vital interest to it but become more flexible in areas that it considers of less importance. The risk is that as new leaders (e.g., China) take charge in some areas, the old rules will be softened so much that the entire system will no longer hold together and will simply disintegrate.

This dilemma cannot be avoided by the United States taking a more assertive role on the global stage. Under the Trump administration, the United States has increasingly pursued an "America First" agenda that has alienated traditional allies. In some cases, like the many trade wars with both allies and competitors, the United States apparently has felt free to break rules it set itself when it helped create the current world order. This tactic is extremely dangerous because history shows that global or regional economic orders tend to suffer soon after the leading nations are allowed to flout their own rules without being punished. For example, the eurozone got into trouble in 2011 and 2012 not because of the excessive debt of Greece and Italy but because in the early 2000s, both France and Germany were allowed to break the Maastricht Treaty's deficit limits without being punished for it. This example gave smaller countries in the eurozone license to break existing deficit rules, and neither France nor Germany could criticize them because they had no moral standing to do so.

If the United States—as the leading power in the existing world order—continues to resist challenges by emerging markets while breaking its own rules whenever convenient, it will face increasing resistance from emerging markets. The example of the AIIB shows that China is willing to take on a regional leadership role in Asia outside of existing global institutions (such as the IMF) if it is unable to lead within the existing system. The existing world order, then, is at risk of breaking down under its current weaknesses.

As discussed, the current world order has created more wealth and been a more effective remedy for poverty than any other system in history. We do not know of any economic or political system that is better at generating wealth and reducing poverty than the current one, and dismantling it risks throwing the baby out with the bathwater. What the world needs to do is not revolutionize but improve the current system so that the benefits are shared more widely and more equally. Maybe the answer is to heed what Henry Kissinger (then, the 93-year-old grandmaster of realpolitik) said in 2016:

> To contribute to the establishment of a more stable world order, we need to foster a perception of a joint enterprise that is not just about buying into an American project . . . What we have not yet seen is a new vision of a future world order. (cited in Goldberg 2016)

Conclusions

In this chapter, I discussed the existing economic world order, which has been based on increasing liberalization and globalization of trade and finance. Despite the many criticisms launched against such institutions as the IMF, their policies tend to foster growth in the long run. In fact, a full set of liberalization measures in emerging markets can boost economic growth by 7 pps in six years, or by more than 1 pp per year, on average. Similarly, the efforts of the GATT and later the WTO to liberalize trade in goods and services have helped lift billions of people out of poverty and have boosted economic growth for both developed and developing countries.

But even though we live in a world of low trade barriers, significant potential still exists to boost economic growth through continued efforts to reduce trade frictions and barriers. This potential boost in growth is projected to be about 0.5 pp for most developed countries but could surpass 7 pps per year for Ireland.

Yet, the trend towards further trade liberalization and globalization has stalled since the GFC. The election of populist and domestically oriented politicians in several major countries has suspended efforts to liberalize trade and risks putting globalization into reverse. Given that increased globalization leads to a permanent increase in annual GDP growth for both developed and developing nations, we can expect that a reduction in globalization will reduce economic growth.

Globalization is under attack not only from populist politicians but also from left-leaning intellectuals and politicians, who point to rising inequality as a source of concern and a failure of globalization. Indeed, globalization has increased inequality within countries. Yet, it has also reduced inequality between countries. People in emerging markets have benefited from rapidly rising incomes, while working class people in developed countries have gained little to nothing. These distributional effects of globalization have been ignored by economists and politicians for too long, and today, we face a political backlash to globalization and economic cooperation that risks the loss of benefits we have gained, and could continue to gain, through globalization.

As this chapter has shown, global economic cooperation has been the best tool for generating economic growth and wealth that we have ever developed. Reversing globalization in the name of decreasing inequality would be a mistake. Instead, we need to find a way to reform economic cooperation and economic policy so that the benefits of globalization are distributed more equally than they are today.

Bibliography

Abiad, A., N. Oomes, and K. Ueda. 2008. "The Quality Effect: Does Financial Liberalization Improve the Allocation of Capital?" *Journal of Development Economics* 87 (2): 270–82.

Aghion, P., N. Bloom, R. Blundell, R. Griffith, and P. Howitt. 2005. "Competition and Innovation: An Inverted-U Relationship." *Quarterly Journal of Economics* 120 (2): 701–28.

Ahn, J., E. Dabla-Norris, R. Duval, B. Hu, and L. Njie. 2019. "Reassessing the Productivity Gains from Trade Liberalization." *Review of International Economics* 27 (1): 130–54.

Bayne, N. 2017. "Challenge and Response in the New Economic Diplomacy." In *The New Economic Diplomacy*, 4th ed., edited by N. Bayne and S. Woolcock, 15–37. New York: Routledge.

Bayne, N., and S. Woolcock. 2017. "What Is Economic Diplomacy?" In *The New Economic Diplomacy*, 4th ed., edited by N. Bayne and S. Woolcock, 1–14. New York: Routledge.

Caliendo, L., and F. Parro. 2015. "Estimates of the Trade and Welfare Effects of NAFTA." *Review of Economic Studies* 82 (1): 1–44.

Devereux, M. P., and S. Loretz. 2013. "What Do We Know about Corporate Tax Competition?" *National Tax Journal* 66 (3): 745–74.

Forslid, R. 2005. "Tax Competition and Agglomeration: Main Effects and Empirical Implications." *Swedish Economic Policy Review* 12 (1): 113–37.

Furceri, D., P. Loungani, and J. Ostry. 2019. "The Aggregate and Distributional Effects of Financial Globalization: Evidence from Macro and Sectoral Data." *Journal of Money, Credit and Banking* 51 (S1): 163–98.

Goldberg, J. 2016. "World Chaos and World Order: Conversations with Henry Kissinger." *Atlantic* (10 November). https://www.theatlantic.com/international/archive/2016/11/kissinger-order-and-chaos/506876/.

Gygli, S., F. Haelg, N. Potrafke, and J.-E. Sturm. 2019. "The KOF Globalisation Index—Revisited." *Review of International Organizations* 14 (3): 543–74.

Hakobyan, S., and J. McLaren. 2016. "Looking for Local Labor Market Effects of NAFTA." *Review of Economics and Statistics* 98 (4): 728–41.

Helpman, E., and P. Krugman. 1985. *Market Structure and Foreign Trade.* Cambridge, MA: MIT Press.

Hoyt, W. H. 1991. "Property Taxation, Nash Equilibrium, and Market Power." *Journal of Urban Economics* 30 (1): 123–31.

IMF. 2014. "Quota Formula—Data Update and Further Considerations." IMF Policy Paper (August).

IMF. 2019. "Reigniting Growth in Low-Income and Emerging Market Economies: What Role Can Structural Reforms Play?" *World Economic Outlook* (October): 93–119.

Johnson, L., L. Sachs, and J. Sachs. 2015. *Investor–State Dispute Settlement, Public Interest and US Domestic Law.* CCSI Policy Paper.

Kharas, Homi, and Brini Seidel. 2018. "What's Happening to the World Income Distribution?" Global Economy & Development Working Paper 114 (April). Brookings Institution. https://www.brookings.edu/wp-content/uploads/2018/04/workingpaper114-elephantchartrevisited.pdf.

Kindleberger, C. P. 2013. *The World in Depression, 1929–1939*, 40th ed. Berkeley, CA: University of California Press.

Lakner, Christoph, and Branko Milanovich. 2016. "Global Income Distribution: From the Fall of the Berlin Wall to the Great Recession." *World Bank Economic Review* 20 (2): 203–32. https://openknowledge.worldbank.org/bitstream/handle/10986/29118/lhv039.pdf?sequence=1&isAllowed=y.

Lee, Y., and R. H. Gordon. 2005. "Tax Structure and Economic Growth." *Journal of Public Economics* 89: 1027–43.

Mazarr, M. J. 2018. *Summary of the Building a Sustainable International Order Project*. Santa Monica, CA: RAND Corporation.

Moons, S. J. V., and P. A. G. van Bergeijk. 2016. "Does Economic Diplomacy Work? A Meta-Analysis of Its Impact on Trade and Investment." *Global Economy* 40 (2): 336–68.

O'Sullivan, C. D. 2008. *Sumner Welles, Postwar Planning, and the Quest for a New World Order, 1937-1943*. New York: Columbia University Press.

Potrafke, N. 2015. "The Evidence on Globalization." *World Economy* 38 (3): 509–52.

PwC. 2017. "The Long View: How Will the Global Economic Order Change by 2050?" PricewaterhouseCoopers. https://www.pwc.com/gx/en/world-2050/assets/pwc-world-in-2050-summary-report-feb-2017.pdf.

Rodrik, D. 2018. "What Do Trade Agreements Really Do?" *Journal of Economic Perspectives* 32 (2): 73–90.

Siegel, D. E. 2013. "Capital Account Restrictions, Trade Agreements, and the IMF." In *Capital Account Regulations and the Trading System: A Compatibility Review*, 67–80. Pardee Center Task Force Report. Boston, MA:, Boston University.

Shevlin, T., L. Shivakumar, and O. Urcan. 2019. "Macroeconomic Effects of Corporate Tax Policy." *Journal of Accounting and Economics* 68 (1).

Spanish Ministry of Foreign Affairs. 2011. "Economic Diplomacy as a Strategy in International Relations." *Miradas Al Exterior* 8 (January–March).

Wilson, J. D. 1991. "Tax Competition with Interregional Differences in Factor Endowments." *Regional Science and Urban Economics* 21 (3): 423–51.

Part II: Geopolitics That Could Matter to Investors

In the first part of this book, I focused on empirical evidence regarding geopolitical events that matter for investors. As a result, Part I was mostly backward looking in nature. In this second part, I will focus on a few geopolitical trends that are observable today and that might or might not have a major influence on financial markets and the global economy over the next decade.

In the chapters that follow, I will look at the increasing competition between the two largest economies in the world: the United States and China. As China has emerged as a major economic power, it has also begun to challenge the United States' dominant political position in the world. So far, the rise of China has been beneficial for China, the United States, and most other countries in the world. But the trade war between the United States and China shows that China's rise has negative side effects that can lead to increased economic and geopolitical tensions between the two countries. The economies of the rest of the world are then caught in the middle between these two economic behemoths and must find a way to optimize their economic growth and their geopolitical influence.

Another hotly debated geopolitical trend is the rise of technology and, in particular, cyber warfare and international cybercrime. Today, wars are increasingly fought in the shadows, not with the mobilization of soldiers but instead with the mobilization of hackers. Whether these hackers are state-sponsored actors hired to advance geopolitical goals or simply criminals motivated by the search for profit does not make much difference for investors. In both cases, investors need to assess the possible risks to investments and to political stability.

Finally, the last two chapters of this book will focus on climate change and the rise of renewable energy. Renewable energy sources, such as solar and wind, are increasingly competitive with fossil fuels around the world. This situation leads to a displacement of fossil fuels in the utility sector, and with this displacement comes the risk that geopolitical power balances shift. Petrostates and international oil majors have to deal with the possibility of declining growth in the demand for oil and ending up with stranded assets, whereas producers of renewable energy need to have energy security insofar as this technology requires a lot of know-how and new materials to be implemented. Some observers warn that the rise of renewables could lead to a geopolitical shift away from petrostates toward the countries that produce important metals used in renewable energy applications, such as cobalt and nickel. The penultimate chapter of this book will explore how realistic such a geopolitical shift could be.

The last chapter deals with the problems created by rising temperatures in our atmosphere. With climate change accelerating, we need to prepare for more frequent and stronger climatic disasters, such as hurricanes and wildfires. The economic impact of these major disasters can be large and show up in unexpected places. As I will explain, the impact of climate change is expected to be rather small when you measure it on a national level. But local areas hit by droughts, hurricanes, and other forms of extreme weather do experience declines in GDP that are larger and longer lasting than those triggered by the Great Recession of 2009. Furthermore, we are unable to reliably assess the economic impact of crossing major tipping points, which means that the risks of climate change to the economy are skewed toward the upside. Unfortunately, unlike other economic risks, climate change cannot be solved at a national level. It is a global risk that requires a globally coordinated solution. If we do not find such a solution, the geopolitical risks from climate change could grow rapidly.

But before we focus on these four geopolitical trends that could matter in the coming decade, we have to be aware that making predictions is difficult. I am well aware that even though I am relying on the most recent academic research on these subjects (which is why I will cite papers primarily from the past few years), the likelihood that someone will read this book in a couple of years and I will have embarrassed myself is high. Geopolitical events often hinge on small, seemingly innocuous developments. A referendum in the United Kingdom that was won by a small margin, 52% to 48%, changed the course of that country's history for decades. The election of Donald Trump as president of the United States did the same for four years. Hence, we need to have some guiding rules for our forecasts that at least reduce the chances of embarrassment. The next chapter will therefore focus on 10 rules of forecasting that we will use as guidelines for the subsequent chapters of this book.

Chapter 5: My Rules of Forecasting

> People don't realize that we cannot forecast the future. What we can do is have probabilities of what causes what, but that's as far as we go.
>
> —*Alan Greenspan*

The Problem with Forecasting Geopolitical Events

Forecasting in the social sciences is much more difficult than it is in the natural sciences. This is not only because the social sciences lack the ability to test theories under laboratory conditions, where all the variables can be controlled, but also because the social sciences deal with people. And people have the nasty habit of changing their minds and acting irrationally from time to time. Even in economics and finance, areas where data are plentiful and forecasting methods have been honed for decades, a survey of the empirical track record of forecasts clearly shows one thing: Economists and investors are horrible at forecasting (Klement 2020).

In the next few chapters, I will focus on the potential future developments of geopolitical events that are currently unfolding. As one might imagine, because political scientists have much less structured data available to them than economists and investors have, their forecasting efforts are much more rudimentary—and often less reliable. As Bressan, Nygård, and Seefeldt (2019) explained, the earliest efforts to forecast geopolitical events, such as wars and the breakdowns of governments, were made shortly after World War II, but the lack of quality data and computing power meant that these efforts were rare and doomed to fail.

In the 1980s, game theoretic models of conflict and geopolitical events were increasingly used to predict real-life outcomes. Thanks to increasingly powerful computers, these approaches could for the first time be tested using real-life data. During this time, some researchers also made the first steps in using artificial intelligence (AI) and machine learning methodologies to analyze news and predict the onset of conflicts (Schrodt 1988). The lessons learned from those days often seem to be forgotten today. Schrodt (2014) listed a series of malpractices he found in modern-day AI-based research of political events, many of which can easily be applied as a criticism of AI-based research in finance and economics.

We Are Getting Better

Nevertheless, significant progress has been made in our ability to forecast the onset of geopolitical conflicts. Especially over shorter time frames of up to two years, early warning systems, such as the one developed by the US government–sponsored Political Instability Task Force, have now achieved relatively good accuracy. Goldstone, Bates, Epstein, Gurr, Lustik, Marshall, Ulfelder, and Woodward (2010) reported both a "Type I error" (falsely predicting a conflict where none exists) and a "Type II error" (falsely predicting no conflict where one exists) frequency of 20% for these models.

Even long-term forecasts are becoming reasonably accurate. Hegre, Karlsen, Nygård, Strand, and Urdal (2013) used data from 1970 to 2009 to predict the likelihood of the onset of armed conflict (either civil war or international wars) in the years 2010–2050. A first model used in a previous study based on data up to the year 2000 was reasonably effective in predicting the onset of conflict in the years 2007–2009. In their 2013 paper, they published a list of the countries most likely to experience some form of armed conflict in 2017, 2030, and 2050. We can now check the accuracy of their country-level forecasts for 2017. **Exhibit 1** shows the five countries with an ongoing conflict in 2009 that had the highest likelihood of a conflict in 2017. It also shows the five countries that had no conflict in 2009 but the highest likelihood of a conflict in 2017. Four of the five countries that were in conflict in 2009 were still in conflict in 2017. Given that these five countries' average likelihood of being in conflict in 2017 was 78%, the model of Hegre et al. (2013) did a good job of predicting the continuation of existing conflicts. Also, with respect to predicting the onset of new conflicts, the model did very well because the

Exhibit 1.   Predicted and Realized Armed Conflicts in 2017

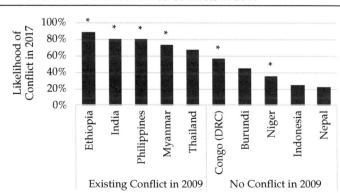

Note: Asterisks denote the countries with an active conflict in 2017.
Sources: Hegre et al. (2013); Uppsala Conflict Data Program Armed Conflict Dataset.

average likelihood of a conflict in 2017 for the five countries with no conflict in 2009 was 37%. Today, two of these five countries indeed have an internal conflict with rebels of the Islamic State.

However, Hegre et al. (2013) had one glaring failure in their predictions. Despite using data up to the year 2009, their model completely failed to predict the Arab Spring that started in Tunisia in 2011 and swept throughout North Africa and the Middle East. Instead, Hegre et al. concluded that their forecasts were "most optimistic for the 'Western Asia and North Africa' region, where the incidence of conflict is predicted to be reduced by almost two thirds, from 27% in 2009 to 6.2% in 2050" (p. 261). As an economist and investment specialist, I take solace in the fact that political scientists are subject to the same catastrophic forecasting failures as we are.

Given this improving but still quite shaky track record of forecasting models in geopolitics, we need to be aware that when we discuss the current geopolitical trends that may influence financial markets and the global economy in the coming years and decades, we should not rely too heavily on numerical forecasts. The best we can do is to infer the likelihood of current events causing some future developments and try to identify the most likely scenarios for the future. But we need to be aware that even with the best models we have and with the most careful reasoning, the longer the time frame of the prediction, the more uncertain the prediction will become. Such events as the Arab Spring or the Global Financial Crisis of 2008 can invalidate even the most sophisticated forecasts within months and make their author look like a fool.[1]

My 10 Rules of Forecasting

Over the years, I have learned that making market and economic forecasts is often a futile exercise if one wants to be overly precise. Instead, the best forecasts are often based on a few input variables and a fundamental understanding of how markets work. I have created a personal list of rules for forecasting financial markets, but as it turns out, these rules have also been very helpful in forecasting geopolitical events. Thus, I provide them here, together with a brief discussion of how to use these rules to analyze geopolitical developments.

The following are my 10 rules of forecasting:

1. **Data matter.** We humans are drawn to anecdotes and illustrations, but looks can be deceiving. Always base your forecasts on data, not on qualitative arguments.

---

[1]I suspect readers will realize on the basis of these sentences that the author of this book is an economist who has years of training in making excuses for failed forecasts.

- **Corollary A:** Torture the data until they confess, but do not fit the data to the story.

- **Corollary B:** Start with base rates (i.e., the historical average rate at which an event happens). The assumption that nothing changes and an event is as likely in the future as it was in the past is a good starting point but is not the end point. Adjust this base rate with the information you have at the moment.

2. **Do not make extreme forecasts.** Predicting the next financial crisis will make you famous if you do it at the right time but will cost you money and your reputation in any other instance.

3. **Reversion to the mean is a powerful force.** In economics, as well as in politics, extremes cannot survive for long. People trend toward averages, and competitive forces in business lead to mean reversion.

4. **We are creatures of habit.** If something has worked in the past, people will keep on repeating it almost forever. This phenomenon introduces long-lasting trends. Do not expect these trends to change quickly, despite mean reversion. It is incredible how long a broken system can survive.

5. **We rarely fall off a cliff.** People often change their habits at the last minute before a catastrophe happens. Yet for behavioral change to happen, the catastrophe must be salient, the outcome must be certain, and the solution must be simple.

6. **A full stomach does not riot.** Revolutions and riots rarely happen when people have enough food and feel relatively safe. A lack of personal freedom is not sufficient to create revolutions, but a lack of food, a lack of medicine, and injustice all are.

7. **The first goal of political and business leaders is to stay in power.** Viewed through that lens, many actions can easily be predicted.

8. **The second goal of political and business leaders is to get rich.** Combined with the previous rule, this explains approximately 90% of all behavior.

9. **Remember Occam's razor.** The simplest explanation is the most likely to be correct. Ignore conspiracy theories.

10. **Do not follow rules blindly.** The world changes all the time, so be aware that any rule might suddenly stop working for a while or even forever.

Astute readers will have noticed that these rules owe a lot to the work of Philip Tetlock (2005) and Tetlock and Gardner (2016). Tetlock (2005) showed that political experts are often bad at forecasting crucial events. Their forecasts are locked into an existing frame of mind that these experts are unable to change.

Civil Strife from the Fall of Communism to the Arab Spring

Toward the end of the 1980s, experts in the intelligence communities of Western countries did not predict that the fall of communism would occur within a few years' time. They essentially followed my Rule 4 and assumed that because people had not risen against communism in more than two decades, they were unlikely to suddenly do so. And admittedly, following Rule 4 served these analysts well for a long time. But younger analysts were able to see the changing environment and realized that communist countries in Central and Eastern Europe had reached a tipping point, where my Rule 6 could be applied. The injustices of these countries together with the perennial shortages of food and medicine were finally serious enough to trigger a civil uprising. Of course, these analysts had to assume that the governments of these socialist European countries would follow Rule 7 and do anything they could to stay in power.

And this is the true surprise of the events of the late 1980s. The government of the German Democratic Republic did not crack down on the growing demonstrations in Leipzig and other cities. The government in the Czech Republic did not crack down on the Velvet Revolution led by Vaclav Havel, nor did governments of Poland and Hungary crack down on the civil uprisings in their countries. When Mikhail Gorbachev abandoned the so-called Brezhnev Doctrine, which stated that the rule of communism should be upheld, if necessary, by force, the local governments in Central and Eastern Europe had no ability to stop the demands for freedom and democracy. Up to today, the peaceful fall of communism can be qualified as one of the biggest geopolitical surprises of the 20th century. By all accounts, if communism were to trigger civil uprisings, one would have expected long-lasting civil wars as a result.

In essence, this is what happened after the Arab Spring of 2011. The Arab Spring was triggered by fast-rising food prices that hit the poorest people the hardest and caused them to revolt (Rule 6). The resulting uprising led to reforms in the political systems in Jordan and Tunisia but created violent conflicts from Algeria to Syria, many of which have lasted up to the present. The example of the Arab Spring shows that peaceful transitions of autocratic regimes to democratic regimes are rare.

Goldstone et al. (2010) showed that the onset of civil war and international conflict can best be predicted by using only four variables (see also Rule 9), the most important of which is the type of political system that has been established in a country. They found that if a country is a full democracy with open and fair elections, the outbreak of civil war is much less likely than in an autocracy. However, as autocracies evolve into full democracies, they have to go through various stages of partial democracy, where elections are *managed*, and rival political factions can form (typically along racial, tribal, or religious lines).

The risk of civil war is significantly elevated in these stages because the various emerging factions tend to engage in a winner-take-all competition for power. Once a faction has gained control over government resources in such transition economies, it often diverts these government resources to line its own pockets (Rule 8). This situation, in turn, triggers widespread feelings of injustice that can cause civil wars (Rule 6).

According to Goldstone et al. (2010), the outbreak of civil war is more than three times likelier in a partial democracy with factionalism than in a full-fledged autocracy. The onset of adverse regime change is more than five times likelier in a partial democracy with factionalism than in an autocracy. These conditions also explain why almost two decades after the United States invaded Afghanistan and Iraq, the latter two countries remain politically unstable and unable to form a functioning democracy.

These statistics from the research of Goldstone et al. (2010) also explain the existence of what Tetlock and Gardner (2016) called "superforecasters"—people who are extremely good at forecasting geopolitical developments. As Tetlock and Gardner (2016) described in an appendix titled "Ten Commandments for Aspiring Superforecasters," these people have learned to break complex problems down into tractable subproblems that can be solved with data analysis and logical reasoning (Rule 1). Then they start with an appropriate baseline estimate of the likelihood of an event (Rule 1, Corollary B). For example, in an autocracy, the likelihood of a civil uprising has historically been x%. This base rate is then adjusted on the basis of new information.

For example, if the autocracy is abolished and a democracy emerges, the probability of a civil uprising first increases and then decreases. Superforecasters adjust their base rates in light of the information about the nature of the emerging democracies. But unlike many pundits in the news, superforecasters do not become overconfident in their forecasts; they adjust base rates only gradually as new information emerges. They refrain from making extreme shifts in their forecasts and arrive at extreme forecasts only when a mountain of evidence has forced them to shift the odds in favor of an extreme outcome (Rule 2). This is why Tetlock (2005) states that superforecasters are often seemingly boring people. But this restraint is the secret to their success. My 10 rules of forecasting, which have served me well in the past, also encourage such restraint.

Conclusion

Forecasting geopolitical developments is even more challenging than making financial market forecasts because the subject matter is (1) more difficult to capture with hard data and (2) more prone to the influence of irrational behavior of individual actors and mass behavior that can change seemingly without warning. This lack of hard data and the complexity of the issues at hand also mean that forecasting tools in political sciences are less developed than in economics and finance. The field is making fast progress, however, and forecasting geopolitical developments is getting increasingly better today. By using a combination of data-driven quantitative forecasting models and scenario analysis based on basic rules of forecasting such as the ones described in this chapter, we can at least qualitatively forecast likely scenarios and future pathways for current geopolitical trends.

Bibliography

Bressan, S., H. M. Nygård, and D. Seefeldt. 2019. "Forecasting and Foresight: Methods for Anticipating Governance Breakdown and Violent Conflict." EU-LISTCO Working Paper No. 2 (September).

Goldstone, J. A., R. H. Bates, D. L. Epstein, T. R. Gurr, M. B. Lustik, M. G. Marshall, J. Ulfelder, and M. Woodward. 2010. "A Global Model for Forecasting Political Instability." *American Journal of Political Science* 54 (1): 190–208.

Hegre, H., J. Karlsen, H. M. Nygård, H. Strand, and H. Urdal. 2013. "Predicting Armed Conflict, 2010–2050." *International Studies Quarterly* 57 (2): 250–70.

Klement, J. 2020. *7 Mistakes Every Investor Makes (and How to Avoid Them)*. Petersfield, UK: Harriman House.

Schrodt, P. A. 1988. "Artificial Intelligence and the Study of International Politics." *American Sociologist* 19 (1): 71–85.

Schrodt, P. A. 2014. "Seven Deadly Sins of Contemporary Quantitative Political Analysis." *Journal of Peace Research* 51 (2): 287–300.

Tetlock, P. E. 2005. *Expert Political Judgement: How Good Is It? How Can We Know?* Princeton, NJ: Princeton University Press.

Tetlock, P. E., and D. Gardner. 2016. *Superforecasting: The Art and Science of Prediction*. New York: Crown.

Chapter 6: The Rivalry between the United States and China

> In China today, Bill Gates is Britney Spears. In America today, Britney Spears is Britney Spears—and that is our problem.
>
> —*Thomas Friedman*

The Return of Great Power Competition

Throughout much of the 19th and 20th centuries, global politics was characterized by a rivalry between great powers for influence. In fact, the term "great power" is typically defined in this context as a country that can exert its military or economic influence everywhere in the world. In the second half of the 19th century, the two dominating great powers of the world were the British Empire and the French Empire, with Germany, Austria-Hungary, the Ottoman Empire, and Russia challenging those two nations in continental Europe and neighboring regions. The rivalry between these great powers led to constantly shifting alliances and a fragile balance that finally collapsed in the early 20th century at the outbreak of World War I.

After the two world wars, great power competition shifted away from the European colonial empires toward a rivalry between the United States and the Soviet Union. But with the fall of the Soviet Union, the United States emerged in the 1990s as the sole great power. No country on the planet could challenge the military or economic power of the United States, and great power competition was pronounced dead. Francis Fukuyama famously even went as far as to call for an "End of History," wherein liberal democracy would be the only relevant political system on Earth (Fukuyama 1992).

But the status of the United States as the sole great power turned out to be short-lived. Although one can argue that militarily, Russia remained a great power because its large nuclear arsenal allowed it to intervene militarily wherever it wished, the country had nowhere near the economic influence of the United States. Meanwhile, in economic terms, China has emerged over the past two decades as another great power and the main challenger of US economic hegemony in the world.

Exhibit 1 shows the GDP of the United States and China together with that of the European Union and Japan since 1980. GDP is expressed in US dollars adjusted for purchasing power parity (PPP), which is why the chart shows China having superseded the United States as the largest economy in the world in 2014. At market exchange rates, the United States is still the largest economy. I use PPP-adjusted GDP in Exhibit 1 because in this discussion, I am concerned with the potential of a country's people to purchase goods and services and to invest their savings. And because most consumption and investing are done locally (especially in the case of China), a PPP-adjusted comparison of the size of different economies is more relevant in this context.

Given that China's GDP rivals and eventually supersedes that of the United States, the country has clearly become a challenger for the United States in not only economic terms but also political terms. That living standards in China are still much lower than in the United States, Europe, and Japan is true (China's PPP GDP per capita is approximately one-quarter of that of the United States), but as a market for global goods and services, China has become a major player. And this economic power has led over time to a more confident political style, particularly under President Xi Jinping. China is demanding its rightful place in the existing world order.

At first, China's emergence as a leading member of the global economic and political elite was welcomed, particularly because after the 9/11 terrorist attacks, the United States believed China would help the West in its efforts to fight global terrorism (Zoellick 2005). But over time, the United States and other leading economies in the world became more skeptical about the Chinese government's increasing political assertiveness (Deng 2014). After the election of Donald Trump as president of the United States, China

Exhibit 1.   Share of World GDP (at PPP Exchange Rates)

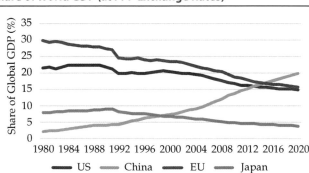

Note: GDP in PPP-adjusted US dollars.
Source: International Monetary Fund (IMF).

increasingly drew the ire of the administration, and tensions between the United States and China escalated drastically, something we will discuss in more detail later in this chapter.

China's Ascent to Economic Superpower. Before we discuss the recent tensions between the United States and China, however, we should review the current state of affairs and the rise of China in a global context. Over the past 30 years, China has gradually opened its economy to the world. It followed in the footsteps of so many emerging markets, most notably the Asian developed economies of South Korea and Japan, which managed to emerge from poverty through the 1960s and 1970s and today have some of the highest living standards in the world.

Just as Japan was in the 1960s and South Korea was in the 1970s, China was competitive thanks to a large labor force that could produce manufactured goods at much lower costs than its Western competitors could. In the beginning, the labor force was largely uneducated, and China gradually became the workshop of the world as it integrated its manufacturing base into the global supply chains of companies from advanced economies. This integration of China into global supply chains led to a massive increase in trade with China. Today, trade flows of goods to and from China amount to 12.9% of global trade, surpassing those of both the United States and Japan, as shown in **Exhibit 2**.

The perception of China as a hub for the production of cheap goods that do not require a lot of skilled labor to manufacture is still widespread in the West. But this view has long been outdated. Consumption as a share of GDP has been rising quickly since 2010 and was 53.6% in 2017. Processing

Exhibit 2. Share of Global Trade in Goods

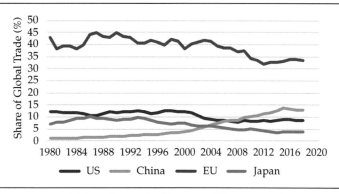

Note: The high share of global trade for the European Union is partly due to intensive trade between EU member countries, particularly in the eurozone.
Source: IMF.

exports—where parts and raw materials are imported into China, assembled into finished goods or inputs for further processing in other countries, and then exported—have declined from 50% of Chinese exports in 2007 to 34% in 2017. Two-thirds of Chinese exports today are goods developed, produced, and finished in China. Processing imports in China—goods and raw materials are imported into China for further processing—have declined even more and today account for just 24% of all Chinese imports (Ahmed 2017). While the country remains the workshop of the world, the part of the Chinese economy consisting solely of assembly is becoming less and less important. Instead, China is increasingly becoming a consumption economy. In 2013, services as a share of GDP overtook manufacturing for the first time ever and now account for more than 50% of China's GDP.

But China is not just integrated into global manufacturing supply chains and the trade of consumption goods; it has also become more integrated into the global financial network. **Exhibit 3** shows the KOF Globalisation Index for trade and financial globalization of the United States and China.

Although the US economy remains far more globalized than the Chinese economy, both Chinese trade and financial services are catching up quickly. Chinese banks are the largest in the world in terms of assets and are now present around the globe. Meanwhile, international banks are increasingly active in China. According to the Bank for International Settlements, US banks had claims against Chinese citizens and businesses totaling $170 billion as of mid-2018. That amounts to 10% of the existing Tier 1 capital of US banks. Banks in the United Kingdom and Singapore are even more exposed to China, with claims amounting to 95% and 277% of Tier 1 capital, respectively. In short, if the Chinese economy gets into trouble, the global trade

Exhibit 3. Globalization in China and the United States Measured by the KOF Globalisation Index

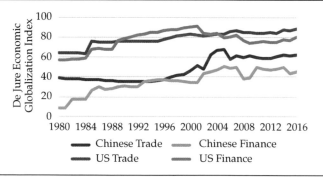

Source: Gygli, Haelg, Potrafke, and Sturm (2019).

in goods is not all that will suffer. We realistically have to expect a financial crisis that could likely spread to Western banks.

What If China Slows Down? China's global integration, together with the sheer size of the country's economy, means that an economic crisis in China will quickly spread around the globe. **Exhibit 4** shows the impact a Chinese growth shock would have on the global economy. The model used here by Ahmed, Correa, Dias, Gornemann, Hoek, Jain, Liu, and Wong (2019) simulates two kinds of Chinese growth shocks: an adverse growth shock and a severely adverse growth shock.

First, a decline in Chinese growth that is in line with the average financial crisis in history (using the experience of both advanced economies and emerging economies as the historical sample) would reduce China's GDP by 4% relative to baseline growth in approximately two years. Exhibit 4 shows

Exhibit 4. Impact of a Chinese Growth Shock

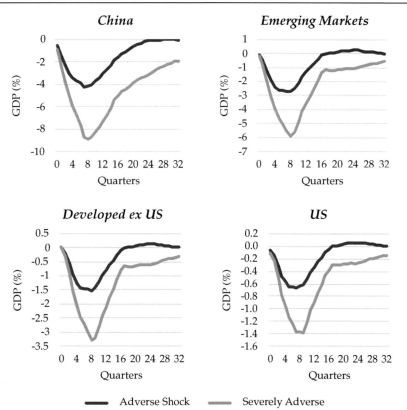

Source: Ahmed et al. (2019).

that such an "adverse growth shock" in China would hit emerging economies the hardest. Emerging markets as a group would suffer a decline in GDP of 2–3 percentage points (pps), whereas advanced economies outside the United States would see their GDP decline by approximately 1.5 pps.

However, countries with greater dependency on exporting to China would be harder hit. Ahmed et al. (2019) estimated that commodity-exporting emerging markets would see their GDP decline by more than 3 pps in two years whereas commodity-importing emerging markets would see their GDP decline by approximately 2 percentage points. And among commodity importers, such countries as South Korea, Germany, and Japan seem likely to be the harder hit advanced economies because of their close export links with China. Given the low trend growth rates of advanced economies in Europe and developed Asia, the impact of such a Chinese growth shock could easily trigger a recession in these countries.

Because the United States exports little to China and depends much less on Chinese demand than other economies do, it would suffer much smaller losses in output, approximately 0.6% of GDP. Normally, such losses would not be enough to cause a recession in the United States, but they could be sufficient if the US economy were already growing at a slow pace when the shock happened.

However, the situation could worsen if China's economy experiences not an average financial crisis but one that is similar to the one the United States experienced after the housing bubble burst in 2006. In this "severely adverse scenario," the Chinese economy would decline by 8.5 pps in two years, a shock that would have much larger ramifications globally.

Exhibit 4 shows that in such a severely adverse scenario, emerging market economies overall would see their GDP decline by approximately 6 pps, while advanced economies outside the United States would suffer GDP reductions on the order of 3–3.5 pps. Again, the United States would be among the least affected countries in such a scenario, but the financial ties between US banks and Chinese borrowers would imply a decline in US GDP that is approximately twice as severe as in the case of the adverse scenario. In short, the economic impact of such a severe financial crisis in China on advanced economies outside the United States and emerging markets would be comparable to the Global Financial Crisis (GFC) of 2008. Now imagine if this happened while the Western economies were still trying to recover from the long-term damage of the Covid-19 pandemic.

Correspondingly, the impact of a growth shock on financial markets ranges from bad to truly horrifying, as shown in **Exhibit 5** (Ahmed et al. 2019):

Exhibit 5.   Impact of a Chinese Growth Shock on Financial Markets

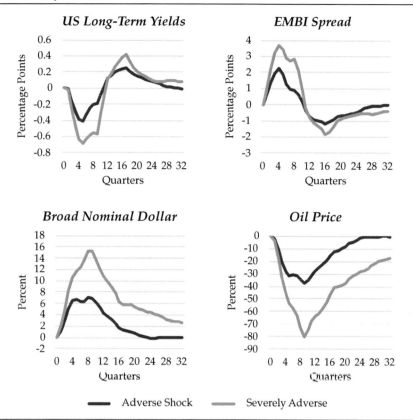

Source. Ahmed et al. (2019).

- Long-term US Treasury yields are expected to decline by 40 bps in the adverse scenario and 60 bps in the severely adverse scenario.

- Emerging market bond spreads (measured as the average spread of the J.P. Morgan Emerging Markets Bond Index [EMBI] Global versus US Treasuries) are expected to jump by 200 bps (adverse scenario) to 300 bps (severely adverse scenario).

- The US dollar is expected to rally by 6% to 12% versus principal developed market currencies over two years. Emerging market currencies would weaken significantly more against the dollar than developed market currencies would. Furthermore, developed market currencies would recover within four years, whereas emerging market currencies might remain weak for much longer.

- Oil prices are expected to drop up to 40% in two years for the adverse scenario and more than 70% in two years for the severely adverse scenario. Industrial metal prices are expected to drop 20% and 50%, respectively.

- Last but not least, stock markets would experience severe bear markets. The S&P 500 Index is expected to drop 15% over two years in the case of a regular China growth shock and up to 40% over two years in the severely adverse scenario. European stock markets are expected to drop 20% and 50%, respectively, whereas emerging market stocks are expected to drop 25% and 55%.

Although such simulations are by no means perfect and are subject to significant estimation errors, they show that a crisis in China would likely trigger a bear market in equities and push Europe and many emerging markets into recession. Meanwhile, a severe financial crisis in China would feel like the GFC for most countries around the world.

Above all, these simulations show that efforts by the United States to hurt China economically are likely to cause significant harm to US and global investors, which, in turn, could lead to even bigger reductions in GDP growth than the ones shown here because adverse sentiment might lead to declining consumption in a second round—something indicated by additional modeling results in Ahmed et al. (2019). A US–China trade war taken to the extremes would sink global financial markets. And investors would take years to recover from such losses.

The Competition between China and the United States Will Be the Dominant Theme. We can, therefore, conclude that denying China its seat at the table of the great powers of the 21st century is impossible. Unfortunately, great power competition has often led to war and economic crises. The rivalry between Germany and Austria-Hungary, on the one hand, and between France and the British Empire, on the other, in the early 20th century led to the outbreak of World War I. The rivalry between the United States and the great powers in Europe led to a trade war that deepened the Great Depression at its onset and sowed the seeds for World War II. And the great power competition between the United States and the Soviet Union after World War II did not end in a great power war, but we came quite close several times.

Great power competition in the 21st century has to find new solutions to these challenges. In the age of nuclear weapons, we cannot allow great power competition between the United States and China to escalate into an all-out military conflict. If we do, the investment implications of such a military conflict will be the last thing on our minds. Thus, we do not have to ponder this outcome as a serious possibility here.

But great power competition between the United States and China could lead to economic war and economic crises. As the discussion thus far has shown, because the network of global connections is so dense, in terms of both trade and financial services, such economic warfare would be an enormously destructive force that would be felt everywhere. The costs for the global economy as well as for any individual country (including the United States) would likely be much bigger than the potential benefits.

That the great power competition between the United States and China will continue to escalate indefinitely seems unlikely. Readers should remember Rule 2 of forecasting from the previous chapter. Making extreme forecasts does not pay off because they almost never come true, and investment strategies that are based on such extreme scenarios can lead to very costly mistakes, indeed. Furthermore, as Rule 3 of forecasting states, mean reversion is a powerful force. The president of the United States faces checks and balances from Congress and the Supreme Court and must run for reelection after four years in office. And the electorate, when given the chance to correct a mistake, does so quite frequently.

At the time of writing, campaigning for the US presidential election is underway, and quite possibly, Donald Trump will not be reelected; if not, he will be succeeded by Joe Biden, who is a more moderate politician. Furthermore, the Phase 1 deal between the United States and China was enacted in January 2020 and has at least temporarily halted the spiral of ever-increasing tariffs. To expect an all-out economic war between the United States and China in the coming years would, therefore, be foolish. What seems more likely is that the trade war between the United States and China will eventually enter a steady state—something I will discuss in more detail later in this chapter.

Made in China 2025 and Beyond

Beyond the current trade tensions between the United States and China, another development is on the horizon that might lead to geopolitical tensions between China and developed countries around the world—one that has garnered much less attention. Although China has become a great power, it remains a middle-income country. The initial gains from a cheap labor force and rapid urbanization have been made. Wages in China have risen to levels that create a competitive disadvantage relative to other emerging markets. According to the Economist Intelligence Unit, the average monthly wage of a Chinese worker in 2018 was $990, compared with $383 for Mexico and $238 for Vietnam (all numbers at current exchange rates). This difference in wages might not lead to a competitive disadvantage if Chinese workers are

　　　　145

more productive, but even if the higher productivity of Chinese workers is taken into account, unit labor costs in China are still 57% higher than in Vietnam and 277% higher than in Mexico. And China's pool of cheap labor is declining rapidly. Today, more than one-half of all Chinese citizens live in cities, and the poverty rate in rural China was 3.4% in 2013, down from 48.8% just 10 years earlier (World Bank 2017).

Given these constraints, growth in China is slowing. After decades of double-digit real GDP growth, it dropped to 6.1% in 2019 and will likely drop significantly in 2020 as a result of the Covid-19 pandemic. Excluding 2020, the slowdown in Chinese growth is in line with the experience of Japan and South Korea from the 1970s to the 1990s, as **Exhibit 6** shows.

But China is at risk of falling into the "middle-income trap." Most emerging economies have not managed to achieve what Japan and South Korea did. After an initial stage when Japan and South Korea caught up with more developed economies thanks to cheap labor, the two countries transformed their economies and increasingly specialized in high-tech manufacturing that allowed them to raise their wealth beyond the levels of middle-income countries. If China wants to keep its seat at the table of great economic powers, it needs to emulate these examples and transform its economy toward higher-value-added industries.

Escaping the Middle-Income Trap. To escape the middle-income trap, China launched its "Made in China 2025" (MIC25) strategy in 2015. It was billed as a signature economic project for the next 10 years and a step closer to the country's ultimate goal of becoming a leading global economic superpower by 2049—the 100th anniversary of the People's Republic of China. This strategy defines 10 industries, including robotics, next-generation

Exhibit 6. China's Growth Slowdown in Context

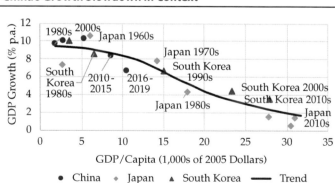

Source: Ahmed (2017).

information technology (IT), energy equipment, and new energy vehicles, in which China wants to develop world leading businesses that dominate their global competition. Currently, many Chinese businesses in traditional high-tech industries, such as aerospace and software engineering, lag behind their Western counterparts. Here the goal is to close the gap, but the country has no ambition to rapidly develop these industries. Being second best seems good enough in these cases, as long as the gap with the West closes gradually.

MIC25 focuses instead on next-generation high-tech industries that are part of the so-called Fourth Industrial Revolution, which include robotics, artificial intelligence, and other fields. MIC25 aims to enable Chinese companies to leapfrog Western competitors and watch them try to catch up.

To achieve the goals of MIC25, China's government has defined a whole range of metrics along which progress is measured. One unofficial key metric is the share of domestic products in key industries. For example, 90% of electric and other new energy vehicles should be from Chinese manufacturers in 2025, and 70% of robots used in China in 2025 should be domestically made, as should 60% of cloud-computing and big data applications. **Exhibit 7** delineates these aspirations.

Additionally, the government has defined more than 100 other measures to assess progress toward the MIC25 goals. These measures range from innovation indicators such as R&D spending, through digitization metrics (broadband penetration is scheduled to rise from 50% to 82%), to environmental goals (CO_2 emissions should be reduced by 40% from 2015 levels). But these goals are not fixed. The government and regional authorities constantly adapt these objectives to a changing environment, accelerating progress where possible and providing more time for development where needed.

Exhibit 7. Unofficial Targets for Products under MIC25

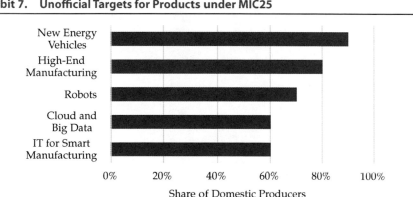

Sources: Wübbeke, Meissner, Zenglein, Ives, and Conrad (2016); Zenglein and Holzmann (2019).

The MIC25 strategy has caused quite a bit of irritation in developed countries because it directly attacks the foundation of economic growth in many of them. Wübbeke et al. (2016) analyzed which developed countries are most threatened by MIC25. Based on the importance of the local manufacturing sector in the overall economy and the importance of high-tech manufacturing in the manufacturing sector, the five countries that face the greatest competitive threats from MIC25 are as follows:

1. South Korea

2. Germany

3. Ireland

4. Hungary

5. Czech Republic

But such countries as Japan, the United States, and the United Kingdom are not far behind. Add to that the idea that China is providing enormous financial resources to companies involved in MIC25 through state-owned banks (in 2016, the China Development Bank pledged $42 billion in financing over five years) as well as a network of more than 1,800 government industrial investment funds (with funds of approximately $420 billion), and one can understand that Western countries are very nervous. In comparison, Germany's Industrie 4.0 program, which was launched with very similar goals in 2011, has total government funding of EUR200 million ($220 million or approximately 5% of the funding of MIC25).

Another cause for concern in the West is the fact that access to the Chinese market remains restricted in many of these next-generation high-tech fields. Facebook and Twitter notably do not operate in China, and Google's search engine is unavailable there as well (though the company maintains a research facility and sells Android smartphones there). In 2015, China adopted a new National Security Law that restricts foreign access to the information and communication technology market on national security grounds. The 2015 Counter-Terrorism Law requires telecom and internet service providers to provide technical support assistance to security organizations investigating terrorist attacks. Finally, China's 2017 Cybersecurity Law further restricts sales of foreign information and communication technology in China and requires foreign technology to be subjected to government security reviews, data to be stored on Chinese servers, and government approval to be granted if data are to be transferred outside China (Office of the Security of Defense 2019). In essence, any modern information and communication technology provider operating in China must provide government authorities access to all its data if it wants to operate in the country.

This criticism of MIC25, together with demands from the United States to drop the plans for MIC25 as part of the resolution of the US–China trade war, led to press reports in late 2018 that China might abolish the program. However, MIC25 appears to be here to stay, though public references to the program have been toned down. **Exhibit 8** shows the changes in wording of major themes of MIC25 that occurred between the public announcement of MIC25 in 2015 and the Government Work Report 2019 (Zenglein and Holzmann 2019).

Laying the Groundwork to Become a High-Tech Nation. China has long laid the groundwork for the transformation of its economy into a high-tech economy. **Exhibit 9** shows that R&D spending has increased from 1.0% of GDP in 2001 to 2.2% of GDP in 2017, overtaking that of the European Union. The number of patent applications is growing exponentially, particularly in such crucial areas as artificial intelligence, but the quality of these patents and the results of the R&D efforts so far seem to be worse than the output of Western countries.

Nevertheless, the pool of highly educated specialists in China is growing fast. The epigraph at the beginning of this chapter from *New York Times* columnist Thomas Friedman alludes to the high social standing of engineers and scientists in China and the reverence provided to them by the public. **Exhibit 10** shows that in 2014, 1.6 million Chinese students graduated from university with a bachelor's degree in a science or engineering field, compared with 742,000 in the United States and 780,000 in the European Union. Expressed as a percentage of the overall population, this is still only approximately one-half the rate seen in the United States but is on par with the European Union. And many of these highly educated engineers and scientists will work in local

Exhibit 8.   The Changing Face of MIC25

Theme	MIC25 (2015)	Government Work Report 2019
Manufacturing superpower	Turn China into a manufacturing superpower with a world-leading manufacturing industry.	Accelerate the establishment of a manufacturing superpower.
Smartification	Make smart manufacturing the major direction to follow.	Expand "smart+."
Quality	By 2025, substantially upgrade the quality of the manufacturing industry.	Promote high-quality development of the manufacturing industry.

Sources: State Council, Xinhua; Zenglein and Holzmann (2019).

Exhibit 9. R&D Spending

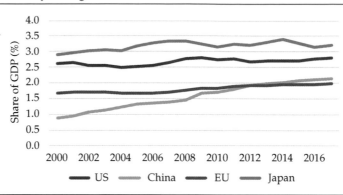

Source: OECD.

Exhibit 10. Graduates with a Bachelor's Degree in a Science or Engineering Field

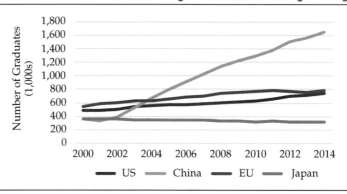

Sources: National Science Foundation; OECD.

factories and research labs to create the technologies of the future. Even if the average level of education of these scientists and engineers is lower than that for the United States and Europe, their sheer number guarantees that China is bound to have the required number of "geniuses" to revolutionize a field.

Finally, China uses restricted access to its market as a bargaining chip to obtain foreign know-how and technologies. Foreign investors are given access to industries that China considers of low strategic importance, such as consumer goods and the automotive industry, and hurdles for joint ventures with Chinese companies and state-owned enterprises are reduced. In return, China aims to gain access to desirable high-tech industries or to attract these industries to China. For example, in the consumer electronics industry, China no longer simply assembles parts that were manufactured abroad but increasingly produces computer chips and other components locally. This means that in recent decades, Chinese companies could upgrade local production with foreign know-how. As a consequence, such companies as Lenovo, Huawei, Haier, and DJI have become well-known brands around the world.

However, some foreign know-how remains elusive for Chinese companies because the businesses that possess it are unwilling to transfer that know-how to China. For example, the elevator company Schindler and the industrial conglomerate Siemens refuse to sell certain high-tech products to China and instead only offer products that are not at the cutting edge of modern technology. In these cases, China tries to get access to this know-how through foreign direct investment (FDI—i.e., acquiring foreign companies with the required knowledge) by hiring specialists from foreign businesses to work in China, by collaborating with Western research institutes and universities where barriers to entry are lower, and via other means (Zenglein and Holzmann 2019).

Western countries react to these efforts very differently. Many Western countries with a strong free-market tradition, such as the United States and the United Kingdom, and countries with limited experience in dealing with Chinese investors tend to welcome Chinese investments. As a result, investment flows from China into these countries tend to be lower but not that much lower than flows from these countries into China (Exhibit 10). Countries that have more experience in dealing with Chinese investors and have more to lose from a loss of local know-how tend to resist Chinese investments much more. The FDI flows between Germany, South Korea, and Japan on one side and China on the other are essentially one-way streets. **Exhibit 11** compares FDI into and from China for some leading industrial countries.

Exhibit 11. FDI Flows with China

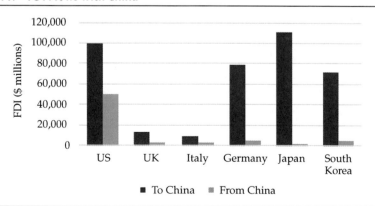

Note: In millions of US dollars, average for 2015–2017.
Source: OECD.

In addition, attempts by Chinese companies to acquire Western high-tech businesses are increasingly the subject of political scrutiny. The 2016 takeover of the world's largest robotics company, KUKA, by China's Midea Group caused significant concern among the German political elite, given KUKA's place at the heart of the Industrie 4.0 initiative. The takeover of Swiss agribusiness company Syngenta by ChemChina in 2017 almost failed because of regulatory concerns in the United States and Europe. And in 2016, the takeover of Western Digital by Tsinghua Unigroup failed after the Committee on Foreign Investment in the United States threatened an investigation.

But Chinese companies' push to become global leaders in next-generation technology will not stop because of such political scrutiny. With a protected home market that generates massive cash flows, many Chinese companies can gradually expand throughout Asia and the rest of the world, where they will compete directly with Western businesses. The impact on Western businesses will be diminishing profit margins and lower sales and earnings growth as well as a gradual diversion of R&D spending from the West to China:

- The Commercial Aircraft Corporation of China, a state-owned aerospace company, will launch its narrow-body C919 aircraft in 2021 and its wide-body C929 aircraft in 2026, putting it in direct competition with Airbus and Boeing. At first, the company will not likely make inroads in Europe and North America, but Chinese and East Asian airlines will increasingly switch to these aircraft.

- Alibaba has begun offering its Alipay payment system in the United States and other countries, giving itself a foothold in the countries dominated by such electronic payment systems as Apple Pay and Google Pay. Additionally, the company allows US retailers to sell their goods on its Chinese e-commerce site, thereby providing them a way to circumvent competition from Amazon. While Americans buy consumer goods made in China, Chinese consumers will in the future increasingly buy goods made in the United States.

- Chinese carmakers that produce electric vehicles are expanding into Europe and the United States. Geely, through its Volvo brand, started selling the Polestar 2 electric car in 2020. This car is in direct competition with the Tesla Model 3. Meanwhile, other Chinese electric car manufacturers, such as BYD, already sell electric buses in the United States and electric cars in Bahrain and Ukraine.

- Seven of the 10 largest companies that produce batteries for electric cars are Chinese, and their combined global market share is 53%. The planned expansion of Chinese battery manufacturing capacity amounts to three times that of the rest of the world. China's leadership in electric vehicles and batteries is so pronounced that Western carmakers, such as BMW and Groupe PSA, have diverted R&D efforts from Europe to China and opened facilities in China to gain access to local know-how—effectively reversing the traditional flow of know-how.

Regional Expansion: The World's Largest Free Trade Zone

Although MIC25 is primarily domestically oriented, a local Chinese high-tech industry clearly needs access to essential raw materials and intermediate goods. Similarly, China, as an export-oriented nation with a growing domestic market, will need easy access to foreign markets for its finished goods. In short, the Chinese high-tech industry has the best chance of succeeding if it is integrated into a global supply chain.

To do this, China needs to ensure that it has easy access to markets. This goal is easier to achieve with regional partners than on a global scale or through global institutions. With respect to partners in Southeast Asia and the Pacific region, China is simply the most desirable bride. When the United States withdrew from the proposed Trans-Pacific Partnership (TPP) in 2017, China was handed a strategic opportunity to enhance its economic influence in the region through its own network of free trade agreements.

Since 2012, the member states of the Association of Southeast Asian Nations (ASEAN), together with their free trade partners (China, India, Japan, South Korea, Australia, and New Zealand), started efforts to harmonize trade agreements between these countries. These efforts, under the title Regional Comprehensive Economic Partnership (RCEP), initially progressed slowly, but with the withdrawal of the United States from the TPP, China and ASEAN countries increased their efforts to develop this loose partnership into a more integrated set of free trade agreements (Tostevin 2019). In late 2019, the members of ASEAN, together with five of their free trade partners—India pulled out at the last minute but is invited to join at any time—agreed to transform the RCEP into the world's largest free trade zone in 2020. Once established, the RCEP will cover 15 countries, with 46% of the world's population and 32% of global GDP. (In comparison, the European Union covers 7% of the world's population and 16% of global GDP, and the North American Free Trade Agreement/United States–Mexico–Canada Agreement [NAFTA/USMCA] covers 6% of the world's population and 18% of global GDP.)

However, the trade liberalization within the RCEP is less pronounced than it is for the European Union or NAFTA/USMCA. Although RCEP member states are expected to gradually lower their tariffs on goods traded between them and other member states, tariffs are not harmonized across the RCEP but are agreed on individually between member states. Also, the RCEP does not cover such sensitive issues as the liberalization of agriculture, workers' rights, and environmental protection (Tostevin 2019). Nevertheless, with the establishment of the RCEP in 2020, Chinese companies will have an incentive to expand their supply chains toward Southeast Asia while developed countries such as Japan, Australia, and South Korea will gain easier access to China. And this will, in the medium to long run, pull these developed countries in the Pacific basin closer to China and farther away from the United States.

Global Connections: The Belt and Road Initiative

But regional expansion of Chinese companies' supply chains and easier access to consumers in Asia are not the end goals of China's ambitious plans. In its efforts to become a global high-tech hub, China aims to expand its reach beyond its neighbors and toward the West. The Belt and Road Initiative (BRI) is meant to do just that. Announced in 2013 and integrated into the constitution of the Chinese Communist Party in 2017, the project is intended to build a global infrastructure network that connects participating countries with China and facilitates trade.

Furthermore, China also offers the possibility of linking the financial institutions of participating countries with Chinese banks and investment companies to provide cheaper financing and a more globalized financial system centered on Chinese banks. In the most ambitious cases, participating countries could even coordinate their economic development policies with China, though so far, no country involved in the BRI has taken this step (Eder 2018).

While the official goals of the BRI include cultural, societal, and economic cooperation, in its final form, the BRI will clearly increase China's economic and political influence significantly in Asia, Europe, and Africa. This prospect of rising Chinese influence in emerging economies and increasingly also in Western Europe has led to some irritation in the United States and other countries as China's BRI investments have come closer and closer to Western Europe and North America. For example, in 2018, Greece became a member of the BRI, and the Chinese company COSCO renovated and began to run Greece's largest port, in Piraeus. And in March 2019, Italy became the first G–7 country to join the BRI, in hopes of attracting substantial Chinese investments in its infrastructure.

What started as a regional initiative among emerging markets has been constantly expanding in terms of both member states and infrastructure projects. In 2017, for example, an Arctic maritime route between China and Europe was included in the BRI, and China intends to expand its BRI to Latin America in the future, as shown in **Exhibit 12**.

Though the BRI was officially announced in 2013, it is still in its early days. As Eder and Mardell (2019) reported, China is seemingly following a phased approach to the development of the BRI. In the first stage, the country was focusing primarily on investments in energy generation and power transmission projects. In the first six years of the BRI, two-thirds of investments (close to $50 billion) were made in the power infrastructure sector, but only $15 billion in transport infrastructure projects and $10 billion in the Digital Silk Road, which is meant to establish a better information and communication infrastructure in participating nations, as shown in **Exhibit 13**.

With respect to energy infrastructure projects, China seems to have a preference for green energy (which includes hydroelectric power plants as well as wind and solar plants). This segment has attracted the most contracts and the biggest investments, particularly in Africa and Scandinavia. However, China also finances and builds a large number of coal power plants and other fossil fuel power plants. The financing of coal power plants seems to be a way of supporting the domestic coal industry. Because a goal of MIC25 is to reduce the CO_2 intensity of the Chinese economy by 40% between 2015 and 2025, coal plants are rapidly being phased out in China. The Chinese

Exhibit 12. The BRI

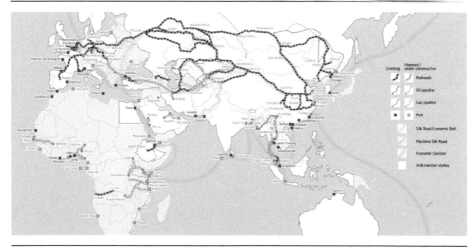

Source: Mercator Institute for China Studies (MERICS).

Exhibit 13. BRI Investments Completed by Mid-2019

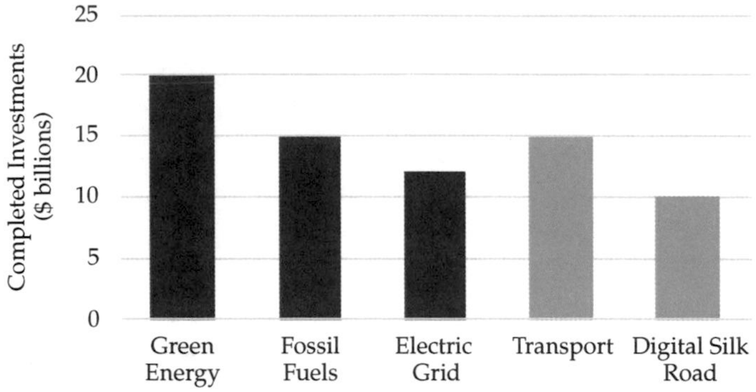

Source: Eder and Mardell (2019).

coal industry is, therefore, under significant economic stress, and exporting this energy source to other emerging markets can help mitigate this stress. Nevertheless, one should not expect China to promote fossil fuels too much in its BRI. The word "coal," for example, appears only once in the BRI's two foundational documents (Eder and Mardell 2019).

The efforts to finance energy infrastructure in BRI member countries imply that Western companies that are trying to operate in these countries face tremendous competitive pressures. Thanks to ample government and bank financing for such projects, Chinese companies are often able to offer cheaper financing and less restrictive conditions on such projects than Western sponsors can offer. As a result, the market share of Chinese companies in BRI member countries is growing slowly but steadily at the expense of Western providers.

So far, this has happened primarily in the energy and energy infrastructure sector, but these investments will lay the foundation on which to expand into transport infrastructure and industrial projects in the future. In fact, the investments in energy infrastructure projects in the first phase of the BRI will allow China to boost the local industrial capabilities of BRI member countries that will gradually become part of the global supply chains centered on Chinese high-tech companies built under MIC25.

BRI's Sometimes Controversial Financing. One of the main questions for the BRI is how to finance the massive investments planned in the coming decades. Identifying the total investments made in the BRI so far or in the future is virtually impossible because China has a multitude of channels through which financing is funneled, some of which are highly opaque to outsiders. **Exhibit 14** summarizes what we currently know about the four main financing channels of the BRI.

The biggest investments are typically made via loans from Chinese commercial banks, which are expected to provide loans of $60 billion per year to companies and countries participating in the BRI. The largest official lender is the Asian Infrastructure Investment Bank (AIIB), which I will discuss in more detail in the next section. The AIIB has paid-up capital of $100 billion and is expected to provide loans in the range of $10 billion to $15 billion per year throughout the 2020s. The New Development Bank (NDB), founded in 2015 and formerly known as the BRICS Development Bank, also has $100 billion in paid-up capital and will be able to provide loans in the range of $5 billion to $7 billion per year in the 2020s. Because the member states of the NDB are Brazil, Russia, India, China, and South Africa only, these investments will focus on these five countries (or rather four, given that China will likely not request any loans from the NDB). Finally, the Silk Road Fund was established in 2014 and is the Chinese government's official investment fund for sponsoring BRI projects. As is clear from Exhibit 14, it is only a secondary funding source compared with the AIIB or Chinese commercial banks.

Of course, both the West and existing global economic institutions, such as the International Monetary Fund (IMF) and the World Bank, have been worried about the expansion of the BRI and the sometimes lax financing conditions of BRI projects. The main criticism of the BRI is that it is a form of "debt diplomacy," wherein loans are provided to BRI member countries and companies for projects that are not economically feasible. Once a project fails, the country involved then has to default on its debt to China, at which point China might take control of vital local infrastructure or make other demands.

The most prominent example of this risk is the Hambantota port project in Sri Lanka. This port, which is close to the country's main port in Colombo, was shopped around by the Sri Lankan government for years. Nobody wanted to take it on because it was not considered economically feasible. In the end,

Exhibit 14. Financing Capacity for the BRI

Institutions	Authorized Capital ($ billions)	Possible Lending in Early 2020s ($ billions per year)
AIIB	100	10–15
New Development Bank	100	5–7
Silk Road Fund	40	2–3
Commercial banks		ca. 60

Source: He (2017).

China offered financing for the project with an annual interest rate of 6%–7%. The port was built and eventually failed, as predicted, so that Sri Lanka had to default on the Chinese loans. In 2017, 70% of the port was refinanced in a debt-to-equity swap with China Merchants Port Holdings Company (CMPort), which provided the Sri Lankan government with $1.4 billion to repay its Chinese debt. In return, Sri Lanka maintains ownership of the port but has leased it for 99 years to CMPort, which will invest $700 million to $800 million in the port to modernize and revitalize it.

The Hambantota port project acts as a warning to other BRI members accepting Chinese loans, but it also shows that China has remarkable flexibility in accepting payments. In fact, the sale of a project to a Chinese company seems to be the exception rather than the rule. When a debtor gets into distress, Chinese lenders are typically willing to accept payments other than cash, such as commodities or leases of existing infrastructure, as in the case of the Hambantota port. This makes Chinese loans more interesting in the eyes of many emerging markets than loans from the World Bank and other Western institutions because the borrowers are often asset rich but cash poor. As a result, they would have to ask for debt forgiveness or debt restructuring if they received loans from the World Bank or Western countries, whereas they could avoid these situations with loans from China. What the West, therefore, sees as a threat to emerging markets is often perceived as an advantage in these countries.

And in the long run, we have to admit that, despite the risks of excessive debt financing, the BRI will likely be beneficial not just for China but also for the participating member states. Remember from Chapter 4, "International Economic Cooperation," that increased trade provides a clear boost to economic growth through increased exports and increased productivity. But emerging markets often lack the vital energy and transportation infrastructure to take full advantage of the benefits of free trade.

This is where the BRI will be able to help. Because of the lack of data and the relatively small number of infrastructure projects completed outside the energy sector, assessing the economic benefits of the BRI for member countries is difficult. In 2018, researchers from the RAND Corporation made initial efforts to estimate the projected benefits of the buildout in transport infrastructure. Because transport infrastructure is relatively clearly defined, its benefits can be modeled more easily than those of energy infrastructure or communication technology.

The researchers estimated that the existence of a rail connection between two participating BRI countries could increase exports by 2.8% for these countries. The reduction of air distance by 10% (e.g., through modernized airports) increases trade by 0.4%, and a 10% reduction in maritime distance increases trade by 0.1%. Taking all planned transport infrastructure measures together, the expected gains amount to 7.3% of GDP for BRI member countries, or a total of $329 billion. Even EU member states would benefit because they are neighbors of many BRI members and face increased demand from these countries. The expected boost to EU GDP would be 2.6%, or $133 billion (Lu, Rohr, Hafner, and Knack 2018).

Expanding the Existing World Order: The AIIB

A major component of the BRI that warrants a separate analysis is the AIIB, which became operational in January 2016 and provides financing for infrastructure projects to enhance the connectivity between economies. But wait, is that not the job of the World Bank? Indeed, the AIIB is in direct competition with the World Bank, the Asian Development Bank, and other existing institutions of the current economic world order. China is a member of all these institutions but has very little influence compared with the United States and other Western countries, as **Exhibit 15** illustrates. Thus, China has had difficulty influencing decision making in the World Bank and IMF.

As Exhibit 15 shows, China is willing to take on a bigger leadership role in the emerging new world order, but with its rise as a great economic power, it no longer has to play by the rules of the West if it does not want to. If the World Bank and the IMF are unable to reform themselves and grant China more influence, the country can increasingly go it alone and create rival institutions under its leadership.

In an interview with the *Financial Times* in 2015, former Fed chairman Ben Bernanke even claimed that the refusal of the US Congress to accept

Exhibit 15. Voting Rights in the IMF, World Bank, and AIIB

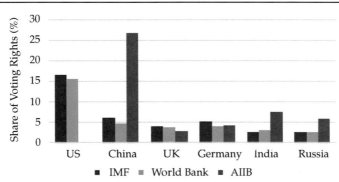

Sources: IMF, World Bank, AIIB.

159

a higher voting share for China in the IMF might have been a trigger for the creation of the AIIB (Pilling and Noble 2015). In this respect, China has done with the AIIB what great powers have done for decades. It is an active member of institutions it deems beneficial for its political and economic interests and refuses to become a member of those institutions it considers not helpful or even dangerous to its interests. The United States has done the same in the past and increasingly so under President Donald Trump (e.g., the withdrawal of the United States from the TPP and the Paris Agreement).

As Ikenberry and Lim (2017) pointed out, the AIIB is an element of geo-economic policy that sits on one end of the spectrum of options ranging from active membership in Western-led international institutions to Chinese-dominated rival institutions. Within the AIIB, China calls the shots because it has 26.6% of voting rights. Additionally, the president of the AIIB, Jin Liqun, is Chinese. With the AIIB's help, China can demonstrate to the world that it is willing to take on more responsibility on a global stage and prove that it can do so responsibly. And the AIIB shows the West that the country can work successfully outside the existing institutions if it is not granted more rights and influence within them.

The AIIB also has many economic advantages for China. The People's Bank of China has the world's largest foreign exchange reserves, predominantly held in US Treasuries. Since the GFC, these Treasuries have had very low yields, and when yields will rise to levels that are commensurate with the returns available in global infrastructure projects is unclear. The AIIB, therefore, allows China to recycle some of its reserves into higher-yielding international projects while keeping control over the timing, size, and destination of the funds. Meanwhile, China does not bear the risks of these projects alone but shares them with the other AIIB member states. Furthermore, the AIIB allows China to provide an outlet for the international expansion of Chinese companies within the BRI. In the long run, the AIIB might even be helpful in expanding the global reach of the renminbi, but so far, this seems to be far off in the future.

The risk the AIIB poses for emerging markets and the West is that China might be tempted to undercut the lending standards of the World Bank or even use the potential recall of AIIB funds as a threat to borrowers to enhance China's political influence in emerging markets. In the long run, such aggressive behavior would undercut China's aim of establishing itself as a responsible great power alternative to the United States.

This is the reason we have not, so far, seen an erosion of lending standards by the AIIB relative to the World Bank or the Asian Development Bank. The AIIB received a AAA rating from the three major credit rating agencies within 18 months of being established, and it relies on the membership of

Western democracies to lend it legitimacy and provide expertise in project due diligence. (Most of the vice presidents of the AIIB are Westerners with extensive knowledge of international project finance.)

Because the AIIB finances most of its activities by borrowing in international debt markets with the contributions of member states as collateral, it must retain a high credit rating and be seen in international markets as a high-quality borrower. Otherwise, the institution would quickly face rising borrowing costs that would undermine the profitability of the financed projects and the AIIB's reputation as a valid alternative to the World Bank. In short, the AIIB is constrained by its Western members because it needs them to provide legitimacy to the institution, and thus it cannot deviate too far from established institutions' lending practices. Although the AIIB is in its early days and still in the process of building its portfolio of projects, Ikenberry and Lim (2017) have empirically analyzed its lending activities and found little difference, so far, between its lending standards and those of the World Bank.

The Reaction of the United States under Donald Trump

As we have seen throughout this chapter, China's increased economic influence globally, together with the country's ambitious plans to escape the middle-income trap, has caused concern in the West. This concern is understandable, given that China's emergence as a great power undercuts the economic influence of Western countries and reduces the profits of Western businesses. No country feels more threatened by the rise of China than the United States because the latter has been the sole leader of the global economy and promoted liberal democracy and a neoliberal economic model for the past three decades. The benefits for the United States in the years since World War II have been significantly higher than the costs, as we saw in Chapter 4.

With China's rise, the United States and its Western allies have lost influence and now fear that the core values on which the existing world order has been built—freedom of expression, democracy, and free markets—will be undermined by China's state capitalist system. That system restricts certain liberties that are taken for granted in the West. On top of that are rising concerns that some business practices of Chinese companies are in violation of international rules. Plenty of accusations that Chinese companies engage in intellectual property (IP) theft have been made, which has led to the slogans that China operates both a "B2B" and a "C2C" business model: "back to Beijing" and "copy to China."

Most Western countries have tried to resolve these challenges with China through existing institutional channels, such as the World Trade Organization (WTO), and through restrictions on Chinese investments in their own countries. With the election of Donald Trump as US president, however, the dispute between the United States and China quickly escalated. Driven by a belief that such protectionist measures as tariffs and quotas can be beneficial for economic growth and create jobs in the United States that had previously been outsourced to emerging markets, the Trump administration started a trade war that escalated throughout 2018 and 2019. **Exhibit 16** shows the value-weighted average import tariffs for Chinese goods into the United States and for US goods into China until mid-2020.

Starting a Trade War. The trade war started with US Section 201 tariffs on solar panels and washing machines imported from China. Section 201 of the Trade Act of 1974 allows the US president to temporarily introduce tariffs and other non-tariff barriers on foreign goods to protect domestic producers of like goods. This rule is in accordance with General Agreement on Tariffs and Trade and WTO rules, but it was rarely used until US solar module producer Suniva fell into bankruptcy in April 2017 and filed a Section 201 complaint with the US government.

On 23 March 2018, the United States introduced additional tariffs on imports of Chinese steel and aluminum under Section 232 of the Trade Expansion Act of 1962, which allows the institution of tariffs if imports of certain goods threaten the national security of the United States. In reaction to the steel and aluminum tariffs, China retaliated with tariffs of its own on 1 May 2018. At that point, the trade war was underway, and it escalated until it caused tariffs of 25% and higher to be imposed on virtually all Chinese imports to the United States and an equivalent amount of tariffs on Chinese imports from the United States, as Exhibit 16 shows.

Exhibit 16.   US–China Tariffs

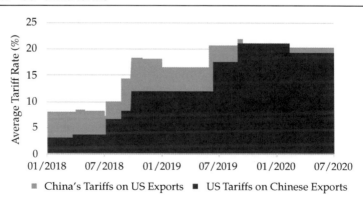

Source: Brown (2019).

With the introduction of the Phase 1 deal, which came into effect on 14 February 2020, the escalation process has come to a halt as of this writing (August 2020). The analysis of Robinson and Thierfelder (2019) can provide a good estimate of the economic impact of the trade war as of the end of 2019. Their analysis assumed that all the tariffs that are in place and announced for the end of 2019 will remain in place throughout 2020 and beyond, which is more or less what the Phase 1 deal stipulates.

Little or No Economic Impact So Far. Given these assumptions, Robinson and Thierfelder (2019) calculated the impact of the trade war on GDP growth in various regions and the change in domestic demand (defined as GDP plus imports minus exports). Their analysis showed that GDP growth will experience a small decline from the trade war in 2020, with US and Mexican GDP reduced by 0.13%, while low-income Asian countries will experience a decline in GDP of approximately 0.05%. This effect is so small that even if the Covid-19 pandemic had not caused the deepest recession in 80 years, it would be hardly visible in the growth statistics of these countries, as **Exhibit 17** illustrates.

The first reason for these small effects is that China did not unilaterally escalate the trade war with the United States but instead restricted its retaliatory actions to the same amount as the US tariffs on Chinese imports. The second reason is that other countries around the world chose not to get involved whenever possible. The Trump administration's proposal to impose tariffs on Canadian and Mexican steel imports created such an outrage that these countries were quickly given exemptions. Ever since, the Trump administration has threatened to introduce tariffs on Western imports (e.g., on European cars),

Exhibit 17. Estimated Impact of US–China Trade War

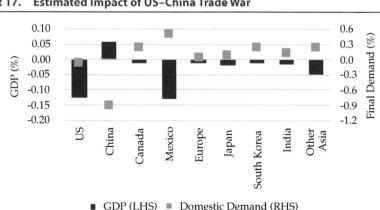

Source: Robinson and Thierfelder (2019).

but with the exception of tariffs sanctioned by the WTO in response to the Airbus subsidies, it has so far not acted on these threats. As a result, the share of global trade affected by the trade war has been relatively small.

This asymmetry in tariffs also creates the seemingly counterintuitive effect of the trade war on China's GDP. According to the model of Robinson and Thierfelder (2019), China's GDP could get a small boost in the order of 0.06% of GDP from the trade war. This effect results from the country's ability to shift exports from the United States to the rest of the world. Robinson and Thierfelder estimated that because of the tariffs, Chinese exports to the United States declined by 14.6% and US exports to China declined by 9.7%. But China can divert its exports to Europe (+6.6%) and Asia (+5.1%), which more than compensates for the loss of exports to the United States. As the rest of the world ignores the US–China trade war, China has an incentive to increase its trade links with the rest of the world and export its products at cheaper prices than those of local competitors in Europe and Asia.

Thus, the price advantage of Chinese goods, together with efforts by the rest of the world to increase trade ties with China and gain access to its market, leads to lower tariff barriers between China and other countries. China has already opened its markets for cosmetics, cars, and other consumer goods to imports from Europe and Japan to dampen the negative effect of higher prices on US imports. In return, Chinese exporters gained better access to these markets.

But this increase in exports also leads to a significant decline in domestic demand (and thus welfare) in China. The increase in exports means that production shifts away from domestic consumption and toward international markets, thus creating a decline in domestic consumption on the order of 0.9%. In the United States, domestic consumption declines because imports from China become more expensive and the United States has little opportunity to substitute these imports with goods from other countries. The decline in imports, therefore, leads to a slight drop in domestic US demand, 0.07%. The true winners seem to be the countries in the rest of the world because they all face higher domestic demand thanks to the improved terms of trade. One can even say that the losers of the US–China trade war are the United States and China, while everyone else wins. One can see this in Exhibit 17.

Because the tariffs raised in the US–China trade war predominantly affect those industries that have globally integrated supply chains, the impact of the trade war on domestic production in China and the United States can vary dramatically from industry to industry. **Exhibit 18** shows that in the United States, the agriculture sector and the manufacturers of final goods are hit the hardest, seeing their production decline by an estimated 0.6%–0.7%.

Exhibit 18. Estimated Impact on Domestic Production

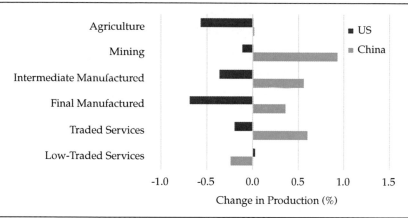

Source: Robinson and Thierfelder (2019).

Services that are typically not internationally traded, in contrast, will hardly see any impact from the US–China trade war. Chinese production in these sectors tends to grow because of the trade war as China successfully diverts its exports to Europe and Asia.

What Is the End Game? How will this trade war play out over time? Will it escalate more and more, dragging other countries into it and eventually causing significant damage to the global economy? Will it end in a stalemate in which the current tariffs remain in place for a long time and neither side makes a move? Or are we heading to a resolution of the trade war and an eventual reduction of tariffs back to the lower levels seen in 2017?

To answer these questions, the Center for Strategic and International Studies, a nonpartisan think tank in Washington, DC, ran a series of simulations of the trade war (commonly known as "war games") in which trade experts took on the roles of the various parties and were asked to act in their self-interest (Goodman, Gerstel, Risberg, Kennedy, and Reinsch 2019).

The participants in the war games behaved as follows:

- The simulations were based on game-theoretical approaches where each actor acts rationally and in her self-interest based on the incentives given to her. In essence, the rise of China as an economic great power creates a situation equivalent to the famous prisoner's dilemma. Both the United States and China would be best off in the long run if they cooperated, but the United States is wary of Chinese influence in the world and thus has an incentive to block this increasing influence. Meanwhile, Beijing is wary of constraints on its economic progress and is willing to defect from the cooperative optimum and establish economic policies outside existing systems, such as those of the AIIB. Thus, each side has an incentive to defect from cooperation, making both sides worse off in the end.

- To force the other side to take certain desirable actions or refrain from undesirable ones, both sides could use escalation and deterrence techniques. These techniques are well studied, particularly in the context of the Cold War, during which nuclear deterrence motivated both the United States and the Soviet Union to avoid starting a nuclear war. One core assumption is that both parties use escalation techniques intentionally, not accidentally.

- Both parties had incomplete information and did not know exactly where the other party's strengths and vulnerabilities were. This means that assessing the exact costs of economic actions before the fact was impossible, opening up the possibility of unintended consequences.

- Finally, within each round of the simulations, both sides could bargain with the other to create a mutually agreeable solution to the trade war. The simulations were run in several rounds, during which both sides were given more information and knowledge about the other. The game was repeated until either a stalemate or a resolution was achieved.

The start dates used in the simulations were 2021, a year after a hypothetical partial trade agreement had been reached between the United States and China, and 2025, after a long period of stasis where both sides stuck to the initial trade agreement but IP theft still occurred on the Chinese side.

Neither simulation ended in a positive resolution of the conflict. Despite the different settings and backgrounds, both parties escalated the trade conflict in a tit-for-tat sequence that led to the partial decoupling of the US and Chinese economies. In the 2021 scenario, both sides tried to escalate the trade war so as to be able to declare victory if the other side made only small concessions. In the 2025 scenario, both sides quickly gave up on achieving a cooperative solution and instead focused on creating alliances to encircle the other side (similar to what happened in the late 19th and early 20th centuries during the great power competition between the British Empire, France, Germany, and Russia).

In both instances, the United States tried to encircle China, though more aggressively so in the 2025 scenario, while China felt threatened by the US efforts to isolate it economically. In both instances, China played defense to retain other countries' willingness to invest in China. This meant that China would typically react to US escalations only in a commensurate way and would use delay tactics to stall further escalations for as long as possible.

China's defensive strategy also meant that the country would, from time to time, agree on partial trade deals to placate the United States and other international investors but avoid structural reforms where possible. On the positive side, both sides increasingly refrained from using tariffs as a measure to escalate the conflict. Instead, the United States increasingly used targeted export bans to prevent the Chinese high-tech industry from acquiring crucial know-how, while China used informal tools to make doing business in China more difficult for US companies (e.g., targeted import checks or online censorship).

The key takeaway from both simulations was that trust increasingly broke down between the United States and China. Both sides were doubtful about the other side's actions, even if they were taken in good faith. As a result, discussions became increasingly difficult, and both sides had incentives to use domestic policy tools to dampen the negative effects of the escalating conflict and to form international relationships with third parties that excluded the opposing side. Furthermore, the need to dampen the negative effects of the conflict meant that the US and Chinese governments had to play an increasingly active role in their domestic economies through regulation, tax incentives, and other forms of government intervention. Thus, we learn that the ongoing trade war poses an increasing risk of market inefficiency and market failure domestically.

Private businesses and third-party countries will play a crucial role. With respect to determining economic and political ties, third-party countries will have to strike a balance between the United States and China and try to remain on each country's good side. But emerging markets especially will feel the pressure to take sides, thus escalating the conflict between the United States and China even further.

Private businesses globally (including those in China and the United States) will thus probably have to deal with a permanent state of heightened political uncertainty. As a result, supply chains will have to become more diversified internationally, which should, in a first step, benefit export-oriented businesses in Europe and the Asia-Pacific region. For example, one would expect some businesses to shift their supply chains from China to India, Vietnam, or Mexico, which could lead to a permanent loss of market share for businesses in China.

The Covid-19 pandemic of 2020 has shown very clearly how dependent Western businesses are on supply chains that originate in China. The rising geopolitical uncertainties, combined with Western companies' desire to "pandemic-proof" their supply chains, will likely accelerate supply chain diversification in the future. The US agriculture industry, however, faces the opposite threat. As China gradually diversifies its supply of agricultural commodities, US farmers will likely lose business with China permanently and have to compete with other agricultural exporters around the globe.

Are We Heading toward a Thucydides Trap?

The rather dire results of the war games on the US–China trade war remind one of the great power competition at the end of the 19th century between the British Empire, France, Germany, and Russia. Under the German chancellor Otto von Bismarck, Germany tried to isolate the British Empire through a net of public and secret alliances. This network of treaties created stability in Europe in the late 19th century and the early years of the 20th century, but it also led to World War I.

First, the British Empire tried to form alliances of its own to counterbalance Germany's efforts. This situation led to an even more complex and fragile web of alliances and dependencies. Once Bismarck was relieved of his role as chancellor and replaced by a government under the leadership of Kaiser Wilhelm II, one that was less capable in international relations (to say the least), this network of alliances led to a fatal chain reaction. When the Austrian crown prince was assassinated by a Serbian in June 1914, Austria-Hungary threatened Serbia with war. Serbia could count on the help of the Russian Empire in case of war, but the Austro-Hungarian Empire, unable to go to war against Russia on its own, was forced to ask Germany for support.

This request meant that in case of war, Germany had to come to the help of Austria-Hungary. When Austria ultimately declared war on Serbia, Russia immediately declared war on Austria, which, in turn, triggered a declaration of war by Germany against Russia. Knowing that the Russian Empire had a military alliance with France, the Germans tried to attack France via a detour through neutral Belgium. Belgium, in turn, could rely on the British Empire as a protector of its neutrality, thus dragging the British Empire into the war. What started as a minor event on the outskirts of Europe spiraled into World War I within a couple of weeks in August 1914. And this war would become the deadliest war up to that point, leaving an estimated 9.5 million soldiers and 8 million civilians dead.

Could an unwanted escalation of a political and economic great power rivalry between the United States and China lead to another world war? As I have discussed, the existence of nuclear weapons means that an escalation of the conflict between these two countries is unlikely to end in outright war, but if it does, we will all have problems bigger than looking after our portfolios.

However, a more limited military confrontation between the United States and China seems at least possible, though not likely. Over the past couple of years, the concept of the "Thucydides Trap," first coined by the historian Graham Allison, has regained popularity. It is named after the ancient Greek historian Thucydides, who claimed that the rise of Athens instilled fear in dominant Sparta and made war inevitable. According to Allison, the past 500 years have seen 16 instances of the rise of a new great power, 12 of which ended in war. The four instances that did not end in military conflict were Spain overtaking Portugal in the 15th century, the United States overtaking the British Empire in the early 20th century, the rise of the Soviet Union during the Cold War, and the rise of Germany as an economic great power in Europe in the 1990s (Allison 2017).

We might be able to take some solace from the fact that three of these four instances of peaceful resolution happened in the 20th century, so we might have learned a lesson from the past to avoid the Thucydides Trap. But as we all know, we learn from history that we do not learn from history and should, therefore, not get too hopeful. Instead, a better approach would be to look for signs of the rising great power undermining the status quo.

As Schweller and Pu (2011) noted, before a rising great power can so much as threaten a military conflict, it must first undermine the authority and dominance of the existing great power. This delegitimization of the existing great power happens through the establishment of a new political or economic order that proves to be stable and prosperous for the members of these new institutions.

If the existing great power resists this new order, all the better for the rising great power, because doing so undermines the existing great power's legitimacy in the eyes of those countries that sympathize with the rising great power. Why align yourself with the existing great power if it is unreliable as a partner and insists on cutting potentially profitable ties with the rising great power? What smoothed the transition from the British Empire to the United States as a global economic superpower and the rise of Germany as a great power in Europe was that in both instances, the rising power had open trade relationships with the existing great power, and this relationship ensured that both the rising great power and the existing great power benefited. Furthermore, these open relationships meant that third parties were not forced to choose one side or the other but could join both at the same time, thus maximizing their benefits.

In short, globalization ensured that the rise of a new great power did not lead to military conflict. Only when globalization broke down did military conflict become inevitable.

These insights also reveal that we should not look for an imminent buildup in military spending by China or the United States. Yes, China is expanding its military capacities, but as a share of GDP, China's military spending remains well below that of the United States, and the military might of the United States is not even remotely threatened by the People's Liberation Army, as shown in **Exhibit 19**. However, as China rises as an economic great power, it not surprisingly also becomes more assertive as a regional military power, putting it in direct conflict with such neighbors as South Korea, Japan, and Vietnam. And because both South Korea and Japan are in a military alliance with the United States, the risk is that unwanted escalation could lead to an armed conflict in East Asia that involves both the United States and China.

The Churchill Trap Is More Likely Than the Thucydides Trap. However, beyond the limited risk of a Thucydides Trap, a much more realistic possibility is what Yang (2018) called the "Churchill Trap"—that the United States and China could repeat the mistakes that Churchill warned of during his famous Iron Curtain speech in March 1946. The United States and the Soviet Union, allies during World War II, quickly became mired in a long-term, low-level economic and political conflict after that war, marked by mutual mistrust and competition for influence among third parties. Such a "new Cold War" between the United States and China is highly likely, as the war games of Goodman et al. (2019) demonstrated.

As Exhibit 19 shows, military spending in the United States was more than twice as high during the Cold War with the Soviet Union as it is today, but what is more important to recognize is that all the participants were economically worse off. Clearly, economic growth was stymied in the socialist

Exhibit 19. Military Spending of the United States and China

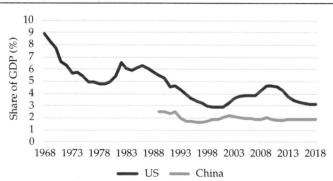

Source: World Bank.

planning economies compared with the capitalist systems in the West, but Western economies were also constrained because they did not have access to the socialist economies and their consumers. They were also diverting resources to military expenditures that would not have been needed if no Cold War had happened. With the end of the Cold War, businesses in the West and the former Warsaw Pact countries could reap the peace dividend and economic growth accelerated for approximately two decades until the GFC.

Avoiding both the Churchill Trap and the Thucydides Trap has, therefore, become the paramount objective of international relations in the 21st century. But doing so is not easy. As Goodman et al. (2019) showed, the key challenge the United States and China face is a decline of trust in the good faith of the other. Goodman et al. emphasized that both sides need to reverse the tit for tat of escalating conflict and start moving in the opposite direction. Such a reverse toward de-escalation can be achieved if both sides show sincerity in their willingness to escalate and in their commitment to de-escalate.

Both the United States and China thus need to commit to unilaterally engaging in de-escalating steps as long as the other side refrains from escalating the situation further or even de-escalates themselves. For example, the United States could promise to reduce tariffs on Chinese steel if China did not cut its imports of US soybeans. If China then complied, the United States would need to follow through with the de-escalation as a sign of goodwill, which could then lead to a demand for a reduction in Chinese import tariffs, which would be met by an equal reduction in US import tariffs, and so on.

Parallel to such a de-escalation strategy, both the United States and China need to collaborate on global issues and become joint leaders of the global economic world order. Such a collaboration would, on the one hand, help build trust between the two parties and, on the other, allow China to play a more important role in the world while remaining aligned with the United States. Finally, such a collaboration between the United States and China on crucial global challenges such as climate change and cybersecurity would ensure that smaller countries would not have to choose between the US and Chinese spheres of influence and could instead work with both great powers at the same time (Yang 2018). Whether such cooperation between the United States and China is possible in the future remains to be seen.

Conclusion

In this chapter, we have seen that China has become an economic great power over the past couple of decades. The sheer size of the Chinese economy and its integration into global supply chains and the global financial system mean that the effects of a severe slowdown of Chinese growth would no longer be limited to China or its neighbors but would lead to a significant global slowdown and, in the worst case, to another financial crisis.

But the Chinese economy faces significant challenges over the coming years. China has tried to escape the middle-income trap by fostering a local high-tech industry that directly competes with high-tech businesses in Japan, Europe, and North America. Furthermore, China has attempted to build a global supply chain centered on Chinese businesses with the help of the BRI. These efforts to foster growth in China have led to significant irritation and concern in the West.

The pushback against Chinese efforts to modernize its economy had primarily come from within traditional political channels, until the United States under President Trump intensified the conflict with the help of unilaterally imposed tariffs. This US–China trade war has escalated, and currently, we see little hope for a de-escalation to the status quo ante. Instead, a long-term stalemate, during which partial agreements on trade will be made and no further escalation happens, seems the most likely outcome for the coming years.

But game-theoretical simulations show that such a stalemate is unlikely to persist for a long time. Instead, the risk of another escalation of the conflict persists, which would lead to a gradual decoupling of the US and Chinese economies and could trigger a new Cold War between the two countries. Such a new Cold War would make all participants worse off, so its avoidance should be the main concern of international relations between the two countries in the coming decades. In the end, a trend toward increased globalization in the 20th century is what has helped prevent the escalation of great power conflict into outright war, and international cooperation between the United States and China seems to be the best solution for the prevention of a new Cold War between the two countries.

Bibliography

Ahmed, S. 2017. "China's Footprints on the Global Economy: Remarks Delivered at the Second IMF and Federal Reserve Bank of Atlanta Research Workshop on the Chinese Economy." Board of Governors of the Federal Reserve System.

Ahmed, S., R. Correa, D. A. Dias, N. Gornemann, J. Hoek, A. Jain, E. Liu, and A. Wong. 2019. "Global Spillovers of a China Hard Landing." International Finance Discussion Papers 1260.

Allison, G. 2017. "The Thucydides Trap." Foreign Policy (9 June). https://foreignpolicy.com/2017/06/09/the-thucydides-trap/.

Brown, C. P. 2019. "US–China Trade War Tariffs: An Up-to-Date Chart." Peterson Institute for International Economics. www.piie.com/research/ piie-charts/us-china-trade-war-tariffs-date-chart.

Curran, E. 2019. "What's the RCEP and What Happened to the TPP?" *Washington Post* (4 November).

Deng, Y. 2014. "China: The Post-Responsible Power." *Washington Quarterly* 37 (4): 117–32.

Eder, T. S. 2018. "Mapping the Belt and Road Initiative: This Is Where We Stand." MERICS. www.merics.org/en/bri-tracker/mapping-the-belt-and-road-initiative.

Eder, T. S., and J. Mardell. 2019. "Powering the Belt and Road: China Supports Its Energy Companies' Global Expansion and Prepares the Ground for Potential New Supply Chains." MERICS. www.merics.org/en/ bri-tracker/powering-the-belt-and-road.

Fukuyama, F. 1992. *The End of History and the Last Man*. New York: Free Press.

Goodman, M. P., D. Gerstel, P. Risberg, S. Kennedy, and W. A. Reinsch. 2019. "Beyond the Brink: Escalation and Conflict in US–China Economic Relations." Center for Strategic and International Studies (September). https://csis-website-prod.s3.amazonaws.com/s3fs-public/publication/ 190925_Goodman_BeyondBrink_WEB.pdf.

Gygli, S., F. Haelg, N. Potrafke, and J.-E. Sturm. 2019. "The KOF Globalisation Index – Revisited." *Review of International Organizations* 14: 543–74.

He, T. 2017. "One Belt, One Road: How Will Partners Profit?" Brink. www.brinknews.com/one-belt-one-road-how-will-partners-profit/?utm_ source=BRINK+Asia.

Ikenberry, G. J., and D. J. Lim. 2017. "China's Emerging Institutional Statecraft: The Asian Infrastructure Investment Bank and the Prospects for Counter-Hegemony." Brookings Institution, Project on International Order and Strategy (April). www.brookings.edu/wp-content/uploads/2017/04/chinas-emerging-institutional-statecraft.pdf.

Lu, H., C. Rohr, M. Hafner, and A. Knack. 2018. "China Belt and Road Initiative: Measuring the Impact of Improving Transportation Connectivity on Trade in the Region." RAND Corporation.

Office of the Secretary of Defense. 2019. "Annual Report to Congress: Military and Security Developments Involving the People's Republic of China 2019." https://media.defense.gov/2019/May/02/2002127082/-1/-1/1/2019_CHINA_MILITARY_POWER_REPORT.pdf.

Pilling, D., and J. Noble. 2015. "US Congress Pushed China into Launching AIIB, Says Bernanke." *Financial Times* (2 June). www.ft.com/content/cb28200c-0904-11e5-b643-00144feabdc0.

Robinson, S., and K. Thierfelder. 2019. "Who's Winning the US–China Trade War? It's Not the United States or China." Peterson Institute for International Economics, *Trade and Investment Policy Watch* (blog). www.piie.com/blogs/trade-and-investment-policy-watch/whos-winning-us-china-trade-war-its-not-united-states-or.

Schweller, R. L., and X. Pu. 2011. "After Unipolarity: China's Visions of International Order in an Era of U.S. Decline." *International Security* 36 (1): 41–72.

Tostevin, M. 2019. "Explainer: World's Biggest Trade Pact Shapes Up without India." Reuters (5 November). www.reuters.com/article/us-asean-summit-trade-explainer/explainer-worlds-biggest-trade-pact-shapes-up-without-india-idUSKBN1XF0XY.

World Bank. 2017. "China Systematic Country Diagnostic Report."

Wübbeke, J., M. Meissner, M. J. Zenglein, J. Ives, and B. Conrad. 2016. "Made in China 2025: The Making of a High-Tech Superpower and Consequences for Industrial Countries." MERICS Papers on China 2 (December). https://merics.org/sites/default/files/2020-04/Made%20in%20China%202025.pdf.

Yang, Y. 2018. "Escape Both the 'Thucydides Trap' and the 'Churchill Trap': Finding a Third Type of Great Power Relations under the Bipolar System." *Chinese Journal of International Politics* 11 (2): 193–235.

Zenglein, M. J., and A. Holzmann. 2019. "Evolving Made in China 2025: China's Industrial Policy in the Quest for Global Tech Leadership." MERICS Papers on China 8 (July).

Zoellick, R. B. 2005. "Whither China: From Membership to Responsibility?" *NBR Analysis* 16 (4): 5.

Chapter 7: Data—The Oil of the 21st Century

If you spend more on coffee than on IT security, you will be hacked. What's more, you deserve to be hacked.

—Richard Clarke

Cyber Warfare and Cyber Attacks

We live in a world where nearly every business is connected to the internet and more than one-half of the people on Earth have online access. This widespread access has opened up the possibility of stealing vital information from both private and public sources and of attacking organizations and putting them temporarily out of business. Cybersecurity has become a major concern in the military, political, economic, and cultural fields, as shown in **Exhibit 1**.

In the military and defense realm, cyber warfare is now a top issue, creating a constant shadow war and arms race between countries and state-sponsored actors. Cyber warfare takes several different forms. As a first line of defense, governments have increased their defensive capabilities and are monitoring the potential cyber vulnerabilities of the software and hardware used for military applications. For example, in 2017, a US Army memo to all service members required them to cease all use of drones from the Chinese company DJI and to uninstall all software from that company because of cyber vulnerabilities in their products (Huang, Madnick, and Johnson 2018). In 2019, the US Department of the Interior followed suit and grounded all drones from Chinese manufacturers, as well as any that contained Chinese parts, because of security concerns (Montague 2019). In 2018, journalists rang the alarm bell when they discovered that the software of a fitness tracking app allowed anyone to locate secret US military bases and follow the patrol routes of US military personnel (Hsu 2018).

But more and more countries are no longer restricting themselves to defensive measures alone. According to public testimony to the US Senate Committee on Armed Services by the then director of National Intelligence James Clapper, more than 30 countries have developed offensive cyberwarfare capabilities. Of course, however, he excluded the United States, making that more than 31 countries.

Exhibit 1. Types of Cybersecurity Concerns

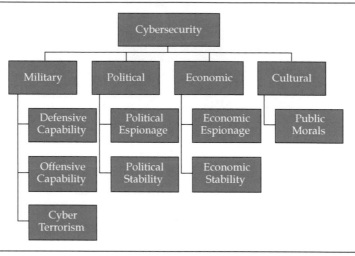

Source: Huang, Madnick, and Johnson (2018).

The list of cyber attacks by states is getting longer by the day. In 2017, Israeli intelligence officials infiltrated the Kaspersky Lab antivirus software and found evidence of Russian hackers using the software to spy on US businesses (Perlroth and Shane 2017). The cyber attacks of the Russian hacker groups Fancy Bear and Cozy Bear, both of which are widely assumed to be aligned with the Russian military intelligence service GRU, are too numerous to count. The Wikipedia pages for these two groups list 32 publicly discovered attacks (as of January 2021), not counting the ones that were never reported in the media.

The United States and Israel are widely thought to be the origin of the Stuxnet worm, first discovered in 2010, that attacked and damaged the Iranian nuclear program but then got out of control. Iran, in response, has created a cyber army that launched attacks against Israel in 2014 (Marks 2014), managed to create a 12-hour power outage in Turkey in 2015 that affected 40 million people (Halpern 2015), and hacked the email accounts of 90 members of parliament in the United Kingdom in 2017 (*Telegraph* 2017). After the 2019 drone attacks on Saudi Aramco facilities, the United States did not retaliate with missile strikes or any other traditional show of military force as it would have done in the past. Instead, it launched a cyber attack against Iranian infrastructure (Ali and Stewart 2019).

A third component of military cybersecurity concerns is the rising threat of cyber terrorism. Clapper, Lettre, and Rogers (2017) reported that international terror groups, such as the Islamic State, have sought to disclose information about US citizens to trigger "lone wolf attacks." Terror groups from al-Qaeda to the Islamic State and the Taliban all use the internet to collect information and organize attacks. Some terror groups, such as Hezbollah and Hamas, already have had considerable success with their cyber attacks in the Middle East.

But cyber attacks are also used to try to achieve political goals. Political espionage, such as the Iranian attacks on British members of parliament or the attacks by Fancy Bear on German politicians in 2014 and 2015, are a constant threat to the political process. Increasingly, rather than trying to steal secrets, state-sponsored hackers try to spread misinformation and fake news to influence elections or undermine public trust in politicians and governments. The most prominent example is the alleged Russian operation to influence the 2016 US presidential election (Mueller 2019).

Numerous cybersecurity concerns also exist in countries that have restricted information in some areas of public interest. For example, in Germany, the sale of Nazi memorabilia is prohibited by law, and authorities therefore must monitor the internet for violations of this law and ban sites that offer such goods for sale. Singapore, Lebanon, and Turkey all ban pornographic and adult entertainment sites to protect public morals and maintain public order (Mitchell and Hepburn 2016).

Cyber Attacks Are a Major Business Risk. Although a deeper dive into the details of these cultural cybersecurity issues would be interesting, the focus for the remainder of this chapter will be on economic cybersecurity issues. Economic cyber attacks run the full spectrum from outright espionage, such as the cyber attacks on US engineering and maritime companies to steal intellectual property (FireEye 2018), to stealing data and money and undermining trust in the reliability and stability of information technology (IT) systems.

The list of cyber attacks on businesses is enormous. Coburn, Daffron, Quantrill, Leverett, Bordeau, Smith, and Harvey (2019) reported that a 2018 survey of 1,300 companies in the United States, Canada, United Kingdom, Mexico, Germany, Australia, Singapore, and Japan showed that two-thirds of respondents were targets of cyber attacks on their supply chain. Government entities seem to be less attractive targets, with only 49% reporting a supply chain attack, compared with 82% of biotech and pharmaceutical companies. If successful, these cyber attacks can cause substantial business interruptions:

- In 2013, phishing emails stole passwords from a Target Corporation vendor and enabled the hackers to install malware in 1,800 stores. The data breach cost Target $200 million, and profits dropped 46% in the fourth quarter of 2013.

- In 2017, the NotPetya malware infiltrated the systems of a range of companies around the world, destroying hard disks and information. Cadbury reported damages of $147 million, Maersk Line of $300 million, and FedEx of $300 million.

- In 2018, the North Korean WannaCry ransomware infiltrated the network of Taiwan Semiconductor Manufacturing Company, causing damages of $170 million.

Kopp, Kaffenberger, and Wilson (2017) reported that the economy-wide cost of cyber attacks could be substantial. While the contribution of the internet to US GDP was estimated to be somewhere between 3.2% and 6.0% in 2015, the costs of cyber attacks could be anywhere between 0.6% and 2.2% of GDP. This means that in the worst-case scenario, the cost of cyber attacks could almost match the lowest estimate of the benefits of the internet.

Given these potentially large costs, cybersecurity, not surprisingly, increasingly is being discussed by investors and corporate analysts. **Exhibit 2** shows the number of companies in the S&P 500 Index that mentioned cybersecurity issues in earnings calls between 2013 and 2018. In 2018, almost 80% of the companies in the S&P 500 mentioned cybersecurity risks, and 26 companies mentioned security breaches in their systems. This public discussion of cybersecurity issues has two goals. First, businesses have to disclose material risks to their businesses. Given the potentially high cost of cyber attacks, addressing these risks in earnings calls is only natural. Second, and more important, businesses are trying to build public trust by openly discussing their investments in cybersecurity and their efforts to protect their businesses from malicious attacks.

Exhibit 2. Number of S&P 500 Companies Mentioning Cybersecurity in Earnings Calls

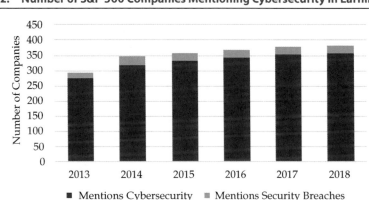

Source: Abbosh and Bissell (2019).

No matter how careful companies are in their efforts to combat cyber attacks, however, they remain vulnerable in two crucial areas. The market for cybersecurity services is dominated by a small number of suppliers, and a security breach in any one of the suppliers could immediately affect a large number of businesses around the world. The infiltration of the Kaspersky Lab software by Russian hackers mentioned earlier is one such example. Kaspersky Lab's anti-malware software is one of the top eight applications on the market, with a market share on Windows systems of 8.1% in 2019 (Liu 2019). In total, these eight providers of anti-malware software cover more than 80% of Windows PCs in the world.

Another area of external concentration risk is in the provision of vital data infrastructure. More and more software providers move their applications onto cloud-computing platforms that not only allow access to data from every mobile device and desktop PC anywhere in the world but also store data in the cloud. Globally, total spending on cloud infrastructure surpassed an estimated $500 billion in 2020, with one-quarter of all businesses spending more than $6 million on cloud services annually (Coborn et al. 2019).

The market for infrastructure as a service is dominated by Amazon Web Services (AWS), which had a market share of 48% in 2018 (Gartner 2019). This means that a severe data breach in Amazon's cloud services would immediately affect a significant share of internet businesses around the world, as **Exhibit 3** shows. In 2018, Amazon got a taste of its vulnerability when its cloud service experienced a series of outages that affected its online store and its Alexa assistant during Amazon Prime Day, the company's second-biggest shopping day of the year. The outages cost Amazon a reported $1.2 million in sales per minute of downtime (Coborn et al. 2019).

Exhibit 3. Market Share of Infrastructure as a Service

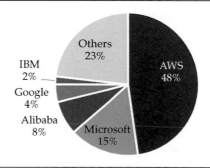

Source: Gartner (2019).

Case Study: From 5G to 6G

Another crucial area for cybersecurity in the coming decade will be the fast-developing communications infrastructure. Starting in 2019, 5G networks were being rolled out around the globe. As in the case of cloud computing, 5G infrastructure is a high-tech product that requires significant know-how and substantial capital to develop. Thus, as **Exhibit 4** shows, the market relies on four different companies, two Chinese (Huawei and ZTE) and two European (Nokia and Ericsson) for wireless telecom infrastructure. Huawei is not only the market leader for 5G infrastructure but also the only manufacturer in the world with sufficient factory capacity to roll out 5G networks in large countries.

Unfortunately, four major Western countries—the United States, Canada, Australia, and New Zealand—have banned Huawei from rolling out 5G networks in their countries because of security concerns (Bryan-Low, Packham, Lague, Stecklow, and Stubbs 2019). In the United Kingdom, Huawei is allowed to operate until 2027, at which point its infrastructure will be banned. Although no proof of Chinese espionage using Huawei equipment has been published, Huawei and other Chinese vendors of 5G technology remain under heightened scrutiny in other countries, including Germany, Japan, and Poland.

This boycott of Chinese hardware poses the risk of creating a technology bifurcation. Because Huawei is the market leader and until early 2019 was the only company with sufficient production capacity, large countries such as the United States face a potential delay of their 5G rollout, compared with China and other countries using Chinese equipment. This delay already puts

Exhibit 4.   5G Market Share Worldwide

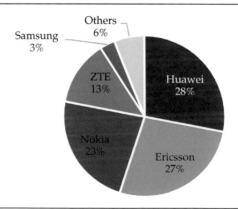

Source: IHS Markit.

the United States and its allies on a backfoot, but it also could lead to the use of slightly different technology standards in the West than in China. Both Western companies and Huawei now have an incentive to develop slightly incompatible technological standards to close their markets to competitors.

As a result, the development of the next generation of wireless communication networks, the 6G standard, might move along different paths. When 6G technology is rolled out in the 2030s, countries could be forced to choose between Western and Chinese technology, thus cementing their economic alliances with either side in the form of crucial communication infrastructure.

To clarify the crucial role 6G networks will play over the next decade, we offer this brief introduction to the technology of communication networks.

The main difference between the current 4G, the new 5G, and the future 6G networks is the frequency of the electromagnetic signals they use to transmit information. The 4G networks typically use frequencies between 1 GHz (gigahertz; 1 billion oscillations per second) and 3.5 GHz. The 5G networks will use frequencies between 24 Ghz and 100 GHz. The 6G networks will go beyond that and use frequencies between 100 GHz and 400 GHz (Ma et al. 2018). The advantage of higher frequencies is that more information can be packed into the signal (i.e., offering higher information density), and thus more information can be transmitted per second.

To give you an idea of the difference the frequency makes on information transmission, consider that under the 4G standard, downloading a two-hour movie onto a smartphone that is working efficiently takes approximately 20 seconds. The transmission rate is approximately 150 Mbps (150 million bits per second). Under the new 5G standard, the transmission rate increases to up to 10 Gbps (10 billion bits per second), making downloading three movies in just one second possible. With 6G, the prediction is that it will allow transmission rates of up to 1 Tbps (1 trillion bits per second), which would allow users to download 300 movies in one second.

Obviously, nobody needs to download 300 movies in one second, but new technologies such as autonomous vehicles, a fully connected global Internet of Things (IoT), and artificial intelligence–powered communication technology will all need transmission rates that are beyond the capabilities of 5G (Lee 2019). Thus, if these long-term technological trends are to have any chance of being realized in the next decade, we need to make rapid progress in determining 6G technology standards and developing new hardware that can cope with these demands (Latva-Aho and Leppänen 2019).

These challenges are tremendous because of the nature of physics. Although higher signal frequencies allow higher transmission rates, the problem is that signal strength declines rapidly with distance for higher frequencies. We are all familiar with this phenomenon in our daily lives when we listen to the radio. Radio signals have very low frequencies, which has the advantage that one can transmit the signal over long distances, and even if many houses or hills are between the sender and the receiver, the signal still arrives in sufficient strength to provide a good listening experience.

Light, in comparison, has much higher frequencies than radio waves, and a simple wall is sufficient to block the signal. In fact, something as ephemeral as water vapor can block light waves after a relatively short distance (that is what happens in a fog). With 6G networks, the first challenge to overcome is developing technologies that can transmit the signals outside a direct line of sight; otherwise, we would need antennas and repeaters literally every few meters in every village, town, and city.

Thus, over the coming decade, the technology race will focus on developing hardware that can combine high transmission rates with long range. Which company will be able to do this best is unclear. For 4G and 5G, the companies involved developed uniform global standards because they all knew they would have to compete with other businesses worldwide, and a unified technological standard would reduce costs. With Huawei boycotted by several countries, it could now design its own 6G infrastructure that is slightly incompatible with the infrastructure developed by Nokia and Ericsson, for example. This would prevent Nokia and Ericsson from competing with Huawei in China and other countries that use Huawei technology. And these slight technological differences would then manifest a slightly different standard for 6G applications in the West and in China, which in turn might affect the ability of businesses to run their applications and software on different 6G networks.

In short, just as railway lines with different gauges hindered international trade and globalization in the 19th century, and differences in radio frequencies forced listeners in different countries to buy different kinds of radios in the 20th century, differences in the communications architecture may hinder trade in the 21st century.

The Vulnerability of Modern Infrastructure

Different technological standards in communications infrastructure not only imply less competition between businesses but also create differences in vulnerability to cyber attacks. Malicious software could damage the infrastructure of one provider but not the other, opening up the possibility for both state-sponsored and private actors to design malware that specifically targets the infrastructure of a single country or an individual provider. Communication infrastructure such as 5G and 6G networks are just a small part of the overall critical infrastructure in a country, but such infrastructure is increasingly interconnected with traditional infrastructure, such as the power grid. Power stations are monitored using modern data technologies, and drones are used to check nuclear and fossil fuel power plants for damage on a routine basis. The signals of these drones are submitted to ground stations using standard 4G and 5G communications networks.

Already today, with globally standardized infrastructure, a successful cyber attack on a country's electricity grid is probably the biggest economic cybersecurity threat imaginable. To understand how severe the economic impact of a successful cyber attack on a country's electric grid could be, the Cambridge Judge Business School's Centre for Risk Studies interviewed dozens of experts to develop three potential scenarios for a cyber attack on the UK electricity grid (Kelly et al. 2016). This exercise provided an instructive example of the potential economic damage of such a cyber attack on industrial countries around the world.

The difficulty of launching a successful large-scale cyber attack on a nation's infrastructure is that it requires enormous know-how, so at present, doing so seems possible only for state-sponsored actors. Having said that, the previous example of the successful infiltration of Turkey's power network by Iranian agents and the subsequent 12-hour power outage in Istanbul and Ankara reveals that such an attack is not beyond the reach of existing state-sponsored entities. While the Iranian attack on the Turkish infrastructure was short-lived, a more devastating attack is possible. The risk is particularly high if the foreign agent is able to penetrate a country's infrastructure with a Trojan Horse that is not immediately recognizable as malware and can spread within the compromised system and then be activated at will (something that the US–Israeli malware Stuxnet did successfully in Iran).

The potential severity of the impact of malicious software can be seen from the 2003 Northeast Blackout, which hit the United States and Canada. In August, a high-voltage cable in Ohio caused a short in the local grid system. Because of a software bug, the local grid operator, FirstEnergy, did not receive the signal that the grid was down, and electricity was not redirected from the local grid to other grids. This triggered a chain reaction that eventually caused total power failures across the Northeastern United States and the southeast of Canada. Over the subsequent two weeks, a total of 55 million people, among them the entire New York City and Toronto metropolitan areas, faced recurrent power outages, a lack of water supply, and potential contamination of drinking water.

One could even imagine that in a state-sponsored cyber attack, a disgruntled employee of National Grid (the government entity responsible for the electric grid hardware in the United Kingdom) could act as a spy for the foreign power and install small pieces of hardware in many different substations in a region (substations are the transformers that change the voltage in the high-voltage power cables used for transmission over long distances to the lower voltages used in factories and households).

In this case, a cyber attack would be even more difficult to stop because the individual pieces of hardware at each substation would need to be identified and disabled manually. Because electric substations are regularly checked for vulnerabilities and physically maintained by trained technicians, the attackers would have to be sophisticated enough to install software or hardware that could remain undetected for weeks before it could be triggered simultaneously. A sequential triggering would likely do no harm to the electric grid thanks to the inherent redundancies in the system that avoid a power outage if the individual substations fail.

The Impact of a Massive Cyber Attack on London. As a base case, the Cambridge Judge study assumed three different scenarios for power outages in substations in and around London, targeting the United Kingdom's economic center, as shown in **Exhibit 5**:

- Scenario S1 is a limited attack that takes approximately 3 weeks to compromise 65 electric substations in and around London and triggers a rolling power outage lasting for approximately 1.5 weeks in total.

- Scenario S2 is a more comprehensive attack that has approximately twice the regional footprint, compromises 95 substations, and lasts approximately 3 weeks before it can be resolved.

- Extreme scenario X1 compromises 125 substations for 6 weeks, including those that serve Heathrow Airport, London's largest airport and a major international traffic hub.

Exhibit 5. Scenarios for Cyber Attacks on UK Infrastructure

Case	Type	Number of substations compromised	Length of cyber attack (weeks)	Length of power outage (weeks)
S1	Optimistic case/ quick recovery	65	3	1.5
S2	Conservative case/ average recovery	95	6	3
X1	Extreme case/ slow recovery	125	12	6

Source: Kelly et al. (2016).

In all three scenarios, the power outages in the substations are launched simultaneously, while malicious software in the system is able to spoof the signal to the control center so that no power outage is detected until customers without electricity start to complain in large numbers to the utility company. Because the control center cannot detect the power outage, it must send a field team to the affected substation, taking valuable time.

Once there, the technicians would not likely have the required expertise in cybersecurity to immediately detect the nature of the problem and the malicious hardware. The field team probably would be able to connect power manually after several hours of work, but only after several substations failed would it become clear that this was not an isolated incident; expert teams would then be sent out to identify the problem. Expert engineers sent to the failed substations then would be able to identify the outage as a cyber attack within 12 to 48 hours and determine a quick fix to override failed substations. The malicious hardware in the substations, however, likely would not be found in such a chaotic situation, enabling the attackers to trigger additional power outages over multiple days.

The repeat rolling blackouts would clearly reveal that the cyber attack is not just a software attack but also relies on hardware, thus triggering a search for hardware in the substations. Within several days to one week, the malicious hardware should be detected, starting a chase to find all the installed malicious hardware across the region.

Because correctly identifying the problem takes several days and then removing the malicious hardware takes several days or weeks, the power outages would affect a large number of people. In the most benign scenario, S1, up to 8.9 million people in the United Kingdom would be without electricity on any given day, as **Exhibit 6** shows. Mobile phone connections and other digital communications would be down for up to 8.6 million people at any given time. Because water utilities could not operate properly because of the power outages (water typically is transported to consumers by electric pumps), the freshwater supply would be disrupted for up to 7.9 million people at any one time, and wastewater removal would be compromised for up to 9.6 million people. Given the size of these disruptions, they would likely create significant chaos in London and its surrounding areas, and the military would need to step in for disaster relief to prevent the spread of diseases.

In the more severe scenario, S2, the situation would be even worse, cutting power for up to 11.3 million people and disrupting wastewater disposal for up to 11 million people. In the most extreme X1 scenario, power would be cut for up to 13.1 million people for up to six weeks, causing severe risk of civil unrest. In each of the three cases, approximately one million railway journeys

Exhibit 6. Peak UK Customers Disrupted in an Infrastructure Cyber Attack

Case	Electricity (millions)	Digital communication (millions)	Water (millions)	Wastewater (millions)
S1	8.9	8.6	7.9	9.6
S2	11.3	11.3	10.4	11.0
X1	13.1	12.8	11.8	12.6

Source: Kelly et al. (2016).

a day would be disrupted, bringing London effectively down to walking pace as commuters either stay home or are forced to walk to work. An estimated 150,000 airline passengers per day would see their flights canceled or severely delayed, except in scenario X1, where the successful attack on Heathrow Airport would more than double this number. The traffic disruptions also imply that the processing of agricultural imports would be delayed, creating the possibility of temporary shortages of certain foods in and around London.

The economic costs of such a cyber attack on the electric grid would be tremendous. In the most benign scenario, S1, direct costs to the UK economy are estimated to be £7.2 billion, and knock-on effects from business disruptions would cause another £4.4 billion in costs, for a total cost of £11.6 billion or 0.4% of UK GDP, as shown in **Exhibit 7**. Note that scenario S1 assumes that this cost is due to a relatively brief disruption of the London infrastructure for several hours a day for approximately 1.5 weeks. Because London's financial sector is large, targeting the electric grid would cause the biggest losses to the financial sector. Direct and indirect losses to the financial sector in scenario S1 would add up to an estimated £1.3 billion, compared with £1.2 billion for the retail sector and £700 million for the health-care sector.

For the more severe scenario, S2, with a disruption of business for approximately three weeks, the total costs to the UK economy would be roughly three times as much and sum to £29 billion, or 1.1% of UK GDP. For the most extreme scenario, X1, the costs of six weeks of power disruptions would amount to 3.3% of UK GDP.

Moreover, in each of these cases, the economic shock likely would spread over time. Higher unemployment, lower consumption, a loss of international trade and tourism, and a significant decline in consumer and business confidence all would conspire to lower economic growth in the quarters and years to come. Kelly et al. (2016) estimated that in scenario S1, the economy would return to trend growth after approximately two years, while in the other two scenarios, the recovery could take up to five years. The total lost output over five years is expected to be £49 billion (1.9% of GDP) in scenario

Exhibit 7. Economic Losses to the United Kingdom from a Cyber Attack on the Electric Grid

Case	Direct losses (£ billions)	Indirect losses (£ billions)	Total losses (£ billions)	% of GDP
S1	7.2	4.4	11.6	0.4
S2	18.0	10.9	29.0	1.1
X1	53.6	31.8	85.5	3.3

Source: Kelly et al. (2016).

S1, £129 billion (4.9% of GDP) in scenario S2, and £442 billion (16.9% of GDP) in scenario X1. In short, scenarios S2 and X1 likely would cause a recession in the United Kingdom, while scenario S1 could push a weak UK economy into recession.

The Cost of Data Breaches for Private Companies

A successful cyber attack on critical national infrastructure is a tail risk, but private businesses have to deal with a constant barrage of small-scale attacks every day. Most of these attacks are launched not by state-sponsored actors or sophisticated hacker groups but instead by criminal groups motivated by money. Increasingly, these criminals do not even have to use malicious software to perform their attacks. Coburn et al. (2019) reported that since 2018, an increase has been seen in so-called living-off-the-land tactics that exploit security loopholes in existing software, such as operating systems, and commonly used office software packages. Such attacks cannot be prevented by traditional anti-malware software because they do not deposit code on the targeted systems, and they reduce the risk of legal ramifications for criminals because tracing their origins is more difficult.

Meanwhile, buying malware on the dark web has become cheaper and cheaper, so that even mildly talented hackers can now launch successful attacks against corporations, multiplying the number of potential attacks. Traditional malware software kits can be bought for $600 to $10,000 per month, while zero-day attack kits that enable living-off-the-land attacks cost from $20,000 for Mac OSX operating systems to $80,000 for Google Chrome and Internet Explorer software.

Given this proliferation of cybercrime, the costs for businesses are rising fast. Bissell and Ponemon (2019) reported that each business globally had to deal with an average of 145 successful security breaches in 2018. Successful security breaches were defined as instances when criminals were able to overcome a company's usual firewall defenses and infiltrate their systems.

As cyber attacks and security breaches become more common, the costs for businesses increase rapidly. In 2018, banks were the preferred targets of cybercrime and incurred costs of approximately $18.4 million per company per year. As **Exhibit 8** shows, the damage to other industries is not far behind. Utility companies are another popular target of cybercriminals because of the potential damage that can be caused by shutting down vital infrastructure, and the costs per utility company averaged approximately $17.8 million in 2018. Software, high-tech, and automotive companies typically are targeted by cybercriminals to extract information and customer data that can be used for malicious purposes.

A company's average loss from cybercrime in 2018 was an estimated $13 million, up 12% from the previous year and up 72% in five years (Bissell and Ponemon 2019). The biggest component of these losses was the loss of information (either by losing client data or losing important internal information), which accounted for almost one-half of the losses incurred from security breaches. Business disruption accounted for roughly one-third of the losses, while lost revenue (e.g., from lost customers or lost bids for new orders) accounted for one-fifth of the losses, as **Exhibit 9** illustrates.

Although the cost for an average company per year does not sound like much, we have to remember that these statistics are averaged over thousands of companies worldwide. Abbosh and Bissell (2019) added everything up and estimated that the total economic loss for global business in the five years from 2019 to 2023 was approximately $5.2 trillion—approximately 2.8% of global corporate revenue and roughly equal to the GDP of the economies of France, Italy, and Spain combined. The estimated forgone revenue over

Exhibit 8. Average Annual Cost of Cybercrime per Company, 2018

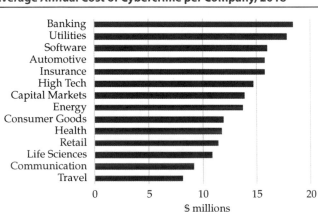

Source: Bissell and Ponemon (2019).

Exhibit 9. Business Impact of Cybercrime

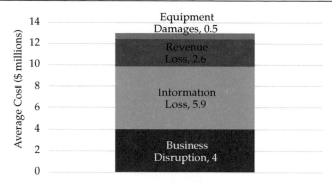

Source: Bissell and Ponemon (2019).

Exhibit 10. Estimated Forgone Revenue Due to Cybercrime, 2019–2023

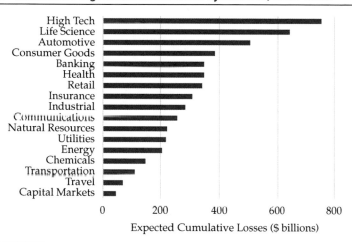

Source: Abbosh and Bissell (2019).

five years was particularly high for high-tech companies ($753 billion), life sciences ($642 billion), and automotive companies ($505 billion). With the exception of the travel industry and capital markets service providers (stock exchanges and so forth), every industry faces revenue losses from cybercrime in excess of $100 billion over five years. **Exhibit 10** illustrates this finding.

Do Stock Markets Care about Security Breaches?

The majority of security breaches lead to small or insignificant losses for a business. As a result, even those security breaches that are publicly announced but not consequential for the business at hand likely do not affect a company's share price for long.

Bischoff (2020) collected information on a series of publicly announced security breaches that led to data losses and business disruptions in US listed companies between 2008 and 2018. We replicate this analysis in **Exhibit 11** and differentiate between small- and midsize security breaches, on the one hand, and severe security breaches, on the other. On the actual day of the announcement, the average stock market reaction was rather muted, with a decline in the share price of less than 1%. In the case of small security breaches, that was about what happened. The share price of companies affected by such smaller breaches was virtually indistinguishable from the share price development of companies unaffected by security breaches.

In contrast, severe security breaches can depress the share price of affected companies for several months. One month after the announcement of a severe security breach, the share price of an affected company declined by 4% on average, and after three months, it was still approximately 2% lower. A major driving force behind this delayed share price reaction after severe security breaches is that the main impact on the business in the medium term seems to be a loss of client trust and hence a loss of business that materializes slowly over time.

Abbosh and Bissell (2019) calculated the average revenue growth of companies affected by severe security breaches in the eight quarters after a breach and compared it with the average revenue growth of companies in the same industry that were not affected by cybercrime. The authors covered the time period 2013 to 2018 and selected 460 unique events in 432 companies worldwide. In the two years after a severe security breach, corporate revenues first declined by approximately 10% on average and then recovered slowly.

Exhibit 11. Share Price Response to Data Breaches

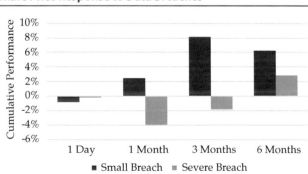

Source: Bloomberg; Bischoff (2018).

After two years, revenues had returned only to the same level they were when the security breach happened. Meanwhile, the revenues of companies that did not suffer a security breach increased by almost 20% in the same time period.

These averages can disguise big individual differences. **Exhibit 12** shows the average share price development in the six months after a severe security breach, along with the top quartile stocks in the sample and the bottom quartile stocks in the sample. Note that every stock in the sample suffered a severe security breach at time 0 in Exhibit 12, but the companies that saw a significant impact on their business (e.g., through declining revenues or declining profits after a need to invest heavily in IT security) could see their share price drop by 10% or more over six months.

In those extreme cases, the share price could remain depressed for a long time, and losses to investors could be substantial. An example case is the October 2015 leak of consumer data at T-Mobile US, which led to the loss of crucial private information of T-Mobile US customers, including Social Security numbers. Another example is the leak of 1.5 million credit and debit card numbers of customers of Global Payments Systems in 2012. In both instances, customer trust in the companies was shaken, leading to a significant decline in share price.

That markets pay careful attention to the details of a security breach can be seen in the case of Sony. On 26 April 2011, Sony announced that 77 million accounts on the Sony PlayStation Network had been compromised, and some credit card data had been leaked. In response to this leak, Sony shares dropped 31% over the subsequent six months and underperformed the NASDAQ by 23%. On 24 November 2014, Sony announced that 10 million employee records had been hacked over the previous year, leading to the loss of some

Exhibit 12. Share Price Response to a Severe Data Breach

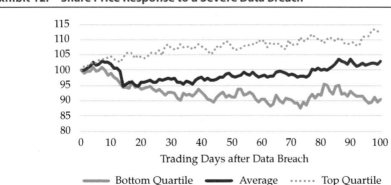

Trading Days after Data Breach

Bottom Quartile — Average ⋯⋯ Top Quartile

Source: Bloomberg; Bischoff (2018).

Social Security numbers. Apparently, employee records do not count for much because Sony's share price was unaffected by this announcement and rallied 42% in the subsequent six months, outperforming the NASDAQ by 37%.

Could Cyber Attacks Cause a Financial Crisis?

A particularly attractive target for cybercriminals and state-sponsored hackers is the financial system. People like to rob banks because that is where the money is. Given the global financial system's high reliance on the internet and IT in general, the modes of attack and the potential targets are manifold:

- The most basic attack is a distributed denial of service (DDoS) attack on a bank, central bank, or service provider. In a DDoS attack, a large number of bots sends so many requests to a website, or to a server belonging to a financial service provider, that it becomes overwhelmed and crashes or grinds to a halt. Disruptions from DDoS attacks are typically short-lived and cause limited damages. For example, on 10 and 11 August 2011, the Hong Kong Stock Exchange news page suffered a DDoS attack. As a result, the trading of seven stocks had to be suspended because on these two days, the companies reported quarterly results that could not be published properly. Another example is a DDoS attack on three banks in Finland (i.e., OP-Pohjola, Danske Bank, and Nordea) in 2014. Their webpages and systems were disrupted, and online services became temporarily unavailable. One bank could no longer process card payments or cash withdrawals from ATMs (Bouveret 2019).

- Payment fraud using the SWIFT system for interbank payments has become a more popular and lucrative way to attack banks. In these attacks, the SWIFT system is hacked, and a fraudulent order to transfer money to an emerging market bank is sent to the victim's account. The most prominent example of such an attack is the attempt by North Korean hackers to steal $951 million from the central bank of Bangladesh. In the end, the hackers managed to steal *only* $81 million, of which $15 million could be recovered (Corkery and Goldstein 2017). Another incident happened on 24 May 2018, when more than 9,000 computers and 500 servers of Chile's largest bank, Banco de Chile, crashed as hackers tried to steal money from the bank through its SWIFT system. The hackers previously had tried to steal $110 million from Mexico's Bancomext. In the case of the Chilean attack, the losses amounted to an estimated $10 million (Cimpanu 2018).

- The potentially most harmful attacks are those targeting central banks. In 2010, a data breach at the Federal Reserve Bank of Cleveland led to the loss of details of 122,000 credit cards, while that same year, the Federal Reserve Bank of New York lost proprietary software worth $9.5 million to hackers in a data breach. In 2013, $13.3 million was stolen from the account of the city of Riobamba at the Central Bank of Ecuador, and thieves who launched 21 cyber attacks on the central bank of Russia tried to steal $50 million in 2016 but managed to steal *only* $22 million (Bouveret 2019).

What makes cyber attacks on banks and financial institutions so treacherous is that the financial system is dependent on a highly complex system of interconnected networks with a few central data hubs. The interconnectedness of the financial network means that cyber attacks targeted in one area or at one company can get out of hand and cause significant damage at other institutions. In June 2017, ransomware targeted at Ukrainian companies spread across the border and caused damages in excess of $1.3 billion to international corporations that had business links with Ukraine. In the financial system, the disruption of one major bank could spread across the system if the bank is a counterparty to other banks in financial transactions, creating liquidity and solvency risks.

Alternatively, central hubs such as clearing houses are charged with reducing counterparty and liquidity risks in the derivatives markets. If a clearing house can be put out of service for a prolonged period, millions, if not billions, of derivative contracts might not be able to be settled, creating large uncertainties and counterparty risks across the system. In the worst-case scenario, a successful cyber attack could take a major central bank offline for an extended period, making it difficult or even impossible for commercial banks to cover their liquidity needs. In this case, international central banks might be able to act as interim lenders, but they typically do not have the required data to directly distribute funding to foreign commercial banks. In effect, such a situation would call for an emergency system in which international central banks would provide funding for the largest international financial institutions. In turn, these financial institutions would act as replacement central banks and distribute this liquidity to their business counterparts where needed.

These extreme examples of a disruption of the global financial system demonstrate that a financial crisis could be triggered by cyber attacks. Traditionally, the triggers of a financial crisis are as follows:

- excess leverage in parts of the economy (e.g., the high amount of mortgage debt that triggered the housing crisis and the global financial crisis of 2008, more than a decade ago);

- disruptions in the bank's maturity transformation business (e.g., a run on the bank for cash or short-term financing could leave banks unable to liquidate illiquid long-term assets, as was the case for the British bank Northern Rock in 2007); and

- the procyclical lending behavior of banks that reduces the price of risk (e.g., the willingness of US savings and loan institutions to invest in high-yield bonds in the late 1980s, leading to the savings and loan crisis).

Today, we face an additional trigger for a financial crisis through cyber-security breaches.

Healey et al. (2018) showed how cybersecurity breaches potentially could lead to a financial crisis through four channels:

- The financial system relies on a few key hubs that process international payments, clear financial contracts, and safeguard assets. A major disruption of any of these key hubs could lead to a widespread breakdown of daily financial activities.

- A breakdown of such key hubs, or more regular but limited outages of everyday banking services such as internet banking or cash withdrawals from ATMs, could undermine public trust in financial institutions and trigger a bank run or significant flows of customer assets from one bank to another, which in turn could lead to a bank default.

- The financial system relies heavily on sensitive customer data. If these data are compromised (not necessarily stolen but maybe just deleted from a bank's system), many banking services will be unavailable for a pro-longed period. The restoration of compromised data is typically possible but can take days or even weeks, during which time a bank would not be able to perform some of its services, causing significant economic damage and a severe loss of trust on the part of customers.

- Banks increasingly rely on cloud-based software and, as we have seen, the communication infrastructure is highly centralized and concentrated as well. Thus, an outage of major cloud-computing providers could lead to banks being unable to provide everyday customer services.

Worse yet, unlike traditional triggers of financial crises, cyber attacks can be timed to cause maximum damage. Theoretically, a cyber attack could be so devastating that it could take a central bank or a major clearing house offline for several weeks, triggering a liquidity crisis and even a solvency crisis. It might be easier for criminal actors to instead wait until the financial system is already under stress (say, in a recession or a minor financial crisis) and then attack vulnerable financial institutions to exacerbate the crisis. In such an environment, trust between financial institutions already would be low. An added cyber attack could create a virtual run on banks that would erode the remaining trust between banks, in a manner similar to the events of autumn 2008, when banks became unwilling to lend to one another in the wake of the Lehman Brothers collapse. Because no one knew who would be next to default on their short-term obligations, banks simply stopped doing business with other banks where possible, and the entire system almost ground to a halt.

Cyber Attacks on Banks Could Be Very Costly for the Entire Economy. The economic losses of such cyber attacks on banks are extremely hard to estimate because they depend very much on the circumstances in which the cyber attack is performed and the nonlinear second-round effects of the attacks (i.e., how quickly and how widely the attack spreads). Bouveret (2019) tried to model the likely impact of such cyber attacks on banks in four scenarios. The "baseline scenario" is one that assumes that cyber attacks happen randomly at the frequency observed between 2011 and 2016 and follow a fat-tailed distribution. In the "severe scenario," the likelihood of an attack happening is approximately twice that of the 2011 to 2016 average. The baseline scenario and the severe scenario assume that cyber attacks remain confined to the targeted financial institution. In a second simulation, Bouveret (2019) assumed that the chance of contagion from one bank to the next is 20%.

Exhibit 13 shows the average loss for the global banking system in the simulations with and without contagion. The baseline scenario without contagion leads to average financial losses to the global financial system of $97 billion, or 9% of the net income of banks worldwide. The losses in any given year would, in 1 instance out of 20 (i.e., a 5% value at risk [VaR]), exceed $147 billion (14% of net income), and the expected shortfall in these cases would be $187 billion, or 18% of net income. Although these numbers look big, they are a fraction of the operational losses banks suffer worldwide, which are estimated at $260 billion to $375 billion each year.

In the severe scenario, however, the potential losses from cyber attacks multiply and become the same as, if not bigger than, operational losses. In the severe case, the average expected loss for banks per year is $268 billion, or 26% of net income, whereas the chance of losses exceeding $352 billion is 5%. In this case, the expected shortfall would be $409 billion. If the cyber attacks are allowed to spread to other banks and institutions, the estimated losses and shortfalls are typically approximately 20% higher, which reflects the 20% likelihood of contagion built into the model.

Given these significant risks to the financial system and the economy overall, financial regulators have focused increasingly on cybersecurity as

Exhibit 13. Estimated Risks from Cyber Attacks on Banks

	Baseline		Severe	
	% of net income	$ billions	% of net income	$ billions
Average loss	9	97	26	268
VaR (95%)	14	147	34	352
Est. shortfall (95%)	18	187	40	409

	With contagion			
	Baseline		Severe	
	% of net income	$ billions	% of net income	$ billions
Average loss	12	127	34	351
VaR (95%)	18	184	43	446
Est. shortfall (95%)	22	229	49	509

Source: Bouveret (2019).

a pillar of financial stability. In June 2016, in conjunction with the Bank for International Settlements (BIS), the Committee on Payments and Market Infrastructures and the International Organization of Securities Commissions, the global regulator of payments and securities regulators,[1] issued "Guidance on Cyber Resilience for Financial Market Infrastructures," a document detailing its members' cybersecurity risks and potential ways to mitigate these risks. In 2017, the BIS published reports on the progress made in four jurisdictions, and in the United States, the Financial Stability Oversight Council recommended practical solutions, such as sharing of cybersecurity information between banks and the regulatory harmonization of a risk-based approach to estimate cybersecurity risks.

Major US banks created the Financial Services Information Sharing and Analysis Center (FS-ISAC), which, together with the Payments Risk Council, performs yearly simulations of cyber attacks against payment processes. In recent years, the efforts of the FS-ISAC to prepare for cybersecurity risks have expanded beyond the borders of the United States and now include banks in Europe, Asia, and Latin America. To date, the efforts to protect the financial system are clearly limited, particularly when compared with the increasing importance of cybersecurity.

---

[1]Yes, regulators have regulators, too.

Blockchain to the Rescue?

Given the rising cybersecurity threats in all areas of the modern economy and the need for the secure transaction of data, we need to devise solutions that are safer than the existing ones. Currently, IT systems are primarily set up in a centralized way, in which a central cloud or a server stores important data. These data are then accessed by individual machines around the world that are connected to the central server by a private or public network. This setup means that if the central server is compromised or taken over by a malicious actor, the entire system is instantly compromised.

Blockchain technology promises a solution to this major vulnerability. In the early 1990s, Haber and Stornetta (1991) created a method to digitally timestamp a document with the help of cryptographic blocks. This method was further developed over time and led to the modern blockchain approach invented in 2008 by the anonymous author who called himself Satoshi Nakamoto in his bitcoin white paper. Bitcoin was the first application to use modern blockchain technology, but cryptocurrencies such as bitcoin are only a small part of the range of blockchain applications.

The basic idea behind blockchain is to create a database that is not centralized but instead is distributed among all the participants who have access to it. To create a blockchain, each participant (commonly called a "node") in the network creates two encryption keys: (1) a public key, which is used by participants to "encrypt" messages and data sent around the network, and (2) a private key, which is used by each participant in the network to "decrypt" the data. Changes made to the database by the different participants are combined in "blocks" that are then encrypted using the public key and sent to neighboring participants in the network. Thus, the blocks are spread around the network through the individual participants and not through a central server.

Once a block is full, individual participants in the network perform what is called a "proof-of-work" operation—essentially a massive number-crunching exercise to provide a verification that the block is genuine. Proof-of-work operations usually are made by brute force and thus are computationally intensive, but they create a solution that is easy to check, thus facilitating verification. This is a crucial step in the blockchain because fraudulent or manipulated data would lead to the incorrect solution and thus a rejection of the block by the other members of the network. Once a member of the network has successfully performed a proof-of-work operation, the solution is sent around the network. If more than one-half of the participants accept the solution, the block is added to the database, and a new block is opened (hence the name "blockchain"). Once a block has been admitted to the blockchain, it can no longer be altered, providing a permanent record of past transactions.

The blockchain approach offers three advantages:

- The blockchain is decentralized; the entire database is copied to each participant in the network and does not rely on a central server or infrastructure.

- The blockchain is transparent; each participant has a copy of the entire database on her computer, and all past actions can be tracked through the timestamps of the past manipulations saved in each block. These timestamps allow past manipulations made to the blockchain to be traced back to the very first day. At the same time, participants are anonymous in the blockchain because the timestamps are unique to each participant, but the cryptographic keys are not linked to real-world identities.

- The blockchain is secure; changing the data in the chain would lead to a faulty proof-of-work operation and a rejection of the block. Once a block is admitted to the chain, it can no longer be altered.

These three advantages of blockchain technology allow the creation of "smart contracts" and "smart properties," which are secured by blockchains but can be changed as needed by the participants.

The first applications for blockchain were in the financial space with cryptocurrencies such as bitcoin, but applications in finance and in health care, for which data protection is crucial, have since mushroomed. Nevertheless, criminals were—as usual—the first to adopt this technology because it allowed anonymity. Today, black markets for drugs and guns on the dark web operate using cryptocurrencies as payments, while ransomware used in cyber attacks usually demands payment in cryptocurrencies as well (Taylor et al. 2020).

Legal and desirable applications for blockchain are likely to grow exponentially over the coming decade, given that the financial and health-care industries are not the only ones with a need for the safe storage and transmission of data. Fernández-Caramés and Fraga-Lamas (2018) demonstrated that the demand for blockchain applications in the IoT is likely to rise. Smart contracts, primarily based on the Ethereum blockchain technology, execute themselves automatically when certain conditions are met. Such smart contracts can be used in international trade and logistics, particularly with emerging markets, in which traditional credit checks and bank connections are less trustworthy, or with mortgages or in crowd-funding activities, in which monies are released only for specific purposes and when certain conditions are met.

In the future, blockchains will be helpful in such IoT applications as sensing, intelligent transportation, and smart living applications. In agriculture, blockchain technology can enhance food safety by tracking farm animals and feed from a farm to the supermarket and consumer tables. Smart grids rely on blockchain technology to protect against malicious attacks against vital infrastructure, such as the electricity grid or power stations.

Indeed, Taylor et al. (2020) showed that from a cybersecurity perspective, IoT applications likely will be the main driver for the adoption of blockchain technology. Thus far, blockchain technology has been used in IoT applications to increase data security and to enable a decentralized deployment of firmware, which can be distributed from application to application without the need for a central server. The firmware cannot be manipulated by individual applications because of the blockchain technology, thereby preventing the manipulation of software. Data can be stored securely in a decentralized way or in a central cloud, where access is given only to members of the network with the right blockchain credentials.

Blockchain technology also can be used to protect local wireless systems by storing and monitoring access to the system in a local database. Finally, a manipulation of the web through the Domain Name System (DNS) is impossible if DNS entries are protected by blockchain technology. Thus, malicious actors can no longer hijack a website or a webserver by manipulating the DNS entry of the webpage in a central database.

Blockchain technology also has limitations, however, that make it difficult if not impossible to use in some applications. Most important, many blockchains are incredibly complex and energy intensive. Bitcoin, for example, has a theoretical maximum of seven transactions per second. VisaNet, Visa's electronic payment system, in contrast, can handle up to 24,000 transactions per second. The volume of transactions needed to drive the global system of credit and debit cards alone is way beyond the limitations of blockchain technology as we know it today (Stinchcombe 2018).

Furthermore, because blocks constantly are added to the chain, the storage space requirements grow quickly. In 2019, the length of the bitcoin blockchain surpassed 250 GB. According to *Digiconomist*, mining bitcoin consumed 73 terawatt-hours or trillions of watt-hours (TWh) of electricity—approximately the same as the annual electricity consumption of Austria—and created a carbon footprint of 34.7 megatons of CO_2, approximately the same as Denmark. Per transaction, bitcoin consumed 641 kilowatt-hours (kWh) of electricity because the proof-of-work calculations are so complex and time-consuming. The electricity used per bitcoin transaction would be sufficient to power a US household for more than three weeks, and the CO_2

Exhibit 14.   Bitcoin Energy Consumption

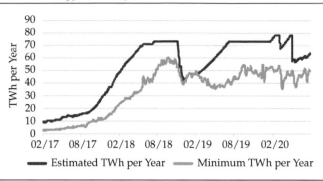

Source: Digiconomist.

emitted by this transaction is approximately the same as the CO_2 generated by 761,333 Visa transactions. Furthermore, because the hardware used to work with bitcoin becomes obsolete within one to two years, the electronic waste created by bitcoin miners is approximately the same as the annual electronic waste created by a country the size of Luxembourg, as **Exhibit 14** illustrates.

More modern blockchain technologies such as Ethereum make lesser demands on energy and storage space. As of 2019, Ethereum mining and transactions consumed 8 TWh of electricity per year (approximately the same amount of electricity as Honduras consumes in a year), and each Ethereum transaction consumes enough energy to power an average US household for a day.

Overall, although blockchain technology holds many promises to increase security and prevent major cyber attacks, it is not without limitations or flaws. Before blockchain technology can become a mainstay in our economy and expand beyond specific niche applications, its limitations in terms of energy need and transaction time need to be overcome. Until then, cybersecurity issues will have to be solved by conventional means, implying that the current arms race between cybercriminals and companies will continue.

Conclusions

In a world in which more than one-half of the Earth's population has access to the internet and both civil and military organizations depend on the internet and computer networks for communication, data storage, and information processing, cybersecurity has become a major issue. Cyber warfare and civilian cyber attacks by criminals with pecuniary motives have become a major threat to the economy, the military, and our political discourse.

State-sponsored actors use cyber attacks to undermine trust in organizations and steal both data and know-how. The resulting damage to the economy and individual businesses can be large, and the damage to public trust in institutions and the media is immeasurable.

Although we have not yet witnessed a major cyber attack with a significant economy-wide impact, businesses are constantly struggling with security breaches costing an estimated $13 million per company per year. For banks and other financial institutions, the costs can be even higher. In 2018, the average bank faced annual damages resulting from cybercrime and data loss of $18.4 million, which means that over a five-year horizon, losses from cyber attacks could reach hundreds of billions annually. In fact, model estimates for the global banking system range from $97 billion to $351 billion per year, depending on the scenario. These losses are significant enough to trigger a financial crisis if key institutions such as central banks or clearing houses are hit. But even if the cyber attacks are insufficient on their own to create a financial crisis, they can be timed in such a way as to further destabilize an already fragile economy.

The worst-case scenario in terms of cybersecurity would be a successful attack on the vital infrastructure of a country. If the United Kingdom were to experience repeated outages of the electricity grid around London for several weeks, the direct economic damage could range from 0.4% of UK GDP to 3.3% of GDP. Over five years, the economic loss of such infrastructure outages could be between 1.5% of GDP and 16.9% of GDP, creating a massive recession in the UK economy. Although such attacks on the national infrastructure of a country are unlikely, they remain possible.

Cybersecurity is thus a major concern for investors and businesses alike and will become more important over time as innovations such as the IoT spread. This means that new defensive technologies, including the use of blockchain to protect data, will have to be developed, although significant technological and economic challenges to these methods remain and will have to be overcome.

Bibliography

Abbosh, O., and K. Bissell. 2019. "Securing the Digital Economy: Reinventing the Internet for Trust." Accenture Strategy. https://www.accenture.com/_acnmedia/thought-leadership-assets/pdf/accenture-securing-the-digital-economy-reinventing-the-internet-for-trust.pdf.

Ali, I., and P. Stewart. 2019. "US Carried Out Secret Cyber Strike in Iran in Wake of Saudi Oil Attack: Officials." Reuters, 16 October. https://

www.reuters.com/article/us-usa-iran-military-cyber-exclusive/exclusive-u-s-carried-out-secret-cyber-strike-on-iran-in-wake-of-saudi-oil-attack-officials-idUSKBN1WV0EK.

Bischoff, P. "How Data Breaches Affect Stock Market Prices. *Comparitech* (blog). https://www.comparitech.com/blog/information-security/data-breach-share-price-2018/.

Bissell, K., and L. Ponemon. 2019. "The Cost of Cybercrime: Ninth Annual Cost of Cybercrime Study." Ponemon Institute and Accenture Security. https://www.accenture.com/_acnmedia/PDF-96/Accenture-2019-Cost-of-Cybercrime-Study-Final.pdf#zoom=50.

Bryan-Low, C., C. Packham, D. Lague, S. Stecklow, and J. Stubbs. 2019. "Hobbling Huawei: Inside the U.S. War on China's Tech Giant." Reuters, 21 May. https://www.reuters.com/investigates/special-report/huawei-usa-campaign/.

Bouveret, A. 2019. "Estimation of Losses Due to Cyber Risk for Financial Institutions." *Journal of Operational Risk* 14 (2): 1–20.

Cimpanu, C. 2018. "Hackers Crashed a Bank's Computers While Attempting a SWIFT Hack." *BleepingComputer*, 8 June. https://www.bleepingcomputer.com/news/security/hackers-crashed-a-bank-s-computers-while-attempting-a-swift-hack/.

Clapper, J. R., M. Lettre, and M. S. Rogers. 2017. "Foreign Cyber Threats to the United States." Joint Statement for the Record before the Committee on Armed Services of the United States Senate, 115th Congress, 5 January. https://www.govinfo.gov/content/pkg/CHRG-115shrg33940/html/CHRG-115shrg33940.htm.

Coburn, A. W., J. Daffron, K. Quantrill, E. Leverett, J. Bordeau, A. Smith, and T. Harvey. 2019. "Cyber Risk Outlook." Centre for Risk Studies, University of Cambridge Judge Business School, and Risk Management Solutions, Cambridge, UK. https://www.jbs.cam.ac.uk/wp-content/uploads/2020/08/crs-cyber-risk-outlook-2019.pdf.

Corkery, M., and M. Goldstein. 2017. "North Korea Said to Be Target of Inquiry over $81 Million Cyberheist." *New York Times*, 22 March. https://www.nytimes.com/2017/03/22/business/dealbook/north-korea-said-to-be-target-of-inquiry-over-81-million-cyberheist.html.

Fernández-Caramés, T. M., and P. Fraga-Lamas. 2018. "A Review on the Use of Blockchain for the Internet of Things." *IEEE Access* 6: 32979–33001.

FireEye. 2018. "Suspected Chinese Cyber Espionage Group (TEMP. Periscope) Targeting U.S. Engineering and Maritime Industries." *FireEye* (blog), 16 March. https://www.fireeye.com/blog/threat-research/2018/03/ suspected-chinese-espionage-group-targeting-maritime-and-engineering-industries.

Gartner. 2019. "Gartner Says Worldwide IaaS Public Cloud Services Market Grew 31.3% in 2018." Press release, Gartner, 29 July. https://www.gartner .com/en/newsroom/press-releases/2019-07-29-gartner-says-worldwide-iaas-public-cloud-services-market-grew-31point3-percent-in-2018.

Haber, S., and W. S. Stornetta. 1991. "How to Time-Stamp a Digital Document." *Journal of Cryptology* 3: 99–111.

Halpern, M. 2015. "Iran Flexes Its Power by Transporting Turkey to the Stone Age." *Observer*, 22 April. https://observer.com/2015/04/iran-flexes-its-power-by-transporting-turkey-to-the-stone-ages/.

Healey, J., P. Mosser, K. Rosen, and A. Tache. 2018. "The Future of Financial Stability and Cyber Risk." Brookings Institution, Washington, DC. https://www.brookings.edu/research/the-future-of-financial-stability-and-cyber-risk/.

Hsu, J. 2018. "The Strava Heat Map and the End of Secrets." *Wired*, 29 January. https://www.wired.com/story/strava-heat-map-military-bases-fitness-trackers-privacy/.

Huang, K., S. Madnick, and S. Johnson. 2018. "Interactions Between Cybersecurity and International Trade: A Systematic Framework." MIT Sloan Research Paper No. 5727-18. MIT Sloan School of Management, Cambridge, MA.

Kelly, S., E. Leverett, E. J. Oughton, J. Copic, S. Thacker, R. Pant, L. Pryor, G. Kassara, T. Evan, S. J. Ruffle, M. Tuveson, A. W. Coburn, D. Ralph, and J. W. Hall. 2016. "Integrated Infrastructure: Cyber Resiliency in Society, Mapping the Consequences of an Interconnected Digital Economy." Cambridge Risk Framework Series. Centre for Risk Studies, University of Cambridge Judge Business School, Cambridge, UK. https://www.jbs.cam .ac.uk/wp-content/uploads/2020/08/crs-integrated-infrastructure-cyber-resiliency-in-society.pdf.

Kopp, E., L. Kaffenberger, and C. Wilson. 2017. "Cyber Risk, Market Failures, and Financial Stability." IMF Working Paper no. 185 (August). International Monetary Fund, Washington, DC.

Latva-Aho, M., and K. Leppänen, eds. 2019. "Key Drivers and Research Challenges for 6G Ubiquitous Wireless Intelligence." 6G Research Visions 1 white paper. 6G Flagship, University of Oulu, Finland.

Lee, J. 2019. "Moving Toward 6G." Presentation at 6G Wireless Summit, Levi, Lapland, Finland, 24–26 March.

Liu, S. 2019. "Market Share Held by the Leading Windows Anti-Malware Application Vendors Worldwide." Statista. https://www.statista.com/statistics/271048/market-share-held-by-antivirus-vendors-for-windows-systems/.

Ma, J., R. Shrestha, L. Moeller, and D. M. Mittleman. 2018. "Channel Performance for Indoor and Outdoor Terahertz Wireless Links." *APL Photonics* 3 (5): 051601.

Marks, J. 2014. "Iran Launched Major Cyberattacks on the Israeli Internet." *Politico*, 18 August.

Mitchell, A. D., and J. Hepburn. 2016. "Don't Fence Me In: Reforming Trade and Investment Law to Better Facilitate Cross-Border Data Transfer." *Yale Journal of Law and Technology* 19 (1): 182–237.

Montague, Z. 2019. "Interior Department Grounds Chinese-Made Drones Amid Review." *New York Times*, 30 October. https://www.nytimes.com/2019/10/30/us/politics/interior-department-chinese-made-drones.html.

Mueller, R. S. 2019. *The Mueller Report: Report on the Investigation into Russian Interference in the 2016 Presidential Election*. Washington, DC: US Department of Justice.

Perlroth, N., and S. Shane. 2017. "How Israel Caught Russian Hackers Scouring the World for U.S. Secrets." *New York Times*, 10 October. https://www.nytimes.com/2017/10/10/technology/kaspersky-lab-israel-russia-hacking.html.

Stinchcombe, K. 2017. "Ten Years In, Nobody Has Come Up with a Use for Blockchain." *Hackernoon*, 22 December. https://hackernoon.com/ten-years-in-nobody-has-come-up-with-a-use-case-for-blockchain-ee98c180100.

Stinchcombe, K. 2018. "Blockchain Is Not Only Crappy Technology But a Bad Vision for the Future." *Medium*, 5 April. https://medium.com/@kaistinchcombe/decentralized-and-trustless-crypto-paradise-is-actually-a-medieval-hellhole-c1ca122efdec.

Taylor, P. J., T. Dargahi, A. Dehghantanha, R. M. Parizi, and K. R. Choo. 2020. "A Systematic Literature Review of Blockchain Cyber Security." *Digital Communications and Networks* 6 (2): 147–56.

Telegraph. 2017. "Iran Blamed for Cyberattack on Parliament that Hit Dozens of MPs, Including Theresa May." 14 October. https://www.telegraph.co.uk/news/2017/10/13/iran-responsible-cyberattack-british-parliament/.

Chapter 8: The Geopolitics of Renewable Energy

> Big things have small beginnings.
>
> —*T. E. Lawrence*

Evolution, Maybe Revolution

Energy revolutions do not happen every day. The last major energy revolution happened more than 100 years ago, when coal was superseded by crude oil as the main source of energy globally. Coal-powered steam engines had been the lifeblood of industry, trains, and ships for more than a century, but in 1895, two German engineers, Gottlieb Daimler and Carl Benz, had the idea of putting a petroleum-powered internal combustion engine into a horse carriage, thereby giving birth to the first practical car.

Because internal combustion engines were more compact, they were easier than bigger steam engines to fit into the small space available in carriages and were thus given preference. But this choice was made initially for practicality reasons, not because the internal combustion engine was more efficient or cheaper. Indeed, in the early years of the car, different drivetrain options competed with each other. Steam-engine cars existed alongside electric cars and internal combustion engine cars. In the end, the gasoline-powered car won the commercial race. Meanwhile, in shipping, the switch from coal-powered steamers to petroleum power was triggered by Winston Churchill's decision after World War I to switch from coal to petroleum as the power source for all British warships, a decision later mirrored by British civilian shipbuilders.

Geoeconomically, the switch from coal to oil as the main source of energy in transportation heralded a multidecade-long decline in coal mining. High-cost producers in England, Wales, German's Ruhr area, and the border areas between France and Germany became uneconomical and finally closed operations in the middle of the 20th century. Coal survived as a power source only for electricity generation and remained the dominant source of such energy until the early years of the 21st century.

With the transition from coal to oil came a transition in geopolitics. The Ruhr area and the border between France and Germany, which had been contested in many wars, became largely irrelevant from a geopolitical perspective (although the Ruhr is still a wealthy industrial region). Instead, the focus shifted to the oil-producing regions of the Middle East—geopolitical backwaters until the 1930s. Today, we face a similar transition, this time from oil as an energy source to nuclear power and renewable energy sources, such as wind and solar power. Just like a century ago, many different technologies are competing for investment, from solar photovoltaic (PV) energy, to wind (onshore and offshore), to geothermal energy and biomass. The list goes on, but today, wind and solar PV seem likely to emerge as the most dominant renewable energy sources of the future, so we focus primarily on these two in this chapter.

Although we call these transitions "energy revolutions," they are more evolutionary than revolutionary in their development. Oil took several decades to supersede coal as the main source of energy in houses, transportation, and industry, and renewables will take several decades to replace oil, gas, and other fossil fuels. Today, wind and solar energy account for approximately 8% of global electricity generation, hydroelectric power stations account for 16%, and other renewables account for approximately 3%. As **Exhibit 1** shows, almost two-thirds of the electricity produced today is still generated using fossil fuels.

Over the next three decades, until 2050, wind and solar are projected to rise to 48% and renewables to increase in total to 62.5% of total power

Exhibit 1.   Share of Renewables in Global Power Generation Mix

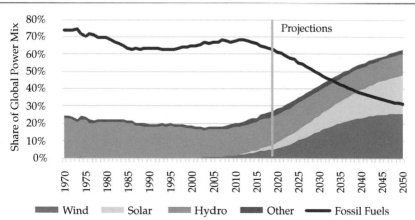

Note: Numbers do not add to 100% because nonrenewables other than fossil fuels, such as nuclear power, are excluded.
Source: Bloomberg New Energy Finance (2019).

generation, according to Bloomberg New Energy Finance (BNEF 2019). Oil will continue to play a role in the economy of 2050, but a much diminished one compared with today. With this diminished role could come diminished importance of the Middle East and other oil-producing regions from a geopolitical perspective—but one should not be so sure about that, as we will learn later in this chapter.

To assess the transition to renewables, we should note that, in some respects, they are very different from fossil fuels. First, renewable energy sources are available everywhere and are not localized the way oil, gas, and coal are. Thus, the need for the kind of transportation infrastructure typically used to transport fossil fuels from their source to the region of end use is reduced in the case of renewables. Crucial transportation chokepoints of today, such as the Strait of Hormuz or pipeline routes, are not something we will necessarily have to worry about in the future.

Some people argue that because renewables can be deployed in a decentralized fashion (every household could theoretically install solar panels on the roof or a windmill in the backyard), the rise of renewables leads, in a sense, to a democratization of energy production and reduces the need for central infrastructure and large-scale utility companies. In reality, economies of scale mean that this democratization process has its limits, but in Germany in 2016, 31.2% of renewable power generation was owned by private investors and was "behind the meter" (International Renewable Energy Agency [IRENA] 2019). In countries with lots of sunshine and high retail electricity prices (looking at you, Australia), solar PV installed on rooftops could become a major source of electricity by 2050.

Another crucial difference between fossil fuels and renewables is important for geopolitical analysis. Fossil fuels are stocks and can be stored easily for a long time. Renewables are flows, which means they never get exhausted and are more difficult to disrupt but also are more difficult to store. Thus, with the rise of renewables comes a need for efficient energy storage systems such as utility-scale batteries. And these technologies, as we will see, might create new geopolitical chokepoints.

Lower Prices Drive Growth of Renewables. Before we dive deeper into the geopolitics of renewables, a word of caution. Projections by major energy and renewable energy organizations such as BNEF, the International Energy Agency (IEA), BP, and IRENA all are subject to significant uncertainty. The rise of renewables depends heavily on GDP growth, the political will to fight climate change, and cost efficiencies resulting from technological progress, all of which are notoriously difficult to predict.

Exhibit 2 shows the estimated annual growth rates of different energy sources until 2040, as projected by BP in 2019. The company ran several different scenarios and made certain assumptions to assess the estimation uncertainty in each sector. It found that the uncertainty around the growth forecasts for oil, coal, and gas was much smaller for each than for renewables. It also found, however, that oil and gas will experience annual growth rates in the range of 1% to 2%, whereas coal demand likely will stagnate. In contrast, annual growth rates for renewables range from 3.7% to 8.4%, with a sample average of 5.5%. Thus, even the most pessimistic scenario for renewables shows annual growth rates that are more than twice as large as the most optimistic case for natural gas and more than three times as large as the most optimistic case for oil.

Renewables are slowly but steadily catching up with fossil fuels as the main source of power generation and eventually will overtake them, but the process is evolutionary, not spontaneous. This is a point on which all forecasters agree, whether they are energy companies or independent think tanks. Forecasts for renewable energy growth, however, have been wrong in the past and will be wrong again in the future.

Whereas forecasts for asset returns or earnings growth tend to be too optimistic for so many other areas of finance, renewables have a long history of surprising to the upside. Analyzing more than a decade of annual forecasts by the IEA for the growth of renewables shows that every year, the IEA had to revise its growth forecasts upward because technological progress had been made so quickly that cost efficiencies were realized much sooner than anticipated.

With these caveats about forecast uncertainty in mind, we can look at the wider implications of this shift to renewable energy sources. Although

Exhibit 2. Expected Annual Growth Rates of Energy Sources

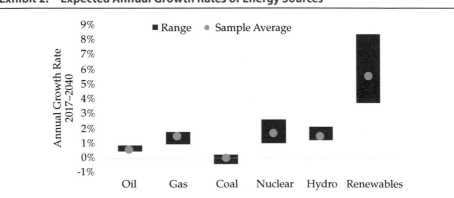

Source: BP (2019).

BNEF projects that 50% of global electricity production will come from wind and solar by 2050, large regional disparities are likely. Europe is taking the lead in this transition. Wind and solar energy are promoted heavily there, with wind energy the preferred source of energy in the United Kingdom and Scandinavia and solar PV in France and southern Europe. BNEF predicts that by 2050, more than 90% of electricity generation in Europe will come from renewable energy sources.

Renewables Have Become the Cheapest Energy Source in Two-Thirds of the World. Meanwhile, China and India will be major players in the renewable energy space, and more than 60% of electricity generated in these two countries in 2050 is expected to come from renewable sources. The carbon dioxide (CO_2) emissions in these countries, however, will continue to rise for several years after 2050. China and India are also the world's biggest users of coal and are responsible for 80% of the coal power plants that have been added in the world in the past five years, as shown in **Exhibit 3**. Even as the rest of the world is phasing out coal, China and India remain hooked on it.

Yet, with its latest five-year plan, China is turning around and increasingly focusing its investments on renewable energy. Between 2016 and 2020, China planned to invest $361 billion into renewable energy generation domestically and create 13 million jobs in the sector (Mason 2017). As we read in chapter 6, China's ambitions with Made in China 2025 and the Belt and Road Initiative concentrate very much on such modern technologies as the generation, storage, and distribution of renewable energy.

Exhibit 3. Coal Capacity Additions, 1950–2019

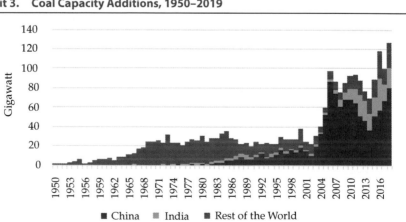

Source: BNEF (2019).

Today, China is the world leader in renewable energy investment by a wide margin. The result of the country's policy shift is that CO_2 emissions will likely peak in China around the year 2027 and then decline to approximately one-half of current levels by 2050. In comparison, India's CO_2 emissions are not expected to peak before 2038 and will then decline only modestly by 2050. India's CO_2 emissions in 2050 are likely to be 50% higher than in 2018 (BNEF 2019).

In the United States, contrary to the rhetoric of the Trump administration, coal is no longer competitive and will be rapidly phased out. This reality, along with the rise of wind and solar energy, means that by 2050, levels of CO_2 emissions from the US power sector will likely be only one-half of those seen in 2018. Nevertheless, the United States will probably remain a laggard in the adoption of renewable energy. BNEF projects that by 2050, only 43% of the electricity used globally will be produced from renewable sources.

The transition to wind and solar is driven not by politics or ideology but simply by economics. In 2014, renewable energy sources were the cheapest source of energy in only one or two countries in the world. In 2019, the least expensive form of energy in two out of three countries worldwide was either wind or solar, even without subsidies. Coal remains the cheapest source of energy in Poland, Turkey, and Malaysia, while natural gas is the least costly form of energy in Russia and Algeria. Even in the United States, wind produced in the plains of Texas is now less expensive than any other form of energy.

As a result, building new gas- or coal-fired power plants in most countries of the world makes no economic sense. If current price trends persist, then shutting down existing coal power plants in China and replacing them with newly built solar and wind power plants will be less expensive in 2027. In the United States, by 2030, building a new wind farm will likely be cheaper than continuing to run an existing gas power plant.

What keeps renewables from growing any faster than they already do is their significant intraday and seasonal variability. The sun shines only during the day, so solar PV plants can produce power only during that time. Wind is not a constant, and the strength of the wind varies from season to season, so that wind energy provides power only part of the year. What is needed is further development of electricity storage technologies, such as batteries and "peaker gas" plants, which can ramp up electricity production quickly in times of fading renewable energy production. These peaker gas plants are the main reason that demand for natural gas, rather than coal or crude oil, is expected to grow at decent rates over the next decades. They provide a complementary energy source to renewables, with relatively low CO_2 emissions.

Fast-Rising Electricity Demand Creates Challenges

Another major challenge for renewables in the coming decades will be the increasing electrification of our societies. Electric vehicles are still more expensive than internal combustion engine cars and require subsidies and tax incentives to be competitive in most countries. But BNEF estimates that between 2022 and 2025, electric vehicles will become cost competitive with internal combustion engine cars. This is the tipping point after which the adoption of electric vehicles should start to accelerate significantly, as **Exhibit 4** shows.

Add to that the increased demand for electricity to power air conditioners in warm, emerging-market countries and the strong growth in GDP and population in those markets, and global electricity demand is expected to increase by 62% over the next three decades. This demand is way beyond the current capacity of power generation and requires estimated investments of $13.3 trillion. How such investments will be financed will be discussed later in this chapter.

Tipping Points and the Inevitable Policy Response

Most forecasters expect the switch from fossil fuels to renewables to be a gradual one, an evolution rather than a revolution. But good arguments can be made as to why we could indeed face a revolution and a rather quick shift in energy use.

Bond (2017) looked at past energy transitions in the United Kingdom and argued that although the new energy source (in these cases, primarily oil and electricity replacing coal) provided only a small fraction of total energy supply, as shown in **Exhibit 5**, investors care about prices, not market shares.

Exhibit 4.   Global Car Sales by Type of Drivetrain

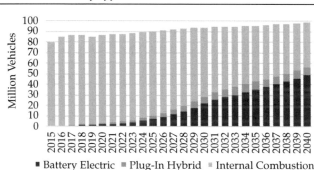

Source: BNEF (2019).

Exhibit 5. Historical Energy Transitions in UK Energy

Area	Fuel Change	Year of Peak Old Demand	Market Share Old Energy	Market Share New Energy
Power	Steam → Electricity	1907	84%	3%
Transport	Coal → Oil	1913	94%	2%
Light	Gas → Electricity	1914	69%	3%
Heat	Coal → Gas	1940	88%	6%

Source: Fouquet (2009).

And prices react to marginal changes in supply and demand rather than to secular changes.

For example, BP reported that the world's total energy consumption in 2017 was 13,511 megatons of oil equivalent (Mtoe),[1] but the annual increase in demand was approximately 225 Mtoe—a growth rate of less than 2%. Given these low growth rates, one might be tempted to think that transitioning from one energy source to another will take a long time. But the rate at which consumers switch is determined by the marginal rate of consumption. If the new energy source is cheaper than the dominating one, then marginal supply and demand will be determined by the production costs of that new energy, and the new energy source will quickly gain market share as long as one additional unit of energy from the new source remains less expensive for consumers than one unit of energy from the old source. In 2015, solar and wind already provided 33% of marginal energy supply globally, whereas fossil fuels accounted for approximately 51% (Bond 2017).

As the marginal energy supply becomes increasingly dominated by renewable energy sources, demand growth for fossil fuels is expected to drop quickly, with potentially hazardous consequences for investors. When demand declined by just 2% for coal in recent years, many coal companies struggled to avoid bankruptcy, and some did not succeed. Once the marginal energy supply is dominated by the new, incoming energy source, investments are rapidly diverted to this energy source, and the transition accelerates. Investors stuck with the old energy source face high price volatility with a potentially secular decline in prices.

Another reason the transition to renewables might become a revolution rather than an evolution is that current trends are by no means sufficient to

---

[1]This amount is equal to approximately 157 petawatt-hours per year, or 157 quadrillion watt-hours per year.

keep CO_2 emissions low enough to ensure that the global average temperature warms by less than 2°C, compared with the levels of the mid-1800s. As **Exhibit 6** shows, the current trajectory keeps us on a less than two-degree path for the next decade or so, after which we would need to restrict CO_2 emissions much more than currently projected. So-called phase II renewables, such as geothermal energy, biomass, and carbon capture and storage (CCS) technologies, will have to be deployed on a large scale to keep us within those limits.

The situation becomes even more challenging if we want to keep global warming within 1.5°C of mid-19th-century levels. In that case, we would need to decarbonize the power sector completely by 2050. A radical shift to renewables, nuclear energy, and other zero-carbon power sources would then be necessary in the mid-2020s.

Today, such a drastic policy change seems unlikely, especially on a global scale. The UN Principles for Responsible Investment, however, argued that a point will come when the effects of climate change will become so visible and salient that public pressure on governments around the globe will increase. Pressure could rise to such a level that politicians will need to change course abruptly and embark on a serious policy shift just to keep their re-election chances intact (Principles for Responsible Investment 2018). In a joint publication, the IEA and IRENA (2017) called for an "unprecedented policy effort" to stay below the two-degree limit with a probability of 66% or higher. The reduction in the use of fossil fuels and their replacement with renewables would have to progress at approximately twice the rate we have seen in recent years (IEA and IRENA 2017).

Exhibit 6. CO_2 Emissions of the Power Sector

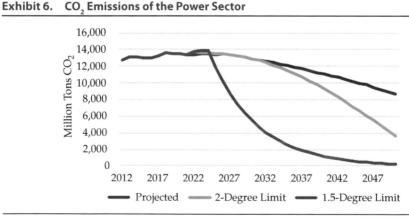

Source: BNEF (2019).

A New Kind of Resource Competition?

Although we could face a drastic shift in climate change policy or investment activity that turns the current transition to renewables into a revolution, we think that looking at the consequences of the current mainstream scenario rather than banking on extreme scenarios is best (see also the rules of forecasting in chapter 5).

One of the areas in which the transition toward renewables might cause geopolitical shifts is in the supply of metals required in solar and wind energy applications. In particular, battery prices have declined rapidly over the past decade and are expected to halve again from current levels by 2025 and then to drop to one-third of current prices by 2030, as **Exhibit 7** shows.

This decline in battery prices creates demand for batteries and, in turn, for the metals used in modern lithium-ion batteries. The most important metals used in the production of batteries are lithium, cobalt, and nickel. Copper, steel, and cement are used heavily in the construction and wiring of solar power plants and windmills. These materials therefore are often the focus of demand analyses in the wake of the shift to renewables. **Exhibit 8** shows the four largest producers of these crucial metals globally. One might ask whether the proliferation of batteries could lead to a geopolitical race for influence in these countries, similar to the race for influence that occurred in the oil-rich Middle East during the 20th century. Especially in the case of cobalt, of which the Democratic Republic of Congo (DRC) owns approximately one-half of global reserves, and Cuba another 7%, these poor countries could possibly become a football in global geopolitics.

Exhibit 7. Lithium-Ion Battery Prices

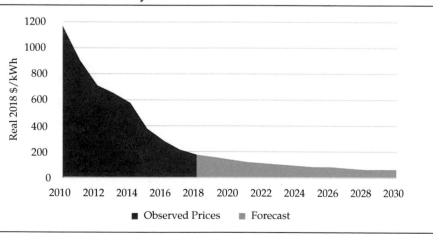

Source: BNEF (2019).

Exhibit 8.   National Origins of Renewable Energy Metals

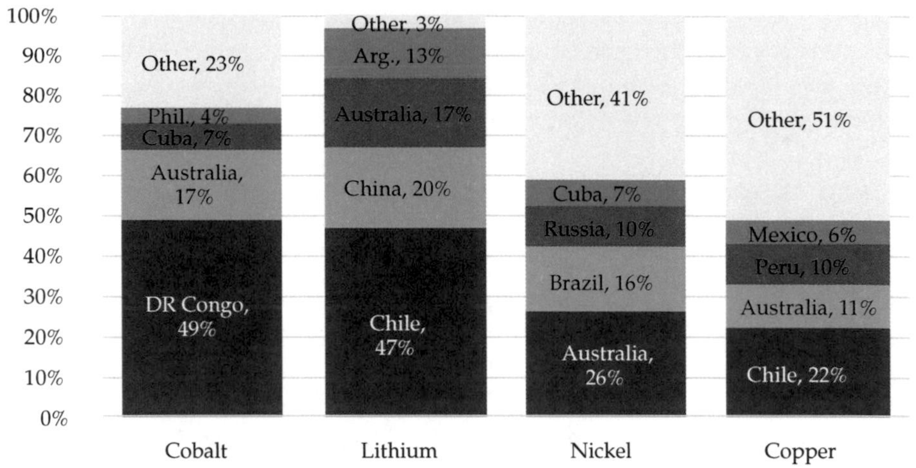

Source: Månberger and Johansson (2019).

For other materials (i.e., lithium and copper), Chile and Australia are effectively the dominant countries of origin, and the potential exists that a production cartel in these metals could control global prices. As we saw in chapter 4, such cartels in copper and other metals have not lasted in the past and quickly were dissolved as some members of the cartel defected and undercut other members' prices.

Furthermore, Overland (2019) showed that geopolitical conflict over these resources is not likely for several reasons. Technological progress is fast, and with it comes a declining reliance on such metals as cobalt, lithium, and copper (Månberger and Stenqvist 2018). Increased recycling and the reuse of old batteries will add to the existing supply of these metals. Furthermore, the value of the metals used in batteries and renewable energy applications in general is much lower than the value of oil and other fossil fuels today (Månberger and Johansson 2019). Price spikes in these metals therefore lead to less strain on governments and businesses and, in turn, less push for political intervention to secure access to these resources. Why send an army when you can simply write a check?

The same is true for the eternally misnamed rare earth metals, which are not actually rare and of which China has little incentive to cut supply, despite being in control of more than 90% of the global supply (see chapter 4 and O'Sullivan, Overland, and Sandalow 2017).

Except for Cobalt, an Adequate Supply of Required Metals Is Available. Furthermore, I agree with the analysis in Overland (2019) that geopolitical conflict over metals is unlikely to materialize simply because, well, they are not truly scarce. **Exhibit 9** shows the projected demand and supply for lithium, sometimes called white gold for its dominance in battery production, over the next five years. Global supply of lithium was 35% higher than global demand for the metal in 2018. By 2025, the supply of lithium is projected to be 70% above projected global demand. If anything, investors should expect lithium prices to drop over the next five years.

The global balance between supply and demand is somewhat tighter in the case of nickel. **Exhibit 10** shows that until 2025, nickel supply is expected

Exhibit 9. Lithium Demand and Supply

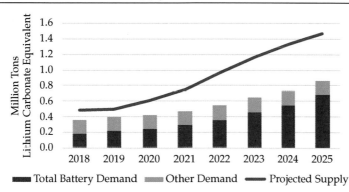

Source: BNEF (2019).

Exhibit 10. Nickel Demand and Supply

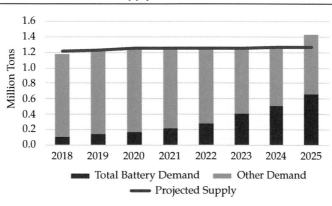

Source: BNEF (2019).

217

to match nickel demand, which means that prices should remain stable or rise slightly. In the short term, production outages in the world's largest nickel mines in Chile, Peru, and Australia could lead to significant price spikes, but little evidence is available for a systemic shortage of nickel in the next few years that could trigger significant price increases.

The only metal facing significant supply shortages in the coming years is cobalt. **Exhibit 11** shows that starting in 2021, global demand for cobalt is expected to exceed global supply. This means that cobalt prices could increase significantly for a while until the point at which recycling becomes economically feasible on a large scale and new mining capacities come onto the market.

We do need to be aware that modern batteries are using less and less cobalt. A lithium-ion battery with a nickel-manganese-cobalt cathode was developed a decade ago (so-called NMC 333) and contains approximately 20% cobalt by weight. Today's state-of-the art NMC 622 batteries contain approximately 12% cobalt by weight, and the next-generation NMC 811 batteries contain only 6% cobalt by weight (Vergine and Van Hyfte 2018). Yet despite this reduced use of cobalt in batteries, the supply shortage is expected to persist until at least the mid-2040s (Månberger and Stenqvist 2018).

Unfortunately, investors have difficulty getting exposure to cobalt mining because the largest mining companies in the world currently have no cobalt operations. **Exhibit 12** shows that only the Swedish mining company Boliden and the Belgian materials company Umicore have a small exposure to cobalt prices. In the case of Umicore, this is primarily driven by the company's recycling business, which should thrive in a world of persistent cobalt shortages and long lead times to develop new cobalt mines.

Exhibit 11.   Cobalt Demand and Supply

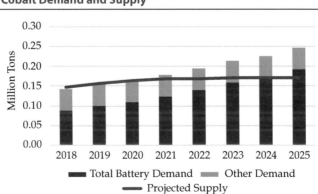

Source: BNEF (2019).

Exhibit 12.   Exposure of Major Mining Companies to Metals Used in Renewable Energy

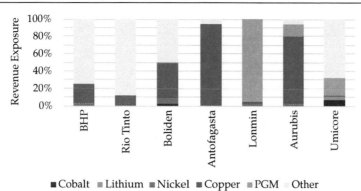

Note: PGM = platinum group metals.
Source: Vergine and Van Hyfte (2018).

Bazilian, Sovacool, and Moss (2017) concluded that given the realities of supply and demand, the fears of a new resource war centered on metals are overblown. Instead, the focus of geopolitics is likely to shift away from access to resources to increased access to technology and supply chains.

Navigating the Energy-Technology Revolution

If we look at the transition from fossil fuels to renewables, it is evident that this is not just an energy transition. The technologies needed to develop renewable energy are much more complex than the technology needed to pump oil and gas out of the ground and refine it into distillates, such as heating oil, gasoline, and kerosene. The shift to renewables thus can be termed an energy technology revolution (ET revolution) in which the countries with the best technology and access to the best know-how and research will have a competitive and geopolitical advantage over the countries that own the resources. Criekemans (2018) postulated that the balance of power could shift away from the owners of resources and toward the countries that own the technology. The future power base of countries will increasingly depend on the countries' ability to combine technology with the natural abundancy of specific renewable energy sources in their region.

In light of this, it is important to note that with respect to one crucial technology, namely batteries, China has already outpaced the rest of the world. **Exhibit 13** shows that in 2019, roughly three-quarters of global manufacturing capacity for batteries was located in China. Europe and other countries in Asia are pushing hard to build additional facilities, but in 2025,

Exhibit 13. Battery Manufacturing Capacity

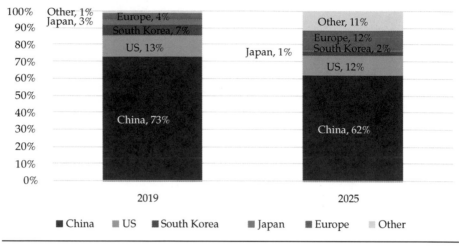

Exhibit 14. Share of Renewables Patents

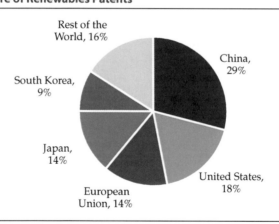

China will still control more than 60% of global manufacturing capacity. China's know-how in batteries and its production capacity are already so dominant that Western car manufacturers are developing new battery technology in research labs in China and rely on Chinese production facilities to drive their future production of electric vehicles (see also chapter 6).

China is also the leader in research and development (R&D) activities in renewable energy. **Exhibit 14** shows that in 2016, 29% of new patents in the renewable energy space were granted to companies and institutions in China, compared with 18% in the United States and 14% in the European Union. China's focus on next-generation technologies means that the country also cooperates intensively with research laboratories and universities in the West to gain access to the know-how there.

China's advantage in renewable energy and batteries, however, might not be as large as the statistics suggest. Arguments have been made that the quality of the patents of Chinese companies is below the quality of patents issued to Western researchers. China still lags the West, and in particular the United States, especially in the area of fundamental research that drives the next generation of breakthrough technologies. The Cleantech Group each year selects the top 100 private companies in the world that are likely to make a significant impact in the coming 5 to 10 years (Cleantech Group 2018). In the 2018 edition, 58 of the 100 companies were based in the United States or Canada and had a combined market valuation of $10.6 billion. In comparison, the United Kingdom had 7 of the top 100 companies, Germany 10, and Israel 5. And China? Three. Of course, this is a statistic about private companies, and the venture capital tradition is simply not as strong in China as it is in the West.

The Cleantech Group also looks at the ability of countries to transform research into economic output in its Global Cleantech Innovation Index (Cleantech Group 2017). It assesses the quality of inputs of innovation such as R&D expenditures, infrastructure for innovation, and government policies to foster innovation in cleantech. The organization then compares these quality measures to a country's output, measured as the number of patents granted, the number of employees in the cleantech industry, the market value of listed and private companies, and the international trade in cleantech products.

Exhibit 15 shows the input score of several countries in the Cleantech Group's 2017 study, along with each one's output score. The higher the score, the more resources available to the cleantech industry in each country. The chart shows that Denmark is the global leader in cleantech innovation, with lots of resources and policies in place to foster cleantech innovation. Yet compared with Finland, Denmark is less efficient in converting these inputs into impactful outputs. The position of the United States on the trend line in Exhibit 15 indicates that the country is roughly average in converting inputs into meaningful outputs. China, on the other hand, is slightly inefficient, as indicated by its position below the trend line. The world's most efficient countries in cleantech innovation are Germany, South Korea, and Singapore, where investors get the best value for their money. In contrast, countries such as India, Australia, and—surprisingly—Norway are among the least efficient countries with respect to cleantech innovation.

Exhibit 15. Efficiency in Cleantech Innovation

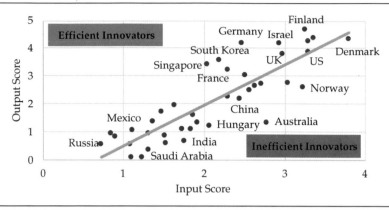

Source: Cleantech Group (2017).

From Phase I to Phase II Renewables. The ET revolution depends not only on economic incentives and R&D efforts but also, to a large extent, on domestic policies in different countries. Renewable energy is a catchall term for a diverse set of technologies and can mean different things to different people. In Europe, renewables predominantly mean wind and solar energy. But in France, nuclear power is an accepted complementary technology to reduce CO_2 emissions and fight climate change, while nuclear power is being phased out in such countries as Germany and Switzerland. In other parts of the world, renewable energy can mean predominantly geothermal energy, as is the case for Iceland, or water, as in Norway and Switzerland.

The advantage of wind and solar energy is that it can be produced in a decentralized manner and on different scales (from single-household rooftop solar PV to large, utility-scale solar arrays). The upfront capital needed to build windmills or solar power plants is relatively low, making such investments ideal for private investors. In countries where large corporations and the government can dedicate significant resources to developing renewable energy, other technologies such as CCS and nuclear power are often seen as a valid alternative to wind and solar, especially with respect to avoiding the intraday and seasonal fluctuations of these mainstream renewable technologies (Paltsev 2016).

The variability in power generation from solar and wind also drives the search for phase II renewables. These new technologies are designed to help alleviate the shortcomings of wind and solar and to provide alternative sources of renewable and zero-emission energy. As we have seen, these phase II renewables will become particularly important if the transition from fossil fuels to renewables speeds up. The most important technologies developed in this area are biomass reactors that generate methane and other flammable gases from organic waste, geothermal reactors that use the heat gradient in the earth's surface, and fossil fuel plants with CCS facilities. Additional popular technologies are concentrated solar power reactors, fuel cell reactors (particularly for use in cars), and subcritical small-scale nuclear reactors, of which a meltdown like the one in Chernobyl is physically impossible.

At the moment, none of these technologies are economically competitive with existing technologies. **Exhibit 16** shows the levelized cost of energy production for a selection of phase II renewables in comparison to the levelized cost of energy of running a gas power plant in China. ("Levelized" refers to the lifetime costs of building, running, and decommissioning the plant divided by the energy the plant produces over its lifetime.) The average cost to produce 1 MWh of electricity is plotted as a function of the capacity factor—that is, the share of time in a year when the plant is actually running and producing electricity. As Exhibit 16 shows, geothermal energy and gas power plants with CCS are competitive with a traditional gas power plant when running at full capacity or close to 100%. Biomass reactors are not far behind.

In a world dominated by wind and solar, these phase II renewables would have to work with capacity factors of 30% or less. And for such low-capacity factors, these phase II renewables are still significantly more expensive than natural gas. As a result, for now, natural gas will remain the power source of choice to complement wind and solar energy. But as we have seen in the past decade, technological progress advances quickly, and in 10 years' time,

Exhibit 16. Levelized Cost of Energy of Phase II Renewable Energy Sources

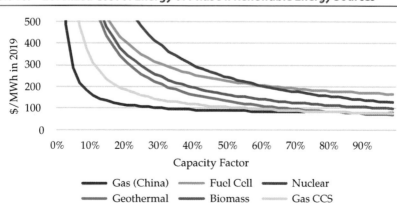

Note: Gas CCS = gas with carbon capture and storage.
Source: BNEF (2019).

CCS technologies or biomass and geothermal energy production might be ready for prime time.

Where Does the Money Come From?

If global electricity demand increases as expected by 62% between 2019 and 2050, who is going to build all the new capacity? And more important, who is going to finance it? According to BNEF (2019), total investments of $13.3 trillion (in 2018 US dollars) will be needed to make this capacity expansion a reality. That amounts to $425.5 billion per year globally. Of this $13.3 trillion, approximately 77% will go to renewable energy sources, primarily solar and wind.

Because energy demand increases most rapidly in Asia, this region will require the most investment. In total, $5.8 trillion needs to be invested in the Asia Pacific region, with China needing $2.9 trillion, India $1.4 trillion, and Southeast Asia $0.6 trillion. Given China's ambitious emission targets, we should expect to see significant resources in that country put to work not only in wind and solar but also in nuclear power, whereas India will be the last major investor in coal power plants and is expected to invest $152 billion in this technology between 2019 and 2050 (BNEF 2019).

In contrast, **Exhibit 17** shows that in Europe, fossil fuels and nuclear energy play only a minor role and are expected to require investments of $135 billion and $171 billion, respectively—nothing compared to the $1.5 trillion investment in onshore and offshore wind. Solar energy investments are likely to amount to only approximately one-half of those made in wind energy, which is understandable given Europe's northerly location.

Exhibit 17. Global Energy Investments by Region, 2019–2050

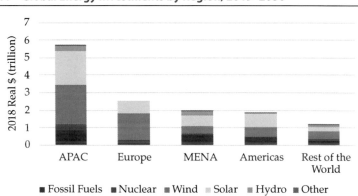

Note: APAC = Asia Pacific; MENA = Middle East and North Africa.
Source: BNEF (2019).

In the Americas, as well as in the Middle East and North Africa, solar power will likely play a more important role, attracting roughly the same amount of investment as wind power (BNEF 2019).

If we look at financing needs by energy source, we see that solar and wind energy require the bulk of financing at $4.2 trillion and $5.3 trillion, respectively, as shown in **Exhibit 18**. This is both good and bad news. The bad news is that the financing needs are quite large, but the good news is that solar and wind power projects are smaller in scale and require less upfront capital expenditure, thereby allowing private and institutional investors to finance individual projects.

The growing shift toward sustainable finance and environmental, social, and governance investing means that private investors are becoming an increasingly important source of capital for solar and wind power plants. A number of firms have listed investment companies similar to REITs that develop and operate wind and solar energy power plants. Like traditional utility companies, such specialized listed investment companies offer stable cash flows and high dividend yields and could become a significant source of investment capital in the future. Private households might also emerge as a major source of small-scale, decentralized renewable energy capacity. Globally, approximately $1.9 trillion is projected to be invested in rooftop solar PV and small-scale batteries by 2050 (BNEF 2019).

What Is the Right Pricing Mechanism? A problem arises, however, with the expansion of wind and solar energy. Because existing solar and wind power plants can generate electricity virtually for free, the expansion of wind and solar power capacity creates downward pressure on wholesale

Exhibit 18.   Global Energy Investments by Energy Source, 2018–2050

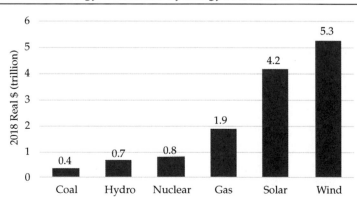

Source: BNEF (2019).

electricity prices. In regions with a large penetration of solar and wind energy, such as California and Germany, we are already witnessing several days a year when wholesale solar power prices become negative; that is, consumers are paid to use the electricity. In 2017, realized solar PV power revenues were approximately one-fifth below the round-the-clock averages for the year (BNEF 2019). At the same time, a heat wave in California or Australia could lead to a scarcity of electricity generated from solar and wind, triggering massive short-term price spikes. Who would invest in an asset that has low to no income and high cash flow volatility?

Thus far, the solution for producers of solar and wind energy has included a combination of free-market prices to exploit scarcity spikes with long-term fixed tariff contracts wherein utility companies purchase solar and wind energy at a fixed cost and in fixed quantities for several years. This ensures that some of the uncertainty about future electricity prices is rolled over to utility companies, while some of it remains on the books of the producer.

Other forms of price formation will likely have to become part of the market mix in the future to provide reasonable certainty to investors that their investments will create positive net cash flows, at least on average, over time. This does not necessarily mean a regulated electricity market in which prices are fixed by the government or a regulatory body. A feasible solution would be to complement free-market pricing with auctions in which capacity is sold at a fixed price for several years.

Such auctions are already commonplace in many countries around the world. In one version, long-term offtake contracts are sold at auction, providing producers of renewable energy with a stable cash flow, while variable electricity production is sold at market prices. One can also think about the reverse situation, in which long-term market prices are negotiated in an unregulated market but variable capacity is auctioned off at guaranteed prices.

Both models can work and reduce the risk for investors while allowing for competitive pricing of electricity. In the end, the process will be a political one, determining which of these solutions for price formation will be implemented. Without such solutions, however, raising the vast sums necessary to expand the global electricity generation capacity to the required extent over the next three decades seems difficult.

The Bottleneck Is the Electricity Grid. The investment requirements do not stop at the ability to generate electricity. We also need to invest in the infrastructure required to transport and distribute electricity. And here comes the shocker. To deliver this electricity to end consumers, another $11.4 trillion in infrastructure investments is needed. **Exhibit 19** shows that

Exhibit 19. Global Investments in Electricity Infrastructure, 2017–2050

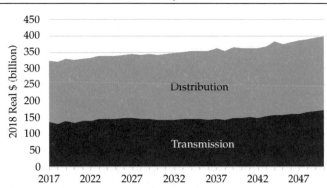

Source: BNEF (2019).

on average, we must spend $148 billion per year on transmission infrastructure and $205 billion per year on distribution infrastructure. Approximately three-quarters of these investments will be required to replace and refurbish old, existing infrastructure that has reached the end of its useful life.

These investments will be focused primarily in industrial countries where the electricity grid is already well developed. Conversely, in emerging markets, a substantial amount must be spent on new transmission and distribution infrastructure, particularly after 2030, when existing grids hit their capacity limits.

In this respect, investors must be aware of the activities of what can easily be called the biggest investment project one has never heard of, namely, China's Global Energy Interconnection, which was set up by the State Grid Corporation of China (SGCC) in 2016 as part of the country's Belt and Road Initiative. It is about to become the biggest investment project in the world and consists of three pillars: (1) an intercontinental backbone network of transmission and distribution grids; (2) large power bases in polar regions, at the equator, and on every continent to integrate distributed power generation from renewable energy sources; and (3) a smart platform that enables energy trade and resource allocation (Cornell 2019).

In a first stage, China promoted the project globally and sponsored R&D in grid infrastructure. This first promotional and explorative stage was expected to last until 2020. Between 2020 and 2030, countries that participate in the Global Energy Interconnection will develop their renewable energy capacity and connect their grids. Finally, from 2030 to 2050, a total of 126,000 km of transcontinental grids will be installed. Each grid will run ultra-high-voltage (UHV) circuits. These UHV circuits were developed in Europe but have been increasingly used in China. Today, Chinese companies are technology leaders in these UHV grids, meaning that building this global grid will benefit Chinese companies and rely on Chinese technology standards—a major source of economic power for the country.

Developing electric grids between 2020 and 2050 allows China to tap into newly built power generation capacity in neighboring countries in Southeast Asia and India. These renewable energy sources are most likely constructed with Chinese solar panels and digitalized distribution technology, in which Chinese companies are world leaders as well, thus providing ample opportunities for growth for Chinese companies.

Additionally, Chinese companies are increasingly investing overseas to secure access to lucrative markets that support continued growth. Between 2013 and 2018, China invested $452 billion overseas in power transactions. Of these investments, power transmission alone accounts for $123 billion. In the European Union, where no regulator is in place to oversee merger and acquisition activity in the power sector, as the Federal Energy Regulatory Commission does in the United States, Chinese companies can invest heavily in local grid companies.

For example, in 2012, SGCC became the largest shareholder in Portugal's electricity grid operator. Chinese state companies own significant grid assets in Italy and Greece, and the country's Three Gorges Corporation wants to expand its stake in the Portuguese utility company EDP (Energias de Portugal). Thus, the Global Energy Initiative is not only a massive investment project that benefits Chinese companies and the recipients of infrastructure investments from China but also a vehicle for soft power that allows China to increase its influence on technological standards and policy making in the areas of infrastructure and global trade (Cornell 2019).

The Decline of Petrostates?

As renewables become more important both in electricity production and transportation, the demand for oil and other fossil fuels is likely to grow at a slower pace. This does not mean that oil demand is going to decline. Most forecasters expect peak oil demand to occur in the mid-2030s, although some think it will not happen before 2060. A typical path of global future oil demand growth is shown in **Exhibit 20** based on data provided by BP.

Demand growth is expected to halve over the next five years, from 1.35 million barrels per day between 2015 and 2020 to 0.65 million barrels per day between 2020 and 2025. The main drivers for this growth deceleration are the decline in demand from the power sector and slower growth in the transportation sector as a result of the greater popularity of hybrid and electric vehicles. By the late 2020s, demand for oil for non-combusted uses

Exhibit 20. Annual Demand Growth for Liquid Fossil Fuels

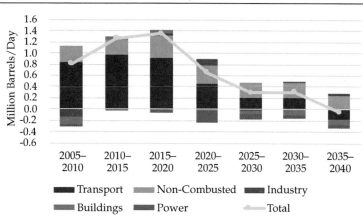

Source: BP (2019).

(primarily plastics, but also pharmaceuticals, paints, and other products) is expected to become the most important driver of demand for crude oil and its distillates. At that point, annual demand growth for crude oil is expected to have declined to essentially zero.

So far, demand growth in emerging markets is still strong because of strong population and GDP growth in these regions. In industrial countries, however, growth has been slowing since before the Global Financial Crisis of 2008. In member countries of the OECD, oil demand has been declining in absolute terms since 2005 and is today at roughly the same level as it was in 1995–1996. Meanwhile, in the European Union, consumption levels have reverted to levels last seen in the mid-1980s (Van de Graaf 2018).

This decline in the rate of demand growth might already be enough to put oil prices under pressure. As we saw in chapter 3, a 1% to 2% shift in the balance between supply and demand leads to a change in oil prices of approximately 10%. Having demand growth slow from approximately 1.5% per year over the past two decades to approximately 0.5% per year over the next two decades could imply a permanent downward trend in oil prices and a significant decline in the revenues of both international oil companies and petrostates. As O'Sullivan et al. (2017) said, this decline in revenues can either trigger economic and political reform in petrostates or create conflict and, in the worst case, trigger civil strife and international wars if the economy of petrostates is not sufficiently diversified.

Who Is Left Stranded? The situation becomes even worse if climate change should force a more aggressive policy response globally. Van de Graaf

(2018) calculated that approximately one-half of the global conventional oil reserves and approximately 80% of unconventional reserves would have to stay in the ground forever if we hope to keep global warming at less than 2°C. **Exhibit 21** illustrates this trend. Canadian tar sands, US shale oil, and Arctic and Antarctic oil deposits should all be left unextracted if we want to have a decent chance of keeping climate change under control. Even if we assume the widespread adoption of CCS technology, approximately 30% of conventional oil deposits would need to remain in the ground.

Middle Eastern petrostates are often claimed to be the areas that will be most affected by this shift in energy demand. This might not necessarily be the case, however, because these countries have the lowest production costs for a barrel of crude oil in the world, as **Exhibit 22** shows. Therefore, these countries could produce oil profitably long after other countries have left the market. What matters for petrostates is the amount of money earned by producing a barrel of crude oil, and this in turn depends on production costs as well as on the market price of oil.

Petrostates essentially have three ways to deal with the challenges of the energy transition and the risk of being left with stranded oil and gas reserves. The first is what Van de Graaf (2018) called "pump and dump." Facing the possibility of dealing with stranded assets, some oil producers—especially those producing at relatively high costs—could decide to sell their oil more quickly than originally planned. Countries that face a high social cost of oil—ones that need oil revenues to finance domestic social safety nets and pension guarantees—also would have an incentive to pump their oil more quickly,

Exhibit 21. Stranded Assets in a 2°C Warming Scenario

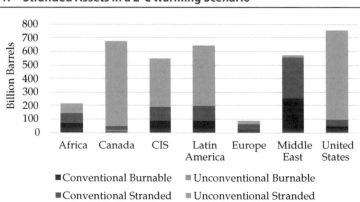

Note: CIS = Commonwealth of Independent States of the former Soviet Union.
Source: Van de Graaf (2018).

Exhibit 22. Estimated Cost Of Production for a Barrel of Crude Oil in 2017

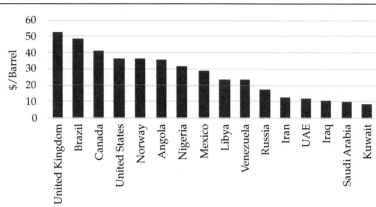

Source: Rystad Energy, CNN.

given that they might face social unrest if they have to cut back on their domestic handouts. This is particularly true for autocratic countries, such as Venezuela and countries in the Middle East, that have extensive social benefits financed by petrodollars.

Countries following a pump-and-dump strategy could trigger a surprise increase in global oil supply that accelerates the decline in oil prices. Oil prices in such a scenario would be unlikely to stay above $50 per barrel for an extended period of time. Paradoxically, these lower oil prices could lead to an increase in demand growth for oil in the coming years.

This scenario seems unlikely to materialize for several reasons. First, materially expanding oil production in a country takes time (often years). Today, most countries, with the exception of Saudi Arabia, are producing at or close to their maximum capacity. Therefore, to increase production permanently, new wells must be drilled and new pipelines built, both of which take time. The only source of crude oil that can be expanded quickly (within months) is shale oil, but it is produced at a relatively high price point, so in a pump-and-dump scenario, this source of supply would not be in play.

Russia, however, seems inadvertently caught in a pump-and-dump strategy. The country has a relatively diversified economy compared with other petro-states. Its manufacturing sector is the 10th largest in the world, and the country has a massive defense sector that is financed primarily by oil and gas revenues. Yet to finance its defense sector and diversify the rest of the economy, the country needs additional revenues. So, in its efforts to wean itself off oil, Russia was forced to increase capital expenditure in the oil and gas sector in recent years at a faster rate than in the rest of the economy. On top of that, as a result of the economic sanctions imposed against Russia since 2014, the country relies even more on energy exports. Today, Russia produces not only more oil than 10 years ago, when oil prices were above $100 per barrel, but also effectively pumps as much as it can (Bradshaw, Van de Graaf, and Connolly 2019).

The second strategy for petrostates to follow during the energy transition is to maximize cash flows by controlling production. In this strategy, OPEC would limit production to keep oil prices at moderately high levels to maximize rents while allowing the global economy to continue to grow. This strategy is essentially the one that OPEC+ (OPEC in coordination with Russia) follows today.

In this scenario, oil prices should hover around $50 per barrel. At an upper limit of approximately $60 per barrel, shale oil production becomes profitable quickly, leading to the expansion of US production. The challenge OPEC faces with this strategy is keeping individual member states from defecting. Some OPEC members produce at much higher costs than Saudi Arabia and other members of the Gulf Cooperation Council (GCC), which gives them an incentive to pump more oil than they agreed to.

This situation already happened in the early 1980s when OPEC introduced production limits that were undermined by several member states that continued to produce more than their quota. The result was a continued decline in oil prices that increased the incentive for these defectors to pump even more oil. In 1986, Saudi Arabia finally stepped in and swamped the market with its oil to enforce discipline on the other OPEC member states.

For investors, of course, the result was that oil prices stayed low for another decade or so until China and other emerging markets had created enough additional demand to push oil prices higher. When, in early 2020, Russia tried to defect from the OPEC+ agreement to cut production, Saudi Arabia again employed this strategy, and Russia had to cave within months and get back in line with OPEC to stabilize the oil price, albeit at much lower levels than before it tried to defect.

The third strategy petrostates can follow is arguably the most sustainable. Facing declining oil rents, petrostates could try to diversify their economies and bolster domestic consumption. The problem is that many petrostates have fallen victim to the so-called Dutch disease, a situation in which the oil sector becomes so dominant that other parts of the economy suffer neglect and become uncompetitive over time.[2]

---

[2]This situation is called the Dutch disease because this kind of scenario occurred in the Netherlands in the 1960s; the Dutch economy has since diversified and prospered.

In these countries, many of which are ruled by an autocratic regime, social cohesion is bought with oil money. To diversify their economy, petrostates need to engage in a long-term strategy to use their wealth to develop their economy rather than spending it on social safety nets and domestic subsidies. If that is not possible, then additional revenues might be raised by selling off some oil assets.

Saudi Arabia tries to follow this diversification strategy. A few years ago, the country introduced Saudi Vision 2030, a strategic plan that aims to increase the role of the private sector in the economy and to diversify the revenues of the state. The IPO of Saudi Aramco was a means to this end. By raising capital from foreign investors, Saudi Arabia could invest the proceeds of the IPO into achieving the goals of Saudi Vision 2030 while simultaneously offloading some of the risks of stranded assets and declining oil rents onto international investors (Bradshaw et al. 2019).

Which strategy each oil-exporting country will take depends on several factors. As Goldthau and Westphal (2019) pointed out, the key variables seem to be the production costs of crude oil and the reserves-to-production (R/P) ratio. Higher R/P ratios imply that a country is forced to be in the oil-exporting business for longer. In this light, recognizing that many of the high-cost producers of oil also have rather low R/P ratios is instructive. Mexico, for instance, is a high-cost producer with an R/P ratio of nine years. Brazil's R/P ratio is 13 years, and Angola's is 16 years. These countries are natural candidates for a pump-and-dump strategy. Other countries with both high production costs and a strong dependence on oil revenues for domestic spending are Venezuela, Nigeria, and Libya.

In contrast, Saudi Arabia's R/P ratio is 60 years, and Iraq's is 90 years (Goldthau and Westphal 2019). Given their low production costs and large reserves, these countries are likely to be in the oil business for the long run. They have an incentive to control output and maximize oil rents while gradually diversifying their economy. Russia is a borderline case. With the lowest production costs outside the GCC and an R/P ratio of 26 years, it could go either way, but as we have seen, for now, the country seems trapped in a pump-and-dump situation.

The irony of these divergent strategies is that OPEC could become more influential again in the future. For decades, OPEC has lacked internal cohesion because different members had different incentives to produce oil. With the transition of the global economy away from fossil fuels, some countries could leave OPEC to follow pump-and-dump and other strategies that they cannot implement under the OPEC quota system. The countries remaining in OPEC most likely would be the low-cost producers of the GCC.

　　　　　　　233

This "core OPEC" would benefit from stronger internal cohesion and thus a better ability to coordinate output and global oil prices.

Geopolitical Hot Spots during the Energy Transition

Given the material impact of the energy transition on petrostates, investors need to consider the risks of failure in any one of these countries. What if the strategy to diversify the economy fails and a country remains hooked on ever-declining cash flows from oil and gas exports? What if a country runs a pump-and-dump strategy and then finally runs out of oil?

The vulnerability of petrostates to the energy transformation depends, on one hand, on the share of government income from fossil fuel production and export and, on the other, on the ability of the economy to generate income from other sources. Inspired by IRENA (2019), we have plotted in **Exhibit 23** every country in the world where fossil fuel rents (income from oil, gas, and coal) make up more than 5% of GDP. We compare the fossil fuel rent with the GDP per capita for each country. GDP per capita is used as a proxy for the robustness of the local economy to declining revenues. If a country is very wealthy, declining oil revenues will still hurt, but the risk of widespread poverty that could trigger civil unrest is smaller than in poorer countries. Remember rule 6 of forecasting in chapter 5? "A full stomach does not riot."

Furthermore, a country can usually achieve a high GDP per capita only if its economy has significant sources of income other than the export of oil and gas. The presence of refineries and oil service companies and of businesses in other sectors mitigates the decline in revenues from the production and export of fossil fuels. In fact, as more and more countries around the world introduce carbon trading schemes that increase the cost of CO_2-producing

Exhibit 23. Vulnerability to the Renewable Energy Transformation

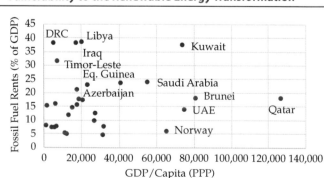

Source: World Bank.

activities, some businesses in the energy sector, such as refineries, might shut down in industrial countries and move instead to the Middle East or another oil-exporting region, where the price of carbon is zero or very low—a possibility that will be further explored in chapter 9. Some petrostates therefore would be able to dampen the decline in oil and gas rents with increased income from oil processing and refining.

Looking at Exhibit 23, we see that Qatar is probably the least vulnerable petrostate, given its extremely high GDP per capita. Other resilient petrostates are Saudi Arabia, Kuwait, the United Arab Emirates (UAE), and Brunei. Despite their high reliance on fossil fuel rents, they have a relatively high GDP per capita. Arguably, inequality is high in many of these countries, and GDP per capita is not distributed as equally as it is in more diversified economies. This adds additional vulnerabilities that we will address.

For now, it is important to note that the most vulnerable countries seem to be the DRC, Libya, Iraq, and Timor-Leste, which all rely heavily on oil and other fossil fuel exports yet remain very poor. This dynamic provides fertile ground for terrorist organizations and a potential trigger for civil war that could spread to neighboring countries, as we saw in 2011 with the Arab Spring.

The potential for social unrest is particularly high in countries that suffer from high inequality, where, for example, only a small elite benefits from the wealth generated by oil and gas exports while the majority of the population suffers from poverty. The situation becomes even worse when a country experiences rapid population growth and thus has a very young population. As the Arab Spring and so many other civil uprisings in history have shown, it is young men (and it is typically men, not women) with nothing to do all day who are prone to start rioting.

Thus, in **Exhibit 24**, I plot the fossil fuel rents of different petrostates along with the latest available youth unemployment rate. Some countries shown in Exhibit 23 have been omitted from Exhibit 24 because they do not publish youth unemployment figures. Furthermore, in many cases, the youth unemployment figures in Exhibit 24 are several years old and might not be too reliable. With these caveats in mind, Qatar is, interestingly, again relatively immune to the risks of the energy transition because it has very low (official) youth unemployment. Saudi Arabia is a borderline case, with a youth unemployment rate of 16.1%, while countries in Africa, such as Egypt, Algeria, the DRC, and Nigeria, all suffer from youth unemployment rates of 20% or higher. In Iran and Iraq, the youth unemployment rate surpasses 30%, putting these countries at extreme risk of social unrest—or even war—should the economy weaken.

Exhibit 24. Potential for Social Unrest Because of the Renewable Energy Transformation

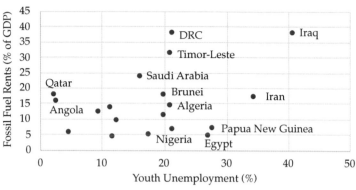

Source: World Bank.

The Options for International Oil Majors

The energy transition leads to new challenges not only for petrostates but also for international oil companies. After all, international oil majors typically produce at higher costs than do the national oil companies of the GCC. Caldecott, Holmes, Kruitwagen, Orozco, and Tomlinson (2018) ran several war games to simulate the strategic options of international oil companies and the likely impact of each on their share price:

- In the first strategy, oil companies could follow a "first-one-out strategy," in which the company would announce its exit from oil exploration and production, try to sell existing high-cost reserves to competitors, and gradually run down the remaining low-cost reserves. Revenues from oil production would be handed back to investors through dividends and share buybacks. During this transition period, the company would transform itself into an oil services company engaged in midstream and downstream activities, become a renewable energy producer, or simply shut down operations altogether. Theoretically, investors should welcome such a strategy because it would provide growth-style cash flows well into the 2030s and reduce the risk of stranded assets.

- The second strategy could be a "last-one-standing strategy," in which the company tries to accumulate as many low-cost reserves as possible to survive a price war between oil majors. This strategy can work for both the company and its shareholders if the company is financially sound and not too leveraged at the beginning because the acquisition of additional reserves likely will lead to a substantial increase in financial leverage.

- Under the third strategy, the company could announce a planned transition of its business model away from oil exploration and production to renewable energy or other energy-related services. In this case, committing to this long-term strategy and resisting pressures from shareholders to increase short-term profits is crucial for the company. The transition will likely take years and reduce profitability in the short run, given that costs increase well before revenues and profits from new business areas do. As the transformation progresses, a legal separation of the legacy business and the new renewables business would likely be necessary. Probably the best example of a company following this strategy is DONG Energy, the former Danish national oil company. Renamed Ørsted, the company successfully transformed itself from an oil company into a pure renewables company in recent years.

- Two final strategies are available for oil companies to follow. A "drift strategy" implies that an oil major continues to drift away from high-cost reserves toward low-cost reserves and other fossil fuels, such as natural gas, but makes no plans for a transition or price war. Another option is the "do-nothing strategy" of pretending that all is well and that nothing needs to change. That both of these strategies are disastrous in the long run should be obvious.

Caldecott et al. (2018) reported that in the war games that simulated the fate of different international oil majors based on stylized facts of real-life companies, those that followed a first-one-out strategy had the least amount of stranded assets remaining when oil demand peaked and finally declined rapidly after the 2040s. Unfortunately, the share price of the companies following such a strategy also collapsed because of the rapid reduction of proven reserves on the companies' balance sheets.

That analysts and investors value an oil company largely based on the value of proven reserves, assuming that all reserves eventually will be sold at market prices, is a fact of life. Investors at the moment therefore do not price in the possibility of stranded assets, so a first-one-out strategy is tantamount to shareholder suicide. What companies need for successful implementation of a first-one-out strategy are shareholders who are long-term oriented and take the risk of stranded assets seriously.

In the war games, companies that followed a drift strategy or a last-one-standing strategy saw relatively stable market valuations but were left with the largest stranded reserves at the end of the simulated period. Continued exploration remained profitable until the mid-2020s, at which point demand slowed rapidly, and the price of carbon increased in many countries, rendering impossible the sale of existing reserves at decent prices and the quick transformation of them into a liability on the balance sheet. Thus, investors face decent performance for several years with such companies but run the risk of a catastrophic collapse of the share price if at some point in the future, some or all of a company's reserves become stranded.

Finally, the most successful strategy in the long run was the planned transformation strategy. Although share prices suffered for several years as costs increased and profitability declined, market valuations for these companies increased after a few years as high growth rates in renewables led to higher earnings growth compared with their peers.

War games are a good way to simulate the potential outcome of different strategic options in a competitive environment, but they remain theoretical. Pickl (2019) investigated what some of the biggest international oil companies are really doing.

Royal Dutch Shell seems to be at the forefront of companies following a planned transition strategy. The company no longer calls itself an "energy company" but rather an "energy transition company" and invests $1 billion to $2 billion per year in electricity generation. The company also bought significant stakes in NewMotion (Europe's largest provider of electric vehicle charging stations), First Utility (a UK electricity company), and Silicon Ranch (a US solar developer). With these investments, Shell is among the largest investors in energy transition technologies in the world. Other companies that follow a planned transition strategy are the French oil major Total, which focuses on investment in renewables as well as refining, chemicals, and shipping; Eni in Italy; and the Norwegian Equinor (formerly Statoil).

BP is a special case among European oil majors. The company was one of the first oil majors to invest in renewables, channeling between $8 billion and $10 billion into renewable energy sources in the first decade of the 2000s, although these investments had to all be written off because the projects were too early and could not be made profitable. The reasons were lack of demand and failure to be price competitive with conventional sources of energy. On top of that, the 2010 oil spill in the Gulf of Mexico forced the company to cut costs and exit the remaining renewables projects. Today, the company is caught in what looks like a drift strategy, but management announced in early 2020 that it wants to engage in a planned transition strategy that is more ambitious than the one followed by Shell.

Unlike their European peers, American oil majors such as Exxon and Chevron follow a last-one-standing strategy that focuses on low-cost oil and gas reserves with limited to no engagement in renewables. The only energy transformation technology to which these companies seem to be willing to commit substantial resources is CCS methods of reducing the emissions of gas and coal power plants. Finally, Brazil's oil major, Petrobras, seems to follow a last-one-standing strategy as well. It potentially is exposing itself to sizeable long-term risks, given that Petrobras has significantly higher production costs than Exxon or Chevron and thus seems poised to lose a potential price war.

Energy Independence for Emerging Markets

Historically, the energy transition from fossil fuels to renewable sources of energy such as solar and wind has been driven by industrial countries in Europe. A look at the global wind energy potential, shown in **Exhibit 25**, reveals why. Most European countries are far north and in the middle of steady winds circling the globe from west to east. The west coasts of Ireland, the United Kingdom, and Norway as well as the North Sea and the North Atlantic face steady winds that are ideal for wind farms, both onshore and offshore. As the costs for windmills dropped rapidly, these countries naturally increased the production of wind energy.

The other major opportunity in the Northern Hemisphere for wind energy lies in the plains of Texas and the American Midwest. Rick Perry, the former US secretary of energy and governor of Texas, realized this economic potential and provided significant government incentives to install wind farms in Texas. Today, Texas is the biggest producer of wind energy in the United States, and wind energy from Texas is the cheapest energy source in

Exhibit 25. World Wind Energy Potential

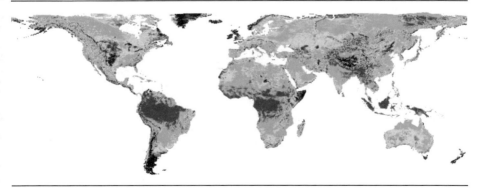

Notes: Blues and greens indicate areas of low potential, and reds indicate areas of high potential. Darker shades of red indicate areas of higher potential for wind energy.
Source: Vaisala, IRENA: Global Atlas for Renewable Energy, Global wind data: VAISALA, 2016.

the country. Houston is no longer just the home of global oil majors but also the home of an ever-increasing number of wind energy companies.

A look at Exhibit 25, however, shows that in the Southern Hemisphere, some of the best places to install wind farms are in emerging markets. The Argentinian Pampas, the Atacama Desert in Chile, and the Horn of Africa are all fertile ground for wind investments. Add in the potential for solar energy, which is obviously highest in the world's deserts and in countries close to the equator, as shown in **Exhibit 26**, and emerging markets clearly have huge potential to benefit from the transition to wind and solar.

BNEF (2018) showed that emerging markets are increasingly driving the transition to renewable energy. In 2017, 63 GW (gigawatts) of renewable energy were installed in industrial countries but 114 GW in emerging markets—mostly in China. And while China, India, Turkey, and South Africa continue to build their coal power capacity, other emerging markets are moving away from coal as a fuel for electricity generation. Investments in renewable energy surpassed $140 billion in 2017, with only $21.4 billion funded from developed countries.

The majority of the funding for renewable energy in 2017 came from local sources. Of 103 emerging markets surveyed by BNEF (2019), only 11 had no official clean energy policy in place. Seventy-four percent of countries had clean energy targets, and 64% gave tax incentives to companies investing in clean technologies. As a share of GDP, the investments in renewable energy in many emerging markets top the investments made in developed markets, such as the United Kingdom and the United States, as shown in **Exhibit 27**.

Mexico illustrates how an emerging market can reduce its dependence on fossil fuels and boost investments in renewables. In 2013, the country

Exhibit 26.   World Solar Energy Potential

Notes: Blues and greens indicate areas of low potential, and reds indicate areas of high potential. Darker shades of red indicate areas of higher potential for solar energy.
Source: Vaisala, IRENA: Global Atlas for Renewable Energy, Global solar data: VAISALA, 2016.

Exhibit 27. Investments in Renewable Energy, 2013–2017

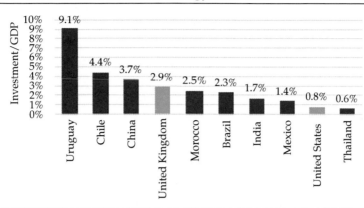

Note: Dark blue bars indicate emerging markets, and light blue bars indicate developed markets.
Source: IRENA.

liberalized its electricity market. Today, the electric grid is run by an independent operator (CENACE), while power generation is subject to market prices. The country also introduced a goal of generating 35% of its power in 2024 from renewable sources. To help achieve this goal, clean energy auctions were introduced, and clean energy certificates were issued to providers of renewables. The result was a massive increase in renewables investments, from $1 billion in 2013 to $6.2 billion in 2017 (BNEF 2018).

Many countries, however, still face considerable obstacles to the development of renewables. Chile has among the highest potential for both wind and solar energy in the world. The Atacama Desert could become an energy production hub for all of South America. Unfortunately, Chile's electricity grid is run by four different operators that are not linked. As a result, electricity generated in the arid north of the country cannot be transported to the big cities in the south, let alone to neighboring countries. In recent years, multi-billion-dollar investments have been made to link the electricity grids of the two largest domestic providers and to connect them to the grid of Peru and other neighboring countries, but much more needs to be done before Chile can meet its potential.

Geopolitical Risks of the Energy Transition

For emerging markets, the energy transition provides many opportunities but comes with its own set of risks. Petrostates, such as many Middle Eastern countries, not only have different incentives than energy importers but also different tools with which to manage the energy transition. And the owners of crucial technologies, most of whom are based in industrial countries in the Northern Hemisphere, fear the loss of intellectual property and cheap competition from emerging markets.

At the moment, therefore, each country manages the energy transition differently and with little international coordination. The UAE, for example, launched its Soft Power Strategy in 2017, which aims to establish bilateral diplomatic links with crucial strategic partners that could become useful during the energy transition (Griffiths 2019).

Although rich in oil, the UAE, like many of its neighbors in the GCC, faces shortages of natural gas supply. Given the area's rapid increase in population, energy demand from private households, much of which is powered by gas, grows fast. Qatar would be the natural hub for local gas supplies because the country has vast gas reserves, but political differences between Qatar and Saudi Arabia, the UAE, and other GCC countries have limited Qatar's ability to deliver gas to its neighbors.

These obstacles have focused the minds of governments in the UAE and other GCC countries, and they are seeking access to gas, nuclear, and renewables technology to develop the countries' domestic power supplies. For example, a bilateral agreement between the UAE and South Korea, in place since 2009, gives the UAE access to nuclear technology. Meanwhile, to increase their influence in the region, both Russia and China are aggressively trying to sell their nuclear technology to Saudi Arabia. In return for access to technology from strategic partners, GCC countries can use their oil as a bargaining chip. No wonder, then, that the strategic partners of the UAE in Asia are China, India, South Korea, and Japan—countries that need Emirati oil and can provide access to crucial technology in return (Griffiths 2019).

Not all emerging markets are as lucky as the GCC and other petrostates. Resource-poor emerging markets must try to improve their economies by building low-cost production centers for renewable energy—in some cases by producing power but also by manufacturing components of solar panels and windmills. Low-cost competition from emerging markets, however, can draw the ire of producers in industrial markets that fear the loss of market share. The tariffs on solar panels that are imported to the United States from China were introduced after the US solar company Suniva filed for bankruptcy in 2017 and complained to the US Commerce Department (see chapter 6).

Because renewables remain a nascent industry, the temptation to introduce trade barriers or protect domestic suppliers from international competition remains high. Thus, the transition to renewable energy increases the risk of a return to government-directed "industrial policies" such as those seen in the 1970s and 1980s.

As Shum (2019) showed, some industrial policies are beneficial and some are harmful. Among the more beneficial policies are those that aim to increase local demand and know-how rather than curtailing supply. Classic examples of such beneficial industrial policies are installation subsidies and feed-in tariffs for renewables. Installation incentives lead to the spread of know-how in renewables technology to small local businesses that install solar panels and windmills. Feed-in tariffs increase demand for solar PV and wind energy that is produced locally and then fed into the electricity grid at subsidized prices. Meanwhile, the question of who supplies solar panels, windmills, and other technology is left to the markets to answer.

The more harmful policies are those that aim to limit supply or protect domestic suppliers against international competition. These policies traditionally take the form of production subsidies and quotas on foreign imports. Under former president Donald Trump, the United States also saw a return to tariffs as a means to protect US manufacturers.

Although such production incentives are politically expedient, they often cause manufacturers to become uncompetitive, then implode once a market is liberalized again, a situation we saw in the early 2010s when European and North American producers of solar panels faced cheaper Chinese competitors and declining domestic demand after government subsidies were curbed. Ironically, in such an imploding market, the temptation to protect domestic manufacturers and jobs becomes even higher for politicians, creating a potentially harmful feedback loop to unwind globalization in the renewables industry. The biggest losers of such a dynamic would be (1) consumers in industrial countries who would have to pay higher prices for renewable energy and (2) manufacturers in emerging markets that would have reduced access to international markets.

Conclusions

In this chapter, we have seen that the rise of renewable energy such as solar and wind has become a fact of life. Wind and solar are the cheapest energy sources (even without government subsidies) in two-thirds of all countries of the world (BNEF 2019). By the late 2020s, wind and solar will likely be cheaper than gas- or coal-powered plants everywhere.

This reality does not mean that we face a rapid decline of fossil fuel as an energy source but rather an evolution in which demand for oil, gas, and coal from the energy sector gradually declines and investments in new capacity are made primarily in the renewables space. Because the transition from fossil fuels to renewables will take many years and peak oil demand is likely to happen only in the mid-2030s or later, investors might be tempted to ignore the energy transition for now.

As this chapter has shown, ignoring the energy transition would be a mistake not just for investors but also for international oil companies and petrostates. Instead, the next decade should be used to diversify the economy of petrostates and the business of international oil majors. Diversification in this context means investing in renewable energy generation that is likely to outgrow oil and gas by a factor of two to three over the next two decades. If this opportunity is missed, geopolitical tension could rise dramatically, particularly in countries that have high production costs for oil and low national income. For international oil majors, not diversifying the business model could even lead to bankruptcy.

The winners of the energy transition will be countries and businesses that have access to the new technologies that drive renewable energy production, because renewable energy production is a high-tech industry. This means that the energy transition is, in reality, an energy-technology transition.

Some countries, including China and Germany as well as those in Scandinavia, have positioned themselves for this energy-technology transition and already have focused their R&D efforts on this industry. The countries that manage the energy transition successfully seem likely to gain considerable geopolitical influence, while the laggards will lose influence. Of course, losing geopolitical influence is not something those countries will take lightly. Instead, we face the risk that countries that are no longer competitive will resort to industrial policies that erect trade barriers or protect inefficient domestic industries from unwanted international competition.

Bibliography

Bazilian, M., B. Sovacool, and T. Moss. 2017. "Rethinking Energy Statecraft: United States Foreign Policy and the Changing Geopolitics of Energy." *Global Policy* 8 (3): 422–25.

BNEF. 2018. "Emerging Markets Outlook 2018: Energy Transition in the World's Fastest Growing Economies." Climatescope, Bloomberg New Energy Finance, London, UK, November. https://global-climatescope.org/assets/data/reports/climatescope-2018-report-en.pdf.

BNEF. 2019. "New Energy Outlook 2019." Bloomberg New Energy Finance, London, UK, 20 August. https://about.bnef.com/new-energy-outlook-2019/#toc-download.

Bond, K. 2017. "Revolution Not Evolution: Marginal Change and the Transformation of the Fossil Fuel Industry." Discussion Paper, University of Oxford Smith School of Enterprise and the Environment, Sustainable Finance Programme, Oxford, UK, February. http://www.divestinvest.org/wp-content/uploads/2017/09/OxfordUniversity.Revolution-not-evolution-SFP-Discussion-Paper-February-2017.pdf.

BP. 2019. "BP Energy Outlook: 2019 Edition." BP Energy Economics, London, UK, 14 February. https://www.bp.com/content/dam/bp/business-sites/en/global/corporate/pdfs/energy-economics/energy-outlook/bp-energy-outlook-2019.pdf.

Bradshaw, M., T. Van de Graaf, and R. Connolly. 2019. "Preparing for the New Oil Order? Saudi Arabia and Russia." *Energy Strategy Reviews* 26: 100374.

Caldecott, B., I. Holmes, L. Kruitwagen, D. Orozco, and S. Tomlinson. 2018. "Crude Awakening: Making Oil Major Business Models Climate Compatible." E3G and the University of Oxford Smith School of Enterprise and the Environment, Sustainable Finance Programme, Oxford, UK, 1 March. https://www.jstor.org/stable/resrep17728.1?seq=1#metadata_info_tab_contents.

Cleantech Group. 2017. "2017 Global Cleantech Innovation Index." Cleantech Group, Oakland, CA, 12 June.

Cleantech Group. 2018. "2018 Global Cleantech 100 Report: A Barometer of the Changing Face of Global Cleantech Innovation." Cleantech Group, Oakland, CA, 24 January.

Cornell, P. 2019. "Energy Governance and China's Bid for Global Grid Integration." *Atlantic Council* (blog), 30 May. https://www.atlanticcouncil.org/blogs/energysource/energy-governance-and-china-s-bid-for-global-grid-integration/.

Criekemans, D. 2018. "Geopolitics of the Renewable Energy Game and Its Potential Impact upon Global Power Relations." In *The Geopolitics of Renewables*, edited by D. Scholten, 37–73. Cham, Switzerland: Springer International.

Fouquet, R. 2009. *Heat, Power and Light: Revolutions in Energy Services.* Cheltenham, UK: Edward Elgar.

Goldthau, A., and K. Westphal. 2019. "Why the Global Energy Transition Does Not Mean the End of the Petrostate." *Global Policy* 10 (2): 279–83.

Griffiths, S. 2019. "Energy Diplomacy in a Time of Energy Transition." *Energy Strategy Reviews* 26: 100386.

IEA and IRENA. 2017. "Perspectives for the Energy Transition: Investment Needs for a Low-Carbon Energy System." International Energy Agency, IEA/OECD, Paris; International Renewable Energy Agency, Abu Dhabi. https://www.irena.org/-/media/Files/IRENA/Agency/Publication/2017/Mar/Perspectives_for_the_Energy_Transition_2017.pdf.

IRENA. 2019. "A New World: The Geopolitics of the Energy Transformation." Global Commission on the Geopolitics of Energy Transformation, International Renewable Energy Agency, Abu Dhabi, January.

Månberger, A., and B. Johansson. 2019. "The Geopolitics of Metals and Metalloids Used for the Renewable Energy Transition." *Energy Strategy Reviews* 26: 100394.

Månberger, A., and B. Stenqvist. 2018. "Global Metal Flows in the Renewable Energy Transition: Exploring the Effects of Substitutes, Technological Mix and Development." *Energy Policy* 119: 226–41.

Mason, J. 2017. "China to Plow $361 Billion into Renewable Fuel by 2020." Reuters, 4 January. https://www.reuters.com/article/us-china-energy-renewables-idUSKBN14P06P.

O'Sullivan, M., I. Overland, and D. Sandalow. 2017. "The Geopolitics of Renewable Energy." Working Paper, HKS No. RWP17-027, John F. Kennedy School of Government Faculty Research Working Paper Series, Harvard University, Cambridge, MA, 26 June.

Overland, I. 2019. "The Geopolitics of Renewable Energy: Debunking Four Emerging Myths." *Energy Research and Social Science* 49: 36–40.

Paltsev, S. 2016. "The Complicated Geopolitics of Renewable Energy." *Bulletin of the Atomic Scientists* 72 (6): 390–95.

Pickl, M. J. 2019. "The Renewable Energy Strategies of Oil Majors—From Oil to Energy?" *Energy Strategy Reviews* 26: 100370.

Principles for Responsible Investment. 2018. "The Inevitable Policy Response: Preparing Financial Markets for Climate-Related Policy/Regulatory Risks." UNEP Finance Initiative, United Nations Global Compact, PRI Association, London, UK. https://www.unpri.org/download?ac=9833.

Shum, R. Y. 2019. "Heliopolitics: The International Political Economy of Solar Supply Chains." *Energy Strategy Reviews* 26: 100390.

Van de Graaf, T. 2018. "Battling for a Shrinking Market: Oil Producers, the Renewables Revolution, and the Risk of Stranded Assets." In *The Geopolitics of Renewables*, edited by D. Scholten, 97–121. Cham, Switzerland: Springer International.

Vergine, E., and W. Van Hyfte. 2018. "Green Solutions under the Hood: The Role of Metals in Energy Transition." Candriam White Paper, New York Life Investments, New York, NY, October. https://s3.amazonaws.com/external_clips/2898532/greenmetals_en_300dpi.pdf?1541220084.

Chapter 9: The Impact of Climate Change

Changes in climate policies, new technologies, and growing physical risks will prompt reassessment of the values of virtually every financial asset. Firms that align their business models with the transition to a net-zero world will reap handsome rewards. Those that fail to adapt will cease to exist. The longer meaningful adjustment is delayed, the greater the disruption will be.

—Mark Carney

Climate Change Skews Us More Than We Might Expect

Climate change is, as I mentioned in the introduction to this book, a global problem and arguably the most pressing problem we face in the 21st century. Yet climate change is also a political hot potato, particularly in such countries as the United States and Australia. On the one hand, the science of climate change is clear. Our global climate is changing, and these changes are going to significantly affect our way of life. The debate is not about whether climate change is real, nor is it about whether climate change is caused by humans. Both of these debates were settled long ago, despite the protestations and fake news campaigns of oil billionaires and conspiracy theorists. That this increase in temperature has been triggered by the rise in greenhouse gases in the Earth's atmosphere has been proven beyond a reasonable doubt.[1]

Our concern in this chapter is the likely economic impact of climate change. And unfortunately, this is where things get really uncertain. As we will see in this chapter, standard economic models of climate change predict a GDP impact that is so small as to be almost negligible. A lot of nonlinear effects are in play, however. Once global warming pushes some processes beyond a tipping point, the resulting damage to the global economy could be

---

[1]What also has been proven beyond a reasonable doubt is that climate change is overwhelmingly driven by human activity rather than by natural variation in solar radiation as past episodes of climate change. I worked for three years as an astrophysicist on a project designed to determine the sun's contribution to climate change, and explaining climate change by solar phenomena is entirely impossible. In fact, back in the day, it was already clear that more than two-thirds of the total climate change seen in the past 150 years had to come from human activity.

much, much higher than anything our standard models predict. For example, the impact of sea-level rise (SLR) on the economy is typically modeled in standard models, but as we will see in this chapter, evidence is increasing that Arctic and Antarctic ice shelves melt faster than previously known and could face a tipping point at which complete destruction of the ice shelf becomes inevitable. In this case, SLR might accelerate to levels far beyond those typically modeled today. And because so many people live in coastal areas, the economic loss due to SLR might quickly become a multiple of what standard models predict.

In other words, this chapter will show that although the economic damage from climate change is currently expected to be manageable and primarily localized, the risks are significantly skewed to the upside and toward much higher levels of damage than we currently expect. We certainly have no reason to be complacent about climate change.

How a Volcano in Iceland Might Have Caused the French Revolution

On 8 June 1783, a volcano called Laki erupted in Iceland. That in itself would not be too big a deal, given that Iceland has plenty of volcanoes that erupt all the time, except that Laki was not your usual volcano, and this eruption was not your usual eruption. For starters, Laki looks nothing like the postcard volcanoes we are used to. It is not a cone-shaped mountain with a crater at the top through which it spits lava and smoke from time to time. Instead, Laki is a crack in the ground 25 km (16 miles) long, with approximately 130 individual craters in it. Imagine the Grand Canyon with mini volcanoes lined up like pearls on a string, and you get an idea of what it looks like.

On that fateful day in 1783, the volcano erupted and blew tons of steam into the air when its magma made contact with groundwater, evaporating it instantaneously. Once the water reservoir had been exhausted, lava rose to the surface and slowly spread across the countryside. This eruption continued for several more days. But what made the eruption special was not the lava emitted from the volcano but the sulfuric aerosols that were ejected and made their way high up in the atmosphere. The volcano continued to eject sulfur for eight months, creating one of the biggest climatic events of the past thousand years.

Exhibit 1 shows the quantity of sulfuric aerosols injected into the atmosphere by volcanoes over the past 300 years. In the chart, I have marked the Laki eruption alongside other prominent volcanic eruptions. Except for the eruption of Mount Tambora in Indonesia in 1815, no volcanic event had a

Exhibit 1. Atmospheric Sulfate Injection from Volcanoes

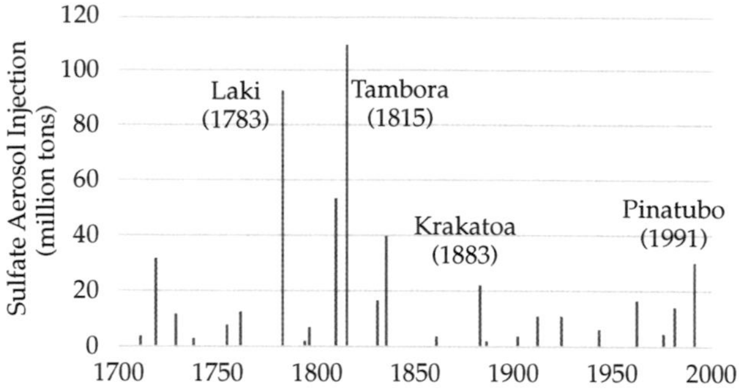

Source: Gao, Robock, and Ammann (2008).

higher sulfur injection. Laki injected approximately four times as much sulfur into the atmosphere as did the famous eruption of Krakatoa in 1883 and approximately three times as much as the eruption of Mount Pinatubo in 1991. And sulfuric aerosols are potent greenhouse gases that have a significant impact on the weather. The sulfur poisoned the wells in Iceland and destroyed harvests. An estimated 20% to 25% of the population of Iceland died as a result of the failed harvests in the subsequent years, and approximately 80% of the sheep and the majority of cows and horses on the island died as well.

But unlike Mount Tambora, Laki was located in Europe, close to the most developed countries in the world at the time. In total, the Laki eruption injected approximately three times as much sulfur aerosols into the atmosphere as the global annual emission of that substance in 2006. Because the aerosols were injected high in the atmosphere, they stayed there longer. Throughout much of the autumn and winter of 1783–1784, a thick haze drifted across Europe, moving from Iceland to Denmark, Berlin, Prague, and finally Paris. The haze was apparently so thick that boats had to stay in their harbors, unable to navigate, and thousands of people died from the smog. Furthermore, the aerosols caused a series of droughts and crop failures across Europe for the next several years.

This, in turn, created widespread poverty and hunger across Europe. Wood (1992) showed that the Laki eruption caused a very hot summer in France in 1785, creating a surplus harvest that led to widespread poverty for rural workers as grain prices dropped. Over the next few years, France was haunted by a series of droughts and severe winters that created famines. Finally, poverty and hunger led to a rebellion of peasants in France in 1789 that we know today as the French Revolution.

Although the Laki eruption certainly was not the sole cause of the French Revolution, it likely contributed to the revolution's outbreak, showing once more that severe climate events can have significant geopolitical consequences. In the case of the French Revolution, the king and queen lost their heads (literally) and were replaced by the First Republic. After that republic failed, Napoleon took the reins as emperor and conquered most of Europe and North Africa, bringing with him a fundamental reordering of European nation-states, laws, and regulations.

Whether climate change and climate events can trigger the outbreak of war remains a debated topic, but at least several prominent examples are known of volcanic eruptions and other natural disasters hastening the decline of civilization in the Americas, Asia, and Africa. Anecdotal evidence points to the possibility that the current civil war in Syria might have been triggered by a severe drought related to climate change. Kelley, Mohtadi, Cane, Seager, and Kushnir (2015) argued that the unusually long drought of 2007–2010 in Syria led to the displacement of a large number of young men and women. Even though Syria is located in what is called the Fertile Crescent, reaching from the south of Turkey to the Nile Delta in Egypt, the country suffered failed harvests for several years in a row. Faced with poverty and potential hunger, many rural workers and farmers moved to the cities to find work. With ample work unavailable, youth unemployment soared in Syria, creating fertile ground for radical Islamists to recruit followers and for others to rebel against the Assad regime.

That climatic events can trigger significant geopolitical events, therefore, is at least possible. But although predicting volcanic eruptions and other natural disasters is impossible, we can anticipate climate change, which gives us warning of increased geopolitical risks from the weather events it creates.

Global Warming and Global Weirding

The key observation in the discussion about climate change is the rising average temperature on Earth, as shown in **Exhibit 2**. The chart is normalized so that the average temperature in the 20th century is set to zero. Average temperatures have clearly risen since the 1960s, and in 2019, the average global temperature was approximately 1°C (1.8°F) higher than the average global temperature of the 20th century.

This increase in global temperature is why climate change is often referred to as "global warming," although that is actually a misnomer. While the average temperature does increase, climate change does not imply that summers are always getting hotter and winters milder. Instead, more energy is trapped in the atmosphere, and this energy leads to more explosive and extreme weather events. These events can take the form of droughts and heat waves,

Exhibit 2.   Global Temperature Anomaly

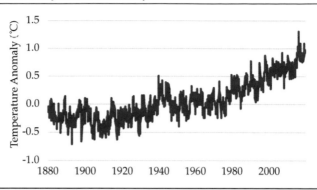

Note: Normalized, 1901–2000 = 0.
Source: US Department of Energy Carbon Dioxide Information Analysis Center.

or they can take the form of massive rainstorms (hurricanes and typhoons), floods, and extreme cold snaps in winter. In essence, we should call it "global weirding" rather than global warming because climate change creates weirder and more extreme weather phenomena.

A plethora of greenhouse gases exists, ranging from carbon dioxide (CO_2) to methane (which is far more potent than CO_2 but has a much shorter life span in the atmosphere) and other gases such as sulfur dioxide and nitrous oxide. Because CO_2 is by far the most prevalent greenhouse gas and the main driver of climate change, we restrict our discussion in this chapter to CO_2 and largely ignore the other gases.

Exhibit 3 shows the atmospheric concentration of CO_2 (measured in parts per million, or ppm) over the past 2,000 years. This is the famous "hockey stick chart," showing that CO_2 concentrations have entered a phase

Exhibit 3.   Atmospheric CO_2 Concentration over the Past 2,000 Years

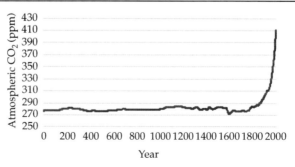

Source: Etheridge (2010) and National Oceanic and Atmospheric Administration (NOAA).

of exponential growth since the Industrial Revolution. In 2015, the concentration of CO_2 in the atmosphere surpassed 400 ppm for the first time ever.

That CO_2 is a powerful greenhouse gas that can render an entire planet uninhabitable can be seen by looking at our closest neighbor in the solar system, Venus. Venus is roughly the same size as Earth (the radius of Venus is approximately 5% less than the radius of Earth) and has similar density and mass. Thus, not surprisingly, perhaps, NASA simulations have shown that approximately three billion years ago, Venus was covered by water and had an average temperature of 11°C (52°F), again very similar to Earth today (Way et al. 2016). But Venus is much closer to the sun than Earth is, so solar irradiation is stronger there.

As a result, the water on Venus's surface evaporated before plants and other life could form. On our planet, these early life-forms began to draw CO_2 out of the atmosphere and transform it into oxygen and other gases. On Venus, the CO_2 concentration did not drop but stayed at high levels. And while Venus remained habitable for approximately 715 million years, the CO_2 created a massive greenhouse gas effect that heated the planet's atmosphere, accelerating the evaporation of water and in turn creating an even stronger greenhouse effect, which led to the dissipation of additional CO_2 from the soil and the evaporating oceans. This runaway greenhouse gas effect made the planet uninhabitable, and today, the temperature on Venus is a balmy 462°C (864°F).

Luckily, the CO_2 concentration on our planet is not even close to that observed on Venus today, but as Exhibit 3 shows, it is higher than at any time in the past 2,000 years and rising fast. Indeed, the CO_2 concentration today is higher than at any other point in humankind's existence. Humans have roamed the Earth for approximately 250,000 years now, but we can trace the CO_2 concentration in the Earth's atmosphere back roughly 800,000 years.

The Antarctic ice shelf is made up of layers of ice that were formed from snow that fell centuries and millennia ago. The deeper one drills into the ice shelf, the farther one can go back in history. As snow fell in Antarctica, tiny air bubbles became trapped in the ice that formed from the snow. By analyzing these air bubbles, one can measure the concentration of CO_2 in the air far back in time. As **Exhibit 4** shows, natural fluctuations in the CO_2 concentration have always occurred and were caused primarily by changes in the surface radiation of the sun. These fluctuations created ice ages (when the CO_2 concentration was low) and warm periods (when the CO_2 concentration was high). What is most obvious from the chart, however, is that today's CO_2 concentration is far above anything we have seen in the past 800,000 years.

Along with this higher concentration of CO_2 comes not only a higher average temperature on Earth but also, as mentioned, an increase in extreme

Exhibit 4.   800,000 Years of CO₂ Data from Antarctic Ice Samples

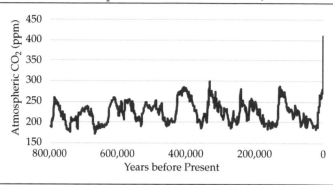

Source: Lüthi et al. (2008), Etheridge (2010), and NOAA.

Exhibit 5.   Frequency of Extreme Climate Events in the United States

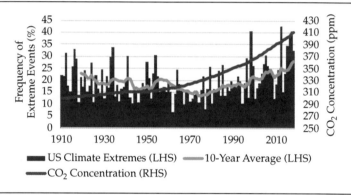

Source: NOAA.

weather events such as floods, droughts, wildfires, and windstorms. **Exhibit 5** shows the number of extreme weather events in the United States since 1910 as measured by the National Oceanic and Atmospheric Administration (NOAA). Since the 1960s, CO_2 concentrations have increased more rapidly, and during that decade, the number of extreme weather events also began to increase.[2]

Climate Change and Investment Risk

As the number of extreme weather events increases because of climate change, the economic damage these events cause also increases. Wouter

---

[2]The 10-year average begins to rise in the early 1970s, indicating that the actual number of events began to increase in the early 1960s.

Botzen, Deschenes, and Sanders (2019) reviewed the empirical and theoretical literature on the economic impact of natural disasters and found that increasing population (particularly in coastal regions), along with economic development, led to rising costs of natural disasters. But the literature by now also shows that, all else equal, climate change leads to stronger storms that cause more damage than past events.

Felbermayr and Gröschl (2014) conducted a panel regression of the economic damages from natural disasters. Controlling for location (poorer countries obviously suffer lower monetary damages than richer countries) and other factors, they found that natural disasters had a significantly negative effect on GDP growth. This relationship also seems highly nonlinear, however, with economic growth dropping far more for major disasters. A disaster in the top 5% of the historic distribution reduced GDP growth by approximately 0.33 percentage points over the subsequent 12 months, whereas a disaster in the top 1% of the historic distribution reduced GDP growth by 6.83 percentage points on average.

Hurricanes—Large and Lasting Economic Damages. A special focus is placed on hurricanes (also called cyclones or typhoons, depending on where they form) in the research on the economic effects of natural disasters. Strobl (2011) investigated the damages caused by hurricanes in the United States and found that in the counties where a hurricane made landfall, GDP growth was reduced by 0.8 percentage points in the first year after the storm and by 0.2 percentage points in the second year.

Different parts of the economy are affected differently. Agriculture, wholesale, retail, and tourism are hit the hardest, whereas the construction sector experiences a boost in activity after a storm because of rebuilding efforts. Another effect of hurricanes is that economic growth and county tax revenues decline because richer people in the affected regions move to other counties (often farther inland), whereas poorer people do not have the means to move and thus remain located in the affected region.

This geographic mobility after a storm has hit a coastal region is an expression of rising risk aversion by the people the storm affects. Ironically, this increased risk aversion can be found in the investment decisions of fund managers. Bernile, Bhagwat, Kecskes, and Nguyen (2018) investigated the performance of equity funds managed by individual fund managers across the United States. They found that fund managers located in a storm area become more risk averse in their funds and reduce volatility significantly. This increase in risk aversion means that their performance declines by 1.7% in the first year after a storm compared with that of fund managers who were personally unaffected by the storm, and declines by 0.7% in the second year. On average, the fund managers take three years to overcome their increased risk aversion.

But cyclones and hurricanes also have long-lasting effects that extend far beyond the immediate impact of the destruction of property. Looking at economic growth in areas hit by 6,700 cyclones globally, Hsiang and Jina (2014) estimated that even 20 years after the incident, GDP remains below the levels of that of comparable regions that were unaffected by the storm. For every additional meter per second in windspeed of a cyclone, GDP per capita was reduced by 0.2% 10 years after the storm hit and by 0.4% 20 years after the storm hit. The effect was similar in size for both rich and poor countries, even though many poor countries tend to experience larger economic damages immediately after a storm because buildings are often not built as durably as they are in rich countries, and building codes are ignored or not as strict.

Exhibit 6 shows the estimated impact on GDP per capita 10 years after a catastrophic event as calculated by Hsiang and Jina (2014). A cyclone in the top 10% of the historical distribution causes damages that reduce GDP per capita in the affected country by 4.4% 10 years after the cyclone hit, whereas a top 1% cyclone causes a drop in GDP per capita of 8.9%. In comparison, 10 years after a civil war ends, GDP per capita tends to be 3% lower, a currency crisis reduces income by 4%, and a banking crisis reduces income by 7.5%. In other words, a severe windstorm has a more pronounced long-term effect than a civil war or a currency crisis, and an extreme storm has a more pronounced effect than a banking crisis. Because these extreme storms are likely to become more frequent as climate change progresses, the economic impact of climate change might well increase rapidly over the next couple of decades—at least locally.

Exhibit 6.   Estimated Impact of Human-Caused and Natural Disasters on GDP per Capita after 10 Years

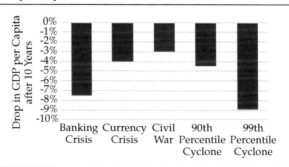

Source: Hsiang and Jina (2014).

Sea Level Rise—A Major Source of Risk for Real Estate. Hsiang et al. (2017) focused on the impact of natural disasters on coastal property because most of the damages in the short to medium term are inflicted on these assets. After all, real estate cannot move out of the way of an approaching hurricane. **Exhibit 7** shows the current average annual damage caused by hurricanes in the US states most affected by these storms. Florida already experiences significant property damage each year because of its geographic location. Now add the threat of rising sea levels because of melting polar ice caps, and the flood risk increases quickly. With the projected SLR until 2100, the average annual damage to property is expected to double in Texas and South Carolina, quadruple in New York State, and almost double in Florida.

If we use a higher estimate of future SLR, the situation quickly becomes worse. If SLR were to end up in the top 1% of the projected range, Florida would lose approximately 4.5% of state GDP every year as a result of floods and windstorms. In New York State, the average annual damage would approach 1% of state GDP. The United States is not alone in facing this risk. Globally, approximately 600 million people live in coastal areas that are 10 meters or less above sea level. Because of rising urbanization and population growth, this number is expected to increase to one billion by 2050. Faster-than-expected SLR brings with it the risk of catastrophic floods and harvest destruction because many fertile lands are located close to the sea.

Climate Risks in Equity Markets. These economic damages directly create additional investment risk across many asset classes. Bansal, Kiku, and Ochoa (2016) argued that global warming creates economic volatility and that this in turn should command a risk premium for investments exposed to these risks. Looking at consumption growth, the authors found that extreme

Exhibit 7. Expected Annual Property Damage Due to Cyclones and SLR in 2100

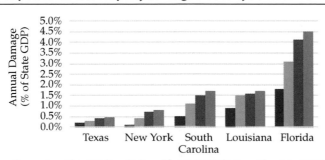

Source: Hsiang et al. (2017).

temperature events (e.g., droughts, extreme heat, cold snaps) trigger an average increase in consumption volatility of 0.18%. As consumption volatility increases, the discount factor for equity valuations should reflect this higher volatility through a higher equity risk premium.

Using a discounted cash flow model with stochastic discount factors, Bansal et al. (2016) measured the contribution of rising temperature to equity valuations and prices in excess of traditional market risks and consumption risks. In their model, they found that virtually all US equity portfolios have a negative beta to long-term temperature fluctuations, but the impact of temperature changes is not homogenous. High book-to-market stocks (i.e., value stocks) tend to have more negative betas than low book-to-market stocks (i.e., growth stocks). This might simply be a reflection of the sector composition of value and growth stocks, given that the industries that are most exposed to heat (and that show the largest sensitivity to temperature changes) are transport, construction, utilities, mining, and oil and gas, all of which currently are classified as value stocks. All these industries have in common that their economic activities are performed primarily outside, and shielding these activities from the impact of heat is difficult, if not impossible.

Averaging across the entire US stock market, Bansal et al. (2016) estimated that the equity risk premium due to rising temperatures is small but not negligible. A 1°C increase in long-term temperature averages increases the risk premium for US equities by an estimated 0.15%. The size of the risk premium is not stable, however, but rather grows as the average temperature rises. For every degree Celsius increase in the starting temperature, the risk premium increases by an estimated 0.18%, so that by 2015, the equity risk premium for US equities affected by rising temperatures was estimated to be in the neighborhood of 0.4%. A back-of-the-envelope calculation with a simple Gordon growth model shows that this 0.4% increase in equity risk premium could lower equity valuations by 10% to 20%.

Going down the path of global weirding rather than global warming, Donadelli, Jüppner, Paradiso, and Schlag (2019) recently investigated the risk premium inherent in UK and EU stocks resulting from the observed increase in temperature volatility. Along with the increase in average temperature, annual and intra-annual temperature volatility also increased.

To test the impact this temperature risk has on stock prices and the risk-free rate, Donadelli et al. (2019) split their observations into two subperiods. For the period 1900–1950, they could not find a risk premium for temperature volatility, but for the period 1950–2015, they found an immediate and highly significant effect of temperature volatility on stock prices and the risk-free rate. A 1°C increase in annual temperature volatility reduced the risk-free rate by a few basis points, but that impact was not statistically significant. In contrast, a 1°C increase in temperature volatility increased the equity risk premium by 0.65% in the United Kingdom and 0.37% in the European Union. Both values were derived after controlling for market risk and consumption risks and were statistically significant. Whether this risk premium for temperature volatility is the same as the one measured by Bansal et al. (2016) for changes in temperature overall is unknown at this point, but markets likely would not price what is essentially the same risk twice.

Scenarios for the Future

Although the investment risks from climate change seem manageable at the moment, they are likely to increase as our planet continues to heat up. Modeling the likely pathway of climate change is therefore important to assess the impact it might have on both geopolitics and the economy. Over the past decade, the main tools used to simulate climate change have been the Representative Concentration Pathways (RCPs) introduced by Moss et al. (2010). These pathways formed the foundation of the most recent Assessment Report of the Intergovernmental Panel on Climate Change (IPCC), published in 2014 (IPCC 2014a), and the Paris climate accord of 2015.

These models make different assumptions about the future development of the emissions of CO_2 and other greenhouse gases. The models are calibrated in such a way that a specific forcing is achieved by 2100. Forcing describes the amount of energy absorbed by the Earth. For example, a forcing parameter of 2.6 watts per square meter corresponds to an increase in the global average temperature of no more than 2°C above the levels seen before the Industrial Revolution. Effectively, this is the level of forcing agreed to as a goal within the Paris climate accord; thus, the RCP2.6 pathway is often used to simulate declared policy goals for the next couple of decades. Higher levels of forcing correspond to bigger increases in temperature and correspondingly more damage caused by climate change. Unfortunately, we are currently moving along the RCP8.5 pathway and are on track to increase the global temperature by 3°C (5.4°F) by 2050 (Schwalm, Glendon, and Duffy 2020). As a result, the RCP8.5 scenario is also often referred to as the baseline or business-as-usual scenario in climate models.

Although the RCPs can inform us about the likely consequences of different climate scenarios, they make no assumption about the feasibility of achieving these pathways. IPCC (2014b) showed formally that socioeconomic and political developments have a significant influence on possible climate paths as well as on the adaptation paths of different countries and societies. Politics and socioeconomic developments could make achieving the Paris climate accord goals impossible or might support these goals.

Shared Socioeconomic Pathways. Riahi et al. (2017) introduced the Shared Socioeconomic Pathways (SSPs) that will be the foundation of the IPCC's sixth Assessment Report, due to be published in 2021. The SSPs provide assumptions about crucial social and economic developments, whereas the RCPs provide assumptions for the required climate change mitigation efforts. Together, these two kinds of pathways form a matrix architecture for simulating the future of climate change.

The main advantage of the SSPs is that they are based on a common set of input parameters used by otherwise-different models around the world. To develop the SSPs, Riahi et al. (2017) began with a set of qualitative narratives for geopolitical and socioeconomic scenarios. These qualitative scenarios were then populated with quantitative projections for crucial socioeconomic drivers, such as population growth, economic activity, urbanization, and education. Specifically, the long-term economic projections included in the SSPs were developed by a team of economists at the OECD who also develop the most frequently used long-term economic forecasts for nearly 200 different countries (Dellink, Chateau, Lanzi, and Magné 2017).

Once the qualitative narratives had been agreed upon, Riahi et al. (2017) tested the basic input parameters with a range of Integrated Assessment Models (IAMs) that derived other important variables, such as land use, energy use, and greenhouse gas scenarios. The different IAMs were tested against each other to determine the range of possible outcomes and to check for consistency between the models.

Finally, for each SSP, Riahi et al. (2017) derived a baseline scenario that assumed no new climate regulation and, crucially, no price on carbon emissions. For each SSP, different RCPs were run to show whether a specific concentration pathway is feasible and, if it is, what measures would be needed to achieve desired outcomes and what stresses these measures would put on society and the economy. The new SSPs allow for a more comprehensive modeling of the interaction between climate change, politics, society, and economy. They are ideal for the purposes of this book and likely will dominate the headlines in coming years.

The following qualitative narratives for each SSP are from Riahi et al. (2017):

SSP1

Sustainability—Taking the Green Road (Low challenges to mitigation and adaptation)

The world shifts gradually, but pervasively, toward a more sustainable path, emphasizing more inclusive development that respects perceived environmental boundaries. Management of the global commons slowly improves, educational and health investments accelerate the demographic transition, and the emphasis on economic growth shifts toward a broader emphasis on human well-being. Driven by an increasing commitment to achieving development goals, inequality is reduced both across and within countries. Consumption is oriented toward low material growth and lower resource and energy intensity.

SSP2

Middle of the Road (Medium challenges to mitigation and adaptation)

The world follows a path in which social, economic, and technological trends do not shift markedly from historical patterns. Development and income growth proceeds unevenly, with some countries making relatively good progress while others fall short of expectations. Global and national institutions work toward but make slow progress in achieving sustainable development goals. Environmental systems experience degradation, although there are some improvements and overall the intensity of resource and energy use declines. Global population growth is moderate and levels off in the second half of the century. Income inequality persists or improves only slowly and challenges to reducing vulnerability to societal and environmental changes remain.

SSP3

Regional Rivalry—A Rocky Road (High challenges to mitigation and adaptation)

A resurgent nationalism, concerns about competitiveness and security, and regional conflicts push countries to increasingly focus on domestic or, at most, regional issues. Policies shift over time to become increasingly oriented toward national and regional security issues. Countries focus on achieving energy and food security goals within their own regions at the expense of broader-based development. Investments in education and technological development decline. Economic development is slow, consumption is material-intensive, and inequalities persist or worsen over time. Population growth is low in industrialized and high in developing countries. A low international priority for addressing environmental concerns leads to strong environmental degradation in some regions.

SSP4

Inequality—A Road Divided (Low challenges to mitigation, high challenges to adaptation)

Highly unequal investments in human capital, combined with increasing disparities in economic opportunity and political power, lead to increasing inequalities and stratification both across and within countries. Over time, a gap widens between an internationally-connected society that contributes to knowledge- and capital-intensive sectors of the global economy, and a fragmented collection of lower-income, poorly educated societies that work in a labor intensive, low-tech economy. Social cohesion degrades and conflict and unrest become increasingly common. Technology development is high in the high-tech economy and sectors. The globally connected energy sector diversifies, with investments in both carbon-intensive fuels like coal and unconventional oil, but also low-carbon energy sources. Environmental policies focus on local issues around middle and high income areas.

SSP5

Fossil-Fueled Development—Taking the Highway (High challenges to mitigation, low challenges to adaptation)

This world places increasing faith in competitive markets, innovation and participatory societies to produce rapid technological progress and development of human capital as the path to sustainable development. Global markets are increasingly integrated. There are also strong investments in health, education, and institutions to enhance human and social capital. At the same time, the push for economic and social development is coupled with the exploitation of abundant fossil fuel resources and the adoption of resource and energy intensive lifestyles around the world. All these factors lead to rapid growth of the global economy, while global population peaks and declines in the 21st century. Local environmental problems like air pollution are successfully managed. There is faith in the ability to effectively manage social and ecological systems, including by geo-engineering if necessary.

Today, we can find the seeds of all these SSPs in the global political landscape:

- SSP1 closely resembles a pathway the United States would take if the proposed Green New Deal becomes a reality. It is also the pathway that the activists of Extinction Rebellion and other organizations advocate for, even if they do not realize it.

- SSP2 resembles the socioeconomic pathway that most countries were on until the rise of populism in the past few years. It is the pathway that most countries probably had in mind when they signed up for the Paris climate accord in 2015.

- SSP3 is the pathway that populist and nationalist politicians around the globe are moving toward. From Jair Bolsonaro in Brazil to

Narendra Modi in India, such politicians place much more emphasis on domestic growth than on environmental protection. Climate
change is considered a far-off or manageable risk at best, a hoax or
distraction at worst.

- SSP4 is the pathway the world would take if we were to continue following the dreams of Silicon Valley entrepreneurs. In this world, the rich
would mitigate the impact from climate change with the help of increasingly expensive technological solutions, with the poor and less educated
increasingly being left behind.

- SSP5 is the pathway US oil majors would like to take because it assumes
that we can continue burning fossil fuels as we have been in the past while
technological innovations, such as carbon capture and storage (CCS),
could mitigate climate change over time.

Which of these pathways (or what combination of them) we will eventually take is unknown today, and we will likely fluctuate between several of
these scenarios. Yet the potential impact on the environment of each of these
pathways is quite different. **Exhibit 8** shows the projected baseline CO_2 emissions for each of the five SSPs. Remember that the baseline scenario assumes
that we do not introduce any new climate regulation.

SSP1 is the pathway with the lowest projected CO_2 emissions, whereas
SSP5 would lead to a dramatic increase in CO_2 concentration in the atmosphere. By 2050, the CO_2 concentration in pathway SSP1 would reach
500 ppm, whereas under SSP5, it would reach 560 ppm. By 2100, the CO_2
concentration under SSP5 would be almost twice that of SSP1.

Exhibit 8.   Baseline Scenarios for CO_2 Concentration

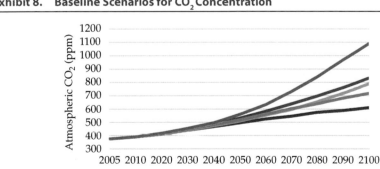

Source: Riahi et al. (2017).

By 2100, however, it would be too late anyway because we need to keep CO_2 concentrations below 450 ppm if we want to keep the global temperature increase below 2°C and achieve the goals of the Paris climate accord. Thus, it should be no surprise that in the baseline scenarios of each SSP, global warming would rise above 2°C quickly and continue to rise into the 22nd century, as **Exhibit 9** shows.

What Policies Are Needed to Fight Climate Change? Given that none of the baseline scenarios can keep climate change under control, we need to simulate different mitigation scenarios that correspond to the different RCPs. To do that, the different climate models need to share some basic assumptions about policies and the range of possible outcomes. After all, it would make little sense to simulate a world in which the socioeconomic pathway followed by different countries is SSP3, with its emphasis on noncooperation and exploitation of natural resources, while at the same time assuming that climate change mitigation successfully employs reforestation as a means to reduce atmospheric CO_2 concentrations.

Thus, the climate models use some shared policy assumptions (SPAs) that define the degree of international cooperation, how much mitigation efforts are enforced and followed, and whether or not some crucial sectors, such as agriculture and forestry, are covered by mitigation efforts. In the past, expanding mitigation efforts to agriculture and forestry was particularly difficult. The resulting SPAs integrated into the simulations are summarized in **Exhibit 10**.

The SPAs are deliberately broad so that the models can make a wide range of assumptions about mitigation strategies. Whether climate change mitigation is achieved through increased energy efficiency or energy conservation, reduction of power generation from fossil fuels, or large-scale development of

Exhibit 9. Baseline Scenarios for Global Temperature Anomaly

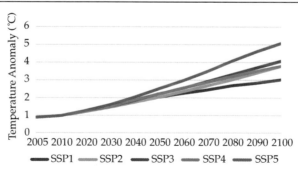

Source: Riahi et al. (2017).

Exhibit 10. Shared Policy Assumptions

Policy stringency in the near term and timing of regional participation	Coverage of land use emissions
SSP1, SSP4	SSP1, SSP5
Early accessions with global collaboration as of 2020.	Effective coverage at the level of emissions control in the industrial and energy sectors.
SSP2, SSP5	SSP2, SSP4
Some delays in establishing global action, with regions transitioning to global cooperation between 2020 and 2040.	Effective coverage of agricultural emissions but limited emissions reduction from deforestation and forest degradation.
SSP3	SSP3
Late accession—higher-income countries join global cooperation between 2020 and 2040 and lower-income regions follow between 2030 and 2050.	Very limited coverage (implementation failures and high transaction costs).

Source: Riahi et al. (2017).

CCS is left for the researchers to figure out. Even geoengineering approaches are fair game. Basically, anything goes.

Nevertheless, not all mitigation scenarios are achievable in all SSPs. Under SSP3, achieving the goals of the Paris climate accord was impossible no matter what Riahi et al. (2017) did with their models. Under SSP5, some models were not able to provide a solution that met the goals of the Paris climate accord, whereas others were.

Despite the wide variety of possibilities for mitigating climate change, the models produced a few results in common (Riahi et al. 2017). To achieve the goals of the Paris climate accord and keep the increase in global temperature below 2°C, the amount of electricity generated from renewable energy sources must be much higher than it is today. The midpoint estimate was for renewables to produce 60% of global electricity by 2050, with a range of 40% to 70%, depending on the model. Contrast that with the baseline projections of the SSPs, wherein none of the five pathways would even come close to this share of renewables in the global energy mix, and in SSP3 and SSP5, the share of renewables in global energy production would even decline.

Another shared result of the different mitigation scenarios is that CCS will have to play an important role if we want to achieve the goals of the Paris climate accord. Estimates for the amount of CO_2 captured and stored by CCS range from 200 gigatons (Gt) to 1,800 Gt between today and 2100. Another important carbon sink (i.e., a technology that reduces CO_2 in the atmosphere)

Exhibit 11. Scenarios for CO$_2$ Concentration under the Paris Climate Accord

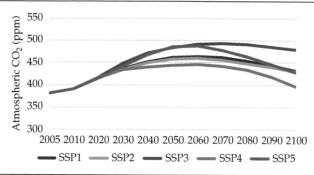

Source: Riahi et al. (2017).

will be reforestation and the revitalization of existing forests. These reforestation efforts are particularly important for SSP1, SSP2, and SSP4 if we want to be able to effectively mitigate climate change under these pathways.

If we can successfully mitigate climate change, then the CO$_2$ concentration in our atmosphere could follow the pathways shown in **Exhibit 11**. Note that SSP3 does not achieve the Paris climate goals, so we show the best possible result under SSP3 in that chart. For all other SSPs, the results shown in the chart correspond to limiting the increase in global temperature to less than 2°C by the year 2100.

For SSP5, however, the global temperature anomaly will likely surpass that level, at least temporarily (see **Exhibit 12**), because in SSP5, the world continues to burn a lot of fossil fuels. Only with the large-scale introduction

Exhibit 12. Scenarios for Global Temperature Anomaly under the Paris Climate Accord

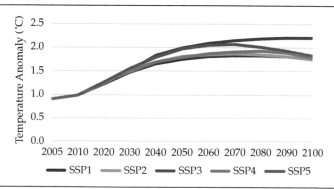

Source: Riahi et al. (2017).

of CCS technology and massively higher prices for CO_2 will the incentives be sufficient to take CO_2 out of the atmosphere again and reduce the concentration of CO_2 and the global average temperature.

Can We Innovate Ourselves Out of Our Problems?

This brings us to the question of whether we can reduce the emission of CO_2 and other greenhouse gases over time. Our experience with the development and rollout of renewable energy shows that the potential for technological advances in green technology not only is vast but also has been consistently underestimated by experts in the past. This should make us optimistic that we will, over time, develop the technological solutions to mitigate climate change and achieve the goals we set for ourselves, even if today we appear poised to miss these goals by a wide margin.

Technological progress must overcome our current limitations as well as the growth in economic activity and population we will face in future decades. In the beginning, as societies develop, their emissions of pollutants increase. The combination of population growth and strong economic growth leads to a substitution of low-carbon activities and technologies with high-carbon technologies.

Think of China. As the country became richer, people abandoned bicycles in favor of cars, which increased the quantity of pollutants in the air dramatically. Add to that the development of a large industrial base, and the end result is that cities in China are plagued by endless smog. But as the costs to society from these pollutants increase, so, too, does the incentive to clean up that mess and invest in clean technologies. Because strong economic growth increases income, the country also has the financial means to invest in these green technologies. China's pivot from fossil fuels to renewables is a case in point.

The pattern of pollutant emissions first rising, then peaking, and finally declining again in an inverted U-shape as a country (or the world) becomes wealthier is known as the environmental Kuznets curve (EKC). A stylized version of the curve appears in **Exhibit 13**. First introduced in the early 1990s, it has since become a standard model against which to test the empirical evidence.

Stern (2017) reviewed the literature on the validity of the EKC over the past 25 years and found mixed results. He found an inverted U-shape for the concentration of some pollutants, such as sulfur components, but not for emissions of other pollutants, such as CO_2. Furthermore, the relationship between GDP per capita and pollutant concentrations seems to have weakened in more recent studies, which more commonly have found a monotonic

Exhibit 13.   The Environmental Kuznets Curve

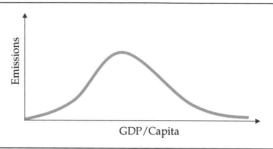

Source: Author's creation.

increase in pollutants no matter the level of income per capita. In contrast, older studies from the 1990s and the 2000s seemed to find more evidence of the EKC hypothesis.

Intuitively, this disparity makes sense if we think about the kind of pollutants that are commonly investigated in these studies. Older studies focused more on classic pollutants, such as sulfur compounds, dust, and carbon particles. Only in the past decade or so has CO_2 become a dominant object of investigation.

If we think back to our rules for forecasting from chapter 5, the fifth rule states that we rarely fall off a cliff. People can change their habits but often do so only at the last minute to avert a catastrophe. For change to happen, the catastrophe must be *salient*, the outcome must be *certain*, and the solution must be *simple*. If you cannot breathe because of the smog in your city, the problem is salient, and you and many other people in your community will advocate for change. In the case of classical industrial pollutants, the outcome of the problem is quite certain because smog causes respiratory problems for many older people as well as infants and young children. Finally, the solution to the problem is simple. Just force factories, cars, and other emitters to include filters in their exhaust systems (or use different inputs, such as unleaded gasoline), and the problem is solved. This approach provides a relatively low-cost solution to a big problem.

The situation is different for CO_2. Because CO_2 is a colorless and odorless gas and is harmless to individuals in low concentrations, we do not notice when the concentration of CO_2 in our atmosphere increases. The very fact that CO_2 concentrations have been rising for 250 years without anyone becoming worried about them is proof that the problem of rising CO_2 emissions is not yet salient.

Only in recent years has climate change become increasingly salient through the prevalence of extreme weather events. This prevalence has given rise to mass environmental movements similar to the rise of the environmental movement in the early 1980s in the wake of acid rain that destroyed forests in Europe. (This was one of the world's first mass environmental movements, and it launched green parties in many Western European countries.)

Because the link between extreme weather events and CO_2 concentration in the atmosphere is not immediately salient to everyone, the current environmental movement faces a lot of pushback from people who advocate for symptomatic treatment of the problem. For example, floods can be prevented by building higher dams rather than by fighting the root cause of the floods.

Furthermore, although rising CO_2 concentrations affect us all, the direct impact on each of us as individuals is uncertain. If you do not live on the coast, you probably care less about hurricanes. If you do not live in a dry area, you probably care less about wildfires and droughts that much. Every problem caused by climate change affects other people but not you, so dismissing the specific problem in question is easy. The alliance to prevent wildfires is relatively small, as is the alliance to prevent hurricanes and floods. Although both try to fight the same root cause, their forces are often not combined.

Finally, the solution to climate change is anything but simple. It requires a widespread redesign of our economy and a drastic shift in consumption habits. As we will see later in this chapter, this shift imposes high costs on large parts of a society in the short term. With these adverse effects comes public resistance to mitigation efforts.

In summary, whether CO_2 emissions will truly follow an inverse U-shape as predicted by the EKC is unclear. Shahbaz and Sinha (2019) recently reviewed the empirical studies on CO_2 emissions from 1991 to 2017. They found that the studies showed no conclusive evidence for or against the EKC in single countries or across countries. For every time period investigated in the literature, one can find studies that confirm the EKC and find an inverted U-shape as well as studies that find monotonically rising CO_2 emissions. One can even find a series of studies that find an N-shaped relationship, in which emissions first increase, then decrease, and then increase again as income per capita rises.

In short, we do not yet know whether the EKC holds, and this means we also do not know whether we will be able to innovate ourselves out of the problems caused by climate change. Furthermore, even if the EKC holds, Shahbaz and Sinha (2019) pointed to one crucial aspect of the EKC that has not been investigated thoroughly. If the EKC is too tall—that is, if pollutants rise to very high levels before mitigation efforts take hold—this could trigger irreversible processes in our climate that are physically impossible to fix within reasonable policy time frames.

The Economic Cost of Carbon

One might be forgiven for giving up hope, given all the uncertainties and unknowns about the future pathways of our society and economy. But this ignores that we do know some things, or at least can estimate them within an acceptable range of uncertainty. And one of the key areas of economic investigation has been the economic cost of rising CO_2 emissions.

Economists around the world agree that climate change and the emission of greenhouse gases like CO_2 are negative externalities that currently are not priced in markets (the studies quoted earlier on the risk premia of temperature changes notwithstanding). And every economist knows that if an externality is not priced, it leads to misallocation of resources and a decline in welfare. Thus, the consensus among economists is that greenhouse gases should be priced through either carbon taxes, cap-and-trade schemes, or emission-trading schemes. Prices for CO_2 should ideally start low and gradually increase so as to not shock the economy. The social cost of carbon is the incremental welfare impact of emitting an additional unit of CO_2 into the atmosphere and thus represents the marginal cost of carbon that should be set by policy makers to maximize welfare.

So far, so good, but how big are the economic and social costs of carbon? Dell, Jones, and Olken (2009) showed that the economic impact of climate change is subject to many competing developments. On one hand, extreme weather events lead to fewer harvest failures, particularly in coastal regions and in poor countries close to the equator, where droughts can severely reduce crop yields. On the other hand, CO_2 is a natural fertilizer for plants. Higher CO_2 concentrations lead to faster growth of most plants and potentially to higher yields. Similarly, while the Earth is getting hotter, energy demand for air conditioning is increasing in hotter regions, whereas areas closer to the poles will experience milder winters and therefore reduced demand for energy for heating.

Which one of these effects will win out is not always clear, but Tol (2018) collected evidence from several studies on the economic impact of climate change. **Exhibit 14** shows that climate change might initially have a positive impact on global welfare and global GDP. As the temperature increases more than 1°C, however, the marginal contribution of climate change to the economy becomes negative, and the total economic impact of climate change starts to drop. For temperature increases above 2°C, the studies show a negative total effect of climate change on global GDP in 2100 relative to that in 2010. Notably, we already seem today to be right at that tipping point at which we have reaped all the benefits of rising global temperatures and now face negative contributions from additional increases.

Exhibit 14. Estimated Impact of Climate Change on Global GDP

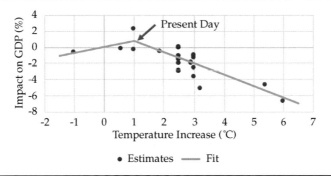

Source: Tol (2018).

Standard Economic Models Predict a Small Economic Impact. The estimated economic costs of climate change are, however, relatively small. The cumulative effect on global GDP between 2010 and 2100 is generally estimated at 1% to 5%, or less than 0.1% per year. These, however, are only the static losses in economic activity. If climate change has a negative impact on economic growth, the costs could accumulate much more rapidly and become much bigger. Research on the impact of climate change on long-term economic growth has so far been minimal, and the results generally have shown an insignificant impact on growth except in poor countries in the "Global South" (Dell, Jones, and Olken 2012). So, why bother with climate change at all if the economic costs over a century are roughly the same as one year's growth?

Every recession costs the economy more than 10 times what climate change costs in any given year. This is why climate change as a problem is not salient to economic decision makers today. But unlike the effects of a recession, the economic costs of climate change are permanent and cumulative (each year is, at least in principle, hotter than the previous one). And the effects are not equally distributed. Dell et al. (2012) showed that poorer countries will face higher costs from climate change than richer countries, primarily because poorer countries tend to be located in hotter regions. Tol (2018) showed the expected economic costs of climate change as a function of the average temperature in a country, as reproduced in **Exhibit 15**.[3] Hotter

---

[3]Canada (–5.4°C), Mongolia (–0.8°C), and Russia (–5.1°C) have negative average temperatures on the Celsius scale. Although economic activities in these countries are located in the warmer areas, the study used average temperatures across the entire country. And because both Canada and Russia have vast areas of land in the Arctic, their average temperature drops below 0°C.

Exhibit 15.   Economic Impact of Climate Change Is Bigger for Hotter Countries

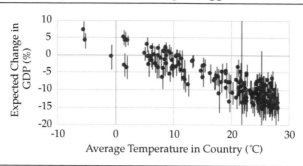

Source: Tol (2018).

countries face disproportionately higher economic costs, and for an increase of the average global temperature of 2.5°C, the majority of countries in the world will face costs in excess of 1.4% of GDP (Dell et al. 2012).

Dell et al. (2012) also looked at the relationship between income per capita and the economic impact of climate change. Unsurprisingly, they found that poorer countries suffer much more than richer countries, as shown in **Exhibit 16**. This is a result of both the geographic location of richer countries, most of which are located in the Northern Hemisphere at medium to high latitudes, and their ability to pay for climate change mitigation measures, as well as their lower reliance on agriculture.

The agriculture sector is most affected by climate change, and in regions where crop yields are already low because of adverse climatic conditions, relatively little is needed to trigger a major harvest failure. Poorer countries in South Asia, Africa, and South America tend to have an economy that

Exhibit 16.   Economic Impact of Climate Change Is Bigger for Poorer Countries

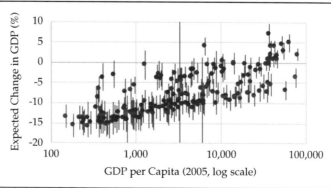

Source: Tol (2018).

depends more on agricultural products and the export of these products. As the planet warms, these countries face climatic situations that are probably new in human history and that we cannot anticipate. In comparison, an industrial country such as the United Kingdom will experience climatic conditions similar to those of Spain as climate change progresses. We have lots of experience of how to live in such a climate (just ask the Spanish), and the United Kingdom has sufficient capital to pay for additional air conditioning and other amenities. In other words, the costs for rich countries tend to be lower, and mitigation is cheaper.

The reason we should care about the economic impact of climate change becomes obvious once we look at climate change through a geopolitical lens. If the poorest countries in the world are hardest hit, economic stress will be concentrated in these countries. And wherever economic stress arises, migration is a natural outcome. Climate change might increase global migration from the poor countries in the south to the rich countries in the north—something we investigate more deeply later in this chapter.

Fighting Climate Change Is Good for the Economy. Another reason we should care about climate change is that it can be avoided, and the economic costs of it can be reduced essentially to zero. Kahn et al. (2019) recently estimated the economic costs of climate change under the RCP8.5 scenario and the Paris climate accord scenario for a range of countries. **Exhibit 17** shows the results for a selection of countries. In their model, GDP per capita faces a decline of 0.5% to 1.0% over the next decade and of 1.0% to 3.0% until 2050, relative to what it otherwise would be. If we manage to achieve the goals set out in the Paris climate accord, the costs of climate change will be effectively zero, and some countries, such as China, will even experience economic gains. This result is due not only to the reduced costs from climate events but also to the boost in productivity from new, green technologies. In short, mitigating climate change is good for business.

What's the Right Price for Carbon? To avoid climate change and the corresponding social and economic damages, we need to put a price on carbon emissions and other greenhouse gases. Unfortunately, this is easier said than done because the fair price of carbon is uncertain and depends, on one hand, on the estimated economic impact of CO_2 emissions and, on the other hand, on the discount rate with which future carbon emissions (and their corresponding damages) are reduced to a present value. If we take a discount rate of 0%, then future damages accrue to the present value at the same rate as current damages, creating a large cost of emitting an additional metric ton of CO_2. If we take a discount rate of 3% or higher, then the future cost of carbon has a relatively small present value.

Exhibit 17. Estimated Impact of Climate Change on GDP per Capita over the Next 10 to 30 Years

Country	2030		2050	
	Paris Agreement	Business as Usual	Paris Agreement	Business as Usual
World	0.0%	−0.8%	−0.1%	−2.5%
Rich Countries	−0.1%	−0.8%	−0.2%	−2.7%
Poor Countries	0.2%	−0.7%	0.2%	−2.2%
United States	−0.2%	−1.2%	−0.6%	−3.8%
United Kingdom	0.0%	−0.3%	0.1%	−1.2%
Germany	0.2%	−0.2%	0.4%	−0.6%
France	0.0%	−0.6%	0.1%	−1.9%
Japan	−0.3%	−1.1%	−1.1%	−3.7%
Australia	−0.1%	−0.6%	−0.2%	−2.3%
Brazil	0.0%	−1.0%	−0.1%	−2.8%
Russia	0.1%	−1.0%	0.3%	−3.1%
India	−0.3%	−1.2%	−0.8%	−3.6%
China	0.5%	−0.6%	0.8%	−1.6%
South Africa	0.0%	−0.7%	−0.1%	−2.5%

Source: Kahn et al. (2019).

The cost of carbon is therefore reduced essentially to the economic damage current emissions cause. **Exhibit 18** shows the social cost of carbon as estimated in Tol (2018), together with the uncertainty around that price. If we apply a 0% discount rate, the cost of emitting a metric ton of CO_2 should be set to $677, whereas a discount rate of 3% gives us an estimate of $43 per metric ton. Today, most countries assume a discount rate of somewhere between 2% and 3%, and the US government uses a social cost of carbon of $12 per ton of CO_2 emissions (tCO2e) to $58/tCO2e, in line with these assumptions. In the European Union, the price of a ton of CO_2 emissions in the Emissions Trading System is $25.

These low prices for carbon emissions are unlikely to be sufficient to incentivize emissions reductions that will keep climate change in check. Within the SSPs, the price of carbon that must be imposed over time is allowed to start low (roughly at current levels) and then gradually increase. Depending on the pathway we take in future decades, the cost of carbon has to increase more or less rapidly to provide enough of an incentive to achieve the goals we set ourselves in the Paris climate accord.

Exhibit 18.   Estimates of the Social Cost of Carbon for Different Discount Rates

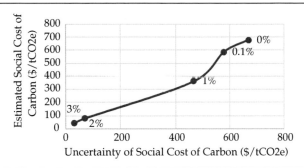

Source: Tol (2018).

Under SSP1, the price of carbon needs to increase to $33/tCO2e by 2030, whereas under SSP2 and SSP5, it needs to rise to approximately $42/tCO2e. Because of the lack of international cooperation and the excessive land use in SSP3, the price of carbon would have to rise to $87/tCO2e by 2030, a cost of carbon not reached under SSP1 and SSP2 before 2050. **Exhibit 19** shows the projected cost of carbon necessary to provide enough incentives to change the direction of the global economy in line with the Paris climate accord for the different SSPs. Not surprisingly, under SSP5, where the use of fossil fuels continues unabated, the price of carbon must rise the most and the fastest, but even under SSP4, the scenario of rising inequality, the cost of carbon must rise dramatically to $185/tCO2e in 2050 and to more than $2,000/tCO2e in 2100. This high cost of carbon is driven by the rising emissions of poor countries that cannot afford the high-tech solutions to climate change developed in the rich countries and therefore must rely on burning fossil fuels.

Exhibit 19.   Scenarios for Carbon Pricing under the Paris Climate Accord

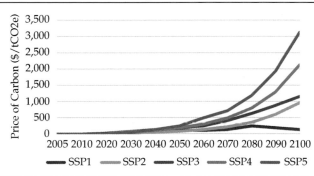

Source: Riahi et al. (2017).

The lesson we can learn from these scenarios is that one of the best investments we can make to reduce the future cost of carbon is in low-carbon infrastructure in low- and middle-income countries around the world. Helping emerging markets build solar and wind power plants and improving the local infrastructure to save energy is likely the best way to help these countries avoid the negative impacts of climate change. When the issue is viewed from this angle, Chinese initiatives such as the Belt and Road Initiative (see chapter 6) are beneficial for us all.

If we compare the projected cost of carbon in the different SSPs to the current cost of carbon shown in **Exhibit 20,** we can see that where implemented, the current price of carbon varies dramatically from place to place. In most countries, the cost of carbon is a few dollars per metric ton. In Japan, it was just $3/tCO2e in 2019, which was way too low to provide any incentives to reduce fossil fuel consumption. In the European Union, the price of carbon is $25/tCO2e, roughly in line with mainstream estimates of the social cost of carbon today and in line with the projections of the SSPs. But such countries as France, Finland, Switzerland, and Sweden have gone well above these values and have introduced carbon taxes ranging from $50/tCO2e to more than $100/tCO2e.

This high price of carbon is intended as an incentive for households and businesses alike to start looking for alternatives to fossil fuels now. In the long run, such efforts could foster a faster transition of these economies and provide businesses an advantage over foreign competitors, even if doing so involves additional costs today.

Exhibit 20.   Current Cost of Carbon as Implemented in Selected Countries

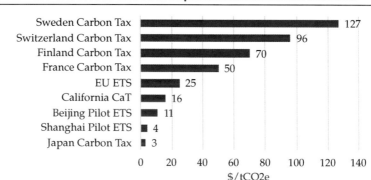

Note: ETS = Emissions Trading System, CaT = Cap and Trade.
Source: Ramstein (2019).

Nevertheless, although these efforts by individual countries are laudable, on a global scale, hardly any CO_2 emissions are currently being priced. Today, less than 20% of global greenhouse gas emissions are priced in one way or another, and with the inception of the nationwide Chinese emissions trading scheme in 2020, the share of priced greenhouse gases will increase to only 20% of global emissions. And of these emissions, roughly one-half are priced at $10/tCO2e or less (Ramstein 2019).

Tipping Points and Black Swans

The economic cost of climate change is expected to be quite low, as we saw in the previous section, but unlike with other economic risk factors, climate change has been underestimated in the past and has the potential to be underestimated today as well. Plenty of black swan events and tipping points could significantly increase the damage.

According to Linden (2019), a climate scientist in the 1990s who predicted that within 25 years, a heat wave could measurably raise sea levels (by 0.5 mm), create temperatures above 0°C (32°F) at the North Pole, and cause desert-like temperatures in Paris and Berlin would have been dismissed as alarmist. Yet all these things happened in 2019. In 1990, the IPCC said climate change would happen slowly and that melting permafrost in the Arctic would not be an issue for at least another century. Yet this is happening today. If we go back to the 1950s, scientists thought climate change happened over time spans of several thousand years. Between the 1960s and 1980s, we learned more about climate change, and the consensus was that it could happen over centuries.

In the early 1990s, however, we got extensive climate data from Greenland and the Antarctic that showed for the first time that climate change could and did happen over much shorter time spans, sometimes years (Weart 2003). As our understanding of the science of climate change improved, the scientific community had to consistently shift its expectations toward the possibility of faster climate change with more devastating effects on our planet. In its 2002 consensus report, the National Research Council had to admit that we do not understand fully how rapidly climate change happened but that it clearly did happen in the past, and we must face the possibility that it will do so again in the future (National Research Council 2002).

DeFries et al. (2019) claimed that modeling these rapid shifts in our economic projections is almost impossible, so they are commonly excluded from the models. The researchers identified several candidates for possible black swan events in climate change modeling:

- The ice sheets in Antarctica and Greenland could enter an irreversible melting pattern that significantly enhances SLR beyond current expectations. Currently, the scientific consensus is that the ice sheets will melt completely over several thousand years and that sea levels will rise by only approximately 1 meter by 2100. But irreversible ice melt could accelerate this SLR to 2 meters and beyond. Indeed, in 2014, scientists estimated that an irreversible collapse of the Western Antarctic ice shield may already have begun, and Rignot et al. (2019) recently reviewed 40 years of satellite images of the East Antarctic ice shield and found that it was not stable but in fact shedding vast amounts of ice. The melting of the East Antarctic ice shield is already responsible for approximately one-third of the SLR caused by melting Antarctic ice. Lenton et al. (2019) also counted the reduction in the Arctic ice fields and accelerated ice loss in Greenland as tipping points that are currently in play.

- Because a hotter atmosphere can hold more water, the frequency and strength of extreme windstorms and heavy rainfall might increase beyond current projections. As a result, coastal regions would experience more frequent destruction, and crops would get flooded more often, increasing the likelihood of famines in poor countries.

- Extreme heat waves might become even more frequent than expected and hit approximately one-third of the world's population once every five years. We already observe more frequent wildfires in the boreal forests of the Northern Hemisphere, and the Amazon rainforest is experiencing droughts and wildfires increasingly often.

- In a warmer climate, some diseases can spread to regions where people and animals do not have a natural resistance to them, creating significant pandemics. We already see the spread among trees in the boreal forests of diseases that are almost impossible to stop, and we humans have to face the spread of tropical diseases such as malaria and dengue fever farther away from the equator.

- Since the 1960s, the Atlantic Ocean currents have been slowing, and warming ocean temperatures not only have destroyed coral reefs but also have changed the climate in large parts of the world. The mild weather in Ireland, the United Kingdom, and much of Northern Europe is almost exclusively owed to the stream of warm water from the Gulf of Mexico that acts like mild air conditioning for Northern Europe year-round. If the temperature difference between the North Atlantic and the Gulf of Mexico drops too much, the risk arises that the Gulf Stream could collapse, in which case, we would have to expect cold weather fronts and blizzards to be able to drift farther to the south in winter, whereas hot weather fronts would be able to drift farther to the north in summer. In short, the temperature extremes in the United Kingdom and Ireland would increase. Similarly, the monsoon season in Asia and Africa could shift or break down altogether if ocean streams in the Indian Ocean break down, creating the potential for massive failed harvests in some of the poorest countries in the world.

- Finally, as we stated earlier, the Arctic permafrost is beginning to melt. Unfortunately, this is a major carbon sink because the ground in this region is full of composted trees and therefore of CO_2. If the Arctic permafrost melts, the CO_2 trapped therein will be released, creating a positive feedback loop that accelerates climate change even more, in turn increasing the speed of the permafrost melt, and so on. How much CO_2 is stored in the permafrost is largely unknown, as is the extent to which the release of this CO_2 would accelerate climate change.

We have only a limited understanding of the physics and chemistry behind all these potential black swans because they were considered highly unlikely until just a few years ago. Lots of resources have been directed toward a better understanding of areas such as ice sheet hydrology and dynamics, coastal erosion and its impact on infrastructure, cascading ecosystem losses, and the compound effect of independent climate disasters (e.g., SLR combined with coastal wildfires). As our understanding of these topics increases, we likely will have to revise our projections for climate change and its economic impact again and again. Unfortunately, history has shown us that the distribution of likely outcomes of these revisions is heavily skewed toward faster climate change and higher economic damages.

The Social Consequences of Climate Change

Economists have defined the social cost of carbon as the marginal cost to society of emitting an additional ton of CO_2. This is a pity because the biggest costs from climate change will not be economic and can hardly be priced. The biggest cost of climate change is the social impact that comes with the economic damages. Hsiang et al. (2017) modeled both the market and non-market economic effects of climate change in the United States. Because the United States is a large country with a broad range of climatic zones reaching from the deserts in the Southwest to the temperate climates in the Northwest, from the continental climate in the Midwest to the tropical climate in the

Southeast, the country can serve as a mini-model of the global trends of climate change.

Modeling the impact of climate change between 2010 and 2100 for a range of factors, Hsiang et al. (2017) showed that just as we would see on a global scale, the hotter and poorer regions of the United States will be harder hit by climate change, whereas the cooler and richer areas will suffer fewer damages. **Exhibit 21**, panel A, shows that the Southeast and the Midwest of the United States will likely experience the biggest reduction in crop yields, whereas the Northwest will likely experience increasing crop yields because of the milder winters. The rising heat in the South will increase mortality rates (especially among older people and small children) and lead to an increase in energy use to power air conditioning (Exhibit 21, panels B and C).

Forced Migration as a Major Source of Conflict. The response to these climatic changes within the United States will be migration away from the southern states to the cooler and more prosperous northern states. As a result, labor supply will likely decline for both indoor jobs (Exhibit 21, panel D)

Exhibit 21. Projected Change in Key Socioeconomic Indicators Due to Climate, 2100 vs. 2010 in the United States

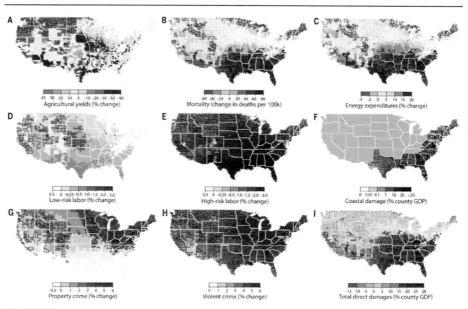

Source: From "Estimating Economic Damage from Climate Change in the United States" by Solomon Hsiang, Robert Kopp, Amir Jina, James Rising, Michael Delgado, Shashank Mohan, D. J. Rasmussen, Robert Muir-Wood, Paul Wilson, Michael Oppenheimer, Kate Larsen, and Trevor Houser. *Science* 30 (June 2017): 1362–69. Reprinted with permission from AAAS.

and outdoor jobs (Exhibit 21, panel E) in these regions. Unfortunately, mass migration will bring its own set of problems to the northern parts of the country. Because the newly arrived immigrants from the southern states will face the possibility of unemployment and a lack of housing, the rate of both property crime and violent crime will likely rise in the northern parts of the United States (Exhibit 21, panels G and H).

I could have made almost the same statements with respect to the global social impact of climate change. The poor countries in the Global South will likely face the biggest decline of crop yields and the biggest increase in energy consumption and mortality rates. Meanwhile, the temperate countries of the north will likely benefit from rising crop yields but also have to deal with the arrival of millions of migrants from the south.

Moore and Shellman (2004) investigated the drivers of forced migration and concluded that violence or fear and persecution is the main factor driving forced migration. Unfortunately, as the example of Syria at the beginning of this chapter showed, climatic events can trigger, or at least contribute to, the outbreak of civil wars and wars. Hsiang, Burke, and Miguel (2013) looked at the findings of 60 studies on the link between conflict and climate change since 1950 and found that all kinds of conflicts increase when temperatures rise or rainfall reaches extremes (either extremely high, causing floods, or extremely low, causing droughts).

In rich countries, these climatic events typically do not cause civil wars, but they increase the likelihood and prevalence of violent crime, police violence, and abrupt changes in political leadership. In poor countries, the stakes are even higher. A one-standard-deviation increase in temperature or precipitation extremes increases the likelihood of the onset of interpersonal violence by 2.3% and the onset of civil wars or wars by 11.1%. If we take only rising temperatures into account, Hsiang, Burke, and Miguel (2013) found that an increase of 1°C (1.8°F) in the average temperature leads to a 2.3% increase in the likelihood of interpersonal violence and a 13.2% increase in the likelihood of civil wars and wars. Because we expect the global temperature average to increase by another 1°C to 2°C by 2050, the likelihood of civil wars and wars in poor countries is going to increase substantially and with it, the potential for large migration to the rich countries in the north.

Abel, Brottrager, Crespo Cuaresma, and Muttarak (2019) found a significant link between climate change and the onset of conflict and then migration for the time period of 2010–2012 (including the Arab Spring in North Africa and the Middle East). They found no such link for the years before or after the Arab Spring, however, indicating that climate change alone is probably not enough to cause civil strife and forced migration.

Instead, climate change must interact with other developments to push a country off the cliff. As for the nations affected by the Arab Spring, they all were in a state of transformation (either economically or demographically, with lots of young people) and thus already more vulnerable to external shocks. These countries also did not necessarily have the infrastructure and resources to deal with climate events, such as severe droughts. All these factors combined to trigger the violent uprisings of the Arab Spring.

This is both good and bad news. It is bad news because it shows us that many countries we identified in the previous chapter as being vulnerable to the decline of petrostates are also vulnerable to the onset of civil war and other wars if extreme climatic events compound the countries' economic transformation process. But it is also good news because it shows that if these countries focus on preparing for climate change, they can avoid the outbreak of civil strife as a result of climatic events. And the rich countries can help the poor countries by financing investments in infrastructure, education, and other resources that help stabilize their societies. Such investments are in the rich countries' best interest because, otherwise, the question will be *when* rather than *if* they will have to deal with millions of migrants on their southern borders.

Unfortunately, current climate policies discussed and implemented in rich countries often fail to consider the unintended consequences they can have on society. The result is that ill-advised climate regulation can lead to protest and violence, even in rich countries. In late 2018, French President Emmanuel Macron introduced a higher fuel tax to help fight climate change. This increase in the fuel tax gave birth to the "yellow vest movement," which started in the countryside, where many people rely on their cars to get to and from work but cannot afford to pay a higher price for fuel. From the countryside, the movement quickly spread to Paris, where it became a mass movement that eventually turned violent and forced Macron to withdraw his proposed fuel tax.

Like every policy measure, climate mitigation policies are likely to have both positive and negative side effects (Markkanen and Anger-Kraavi 2019). The anticipated positive side effects of climate mitigation policies are a reduction of inequality between rich and poor countries as well as in social dimensions such as health outcomes and gender and racial inequality. These positive side effects are increasingly used as a justification for the implementation of climate mitigation policies in countries where economic concerns are of higher importance than fighting climate change.

In the industrial world, the positive side effect of climate mitigation policies is the creation of new jobs in green industries. International Renewable

Energy Agency (IRENA 2019) estimated that globally, approximately 11 million people were employed in the renewable energy sector in 2018, with 3.6 million people in the solar energy industry alone. China provides 39% of global renewable energy jobs, but Brazil is the largest employer in the area of biofuels, with more than 800,000 jobs in this industry. In the United States, approximately 300,000 people are employed in the biofuels industry and 250,000 in the solar energy industry, compared with 50,000 employees in the coal industry. And across the European Union, 1.2 million people are already employed in the renewable energy sector.

The problem, of course, is that although green industries create new jobs, the people who lose their jobs from the transition from fossil fuels to renewable energy are often not qualified for these new jobs, thus creating an effect similar to that of the outsourcing and digitalization trend in the manufacturing sector. Blue-collar workers with low educational attainment are likely to lose from the transition and the transformation of our societies for a greener future.

Inequality is likely to rise both within countries and among countries, unless policies are implemented to mitigate these effects. For example, taxes raised by putting a cost on carbon can be used to finance retraining programs for workers in the fossil fuel industries who lose their jobs as a result of these changes. Government subsidies and tax breaks for employers who hire workers from industries that are in decline or who build factories in areas where many people have lost their jobs because of the decline of fossil fuels are all measures that can mitigate the inequality created by the transition to a greener economy.

Environmental Regulation—An International Competitive Disadvantage?

As we learned in chapter 4, from a geo-economical perspective, countries compete with each other through regulation and taxes. A common claim is that stricter environmental regulation leads to an economic disadvantage for businesses. Two competing theories exist as to how environmental regulation affects businesses, particularly in countries that are at the forefront of climate regulation and that introduced a high price of carbon.

First is the "pollution haven hypothesis," which argues that industries that emit a lot of CO_2 and other greenhouse gases will engage in regulatory arbitrage and move their production facilities from countries with high emission standards to countries and regions with low emission standards. Rising pollution abatement costs and expenditures could make a steel mill in France too expensive to run, thereby forcing the owner of the mill to close it and open another mill in India or another country where the price of carbon is essentially zero.

In the European Union, the introduction of the Emissions Trading System in 2005 has increased the production costs of cement, electricity, iron, and steel by an estimated 5% to 8% (Dechezleprêtre and Sato 2017). Yet evidence in favor of the pollution haven hypothesis in the European Union is limited. Imports of cement, iron, and steel have hardly increased in the European Union after accounting for economic growth, indicating that production was not moved outside the European Union and that cheaper imports from foreign countries did not have a competitive advantage that was large enough to displace domestic production. Conversely, studies in the United States have shown that higher pollution abatement costs and expenditures have led to a small increase in imports of these goods from countries, such as Mexico and Guatemala. In general, tests of the pollution haven hypothesis tend to show no effect, or only a very small one, which is easily dominated by other effects, such as differences in labor costs and tariff barriers.

The second theory about the impact of environmental regulation on the competitiveness of businesses is the "Porter hypothesis" (named after business strategist Michael Porter, who first proposed it). It states that environmental regulation spurs innovation and the search for cost efficiencies and thereby could have a net positive effect on businesses. Some evidence has been found that stricter environmental regulation leads to the search for cost efficiencies and increased investments in research and development of green technologies—at least that is what could be observed in the European Union. But the net effect, considering both higher regulatory costs and increased productivity, is clearly not a benefit for corporations. No empirical evidence has been found in favor of the Porter hypothesis, even though the drive for innovation likely reduces the costs of more regulation (Dechezleprêtre and Sato 2017).

Finally, Fullerton and Muehlegger (2019) have shown that the cost of higher environmental regulation is ultimately borne by consumers and by producers that cannot substitute high-carbon technologies with high-tech, low-carbon technologies. In general, these are the poorer households in a country that cannot afford a new hybrid or electric car and the producers of carbon-intensive goods in poorer countries that cannot afford more modern production facilities. Again, the environmental regulations introduced to transform our economies to a more sustainable model are likely to increase inequality, something that needs to be kept in mind when designing environmental regulations.

Conclusions

In this chapter, we tackled what can be called the ultimate geopolitical risk: climate change. Because climate change is a truly global phenomenon that cannot be restricted to a single country or region, we must all think about its likely impact and ways to adapt to it. Today, we face concentrations of CO_2 and other greenhouse gases that are higher than at any time since we humans first populated this planet. With them comes not only a higher average temperature of our atmosphere but also a higher volatility of the weather, as well as stronger and more frequent weather extremes. The economic cost of weather extremes such as cyclones is high and, even in the long run, comparable to the effects of a currency crisis or civil war. Thus, unsurprisingly, climate risks should command a risk premium in asset markets, and we have seen some indication that rising global temperatures and rising temperature volatility do command a small but non-negligible risk premium for equities.

But extreme climatic events are localized phenomena and thus create significant economic damage in small areas. On a global scale, the direct economic damage from climate change is estimated to be relatively small. In this century, the expected economic damage is roughly the same as one year's growth, although this damage is not equally distributed around the globe.

Both economic and social damages from climate change accrue primarily in poor countries close to the equator, whereas richer countries in the Northern Hemisphere suffer a smaller impact and potentially even small benefits for the agriculture industry. These direct economic impacts are easy to manage for rich countries but much harder for poor countries.

Climate change's main geopolitical risk is thus not necessarily triggered by economic damages but instead by its social impact. Rising temperatures and more frequent and extreme climatic events substantially increase the likelihood of violence in the affected regions, particularly if these regions are undergoing a societal or economic transition or do not have the required infrastructure and resources to mitigate the impact of climate disasters. In the event of dramatic warming or flooding in vulnerable areas, increased violence, famines, and rising poverty would all conspire to create large migrant flows from the poor countries of the global south to the rich countries in the north. Even within rich countries such as the United States, migration from the South to the North is likely to materialize as climate change intensifies. These migrant flows will put additional pressures on the resources and infrastructure of the receiving countries and create rising political pressures that will likely be similar to what we have seen in Europe and the United States in recent years.

These political developments do not bode well for our future because our ability to mitigate and adapt to climate change will depend heavily on the socioeconomic pathways we follow in the coming decades. If we engage in strong international cooperation to mitigate climate change and reduce the global emission of greenhouse gases rapidly, we can keep both the costs of transformation and the expected damages low. But if we instead give in to our nationalistic tendencies and enter a race to the bottom, in which every country fights on its own and puts its national interests above the interests of all others, we not only will accelerate climate change but also increase our economic and social problems to such a degree that we will have to abandon any hope of ever keeping climate change under control. Between these two extremes are several alternatives that provide a middle ground that needs to be explored. The future of climate change and our global economy is not cast in stone, and neither are the geopolitical risks climate change creates. Instead, our job as investors and citizens is to work together in facing these challenges.

Bibliography

Abel, G. J., M. Brottrager, J. Crespo Cuaresma, and R. Muttarak. 2019. "Climate, Conflict and Forced Migration." *Global Environmental Change* 54: 239–49.

Bansal, R., D. Kiku, and M. Ochoa. 2016. "Price of Long-Run Temperature Shifts in Capital Markets." National Bureau of Economic Research Working Paper 22529, Cambridge, MA, August.

Bernile, G., V. Bhagwat, A. Kecskes, and P.-A. Nguyen. 2018. "Are the Risk Attitudes of Professional Investors Affected by Personal Catastrophic Experiences?" SSRN. https://ssrn.com/abstract=3024983.

Carney, M. 2019. "Remarks by Mark Carney Given during the UN Secretary General's Climate Action Summit 2019." UN General Assembly, New York, 23 September. https://www.bankofengland.co.uk/speech/2019/mark-carney-remarks-at-united-nations-climate-action-summit-2019.

Dechezleprêtre, A., and M. Sato. 2017. "The Impacts of Environmental Regulations on Competitiveness." *Review of Environmental Economics and Policy* 11 (2): 183–206.

DeFries, R., O. Edenhofer, A. Halliday, G. Heal, T. Lenton, M. Puma, J. Rising, J. Rockström, A. C. Ruane, H. J. Schellnhuber, D. Stainforth, N. Stern, M. Tedesco, and B. Ward. 2019. "The Missing Economic Risks in Assessments of Climate Change Impacts." Grantham Research Institute on Climate Change and the Environment, the Earth Institute at Columbia University, and the Potsdam Institute for Climate Impact Research, New York, September.

Dell, M., B. F. Jones, and B. A. Olken. 2009. "Temperature and Income: Reconciling New Cross-Sectional and Panel Estimates." *American Economic Review* 99 (2): 198–204.

———. 2012. "Temperature Shocks and Economic Growth: Evidence from the Last Half Century." *American Economic Journal: Macroeconomics* 4 (3): 66–95.

Dellink, R., J. Chateau, E. Lanzi, and B. Magné. 2017. "Long-Term Economic Growth Projections in the Shared Socioeconomic Pathways." *Global Environmental Change* 42: 200–14.

Donadelli, M., M. Jüppner, A. Paradiso, and C. Schlag. 2019. "Temperature Volatility Risk." Ca' Foscari University of Venice, Department of Economics Research Paper Series No. 05/WP/2019, Venice, Italy, February.

Etheridge, D. M. 2010. "Law Dome Ice Core 2000 Year CO_2, CH_4 and N_2O Data." World Data Center for Paleoclimatology and NOAA Paleoclimatology Program, Boulder, CO.

Felbermayr, G., and J. Groschl. 2014. "Naturally Negative: The Growth Effects of Natural Disasters." *Journal of Development Economics* 111: 92–106.

Fullerton, D., and E. Muehlegger. 2019. "Who Bears the Economic Burdens of Environmental Regulations?" *Review of Environmental Economics and Policy* 13 (1): 62–82.

Gao, C., A. Robock, and C. Ammann. 2008. "Volcanic Forcing of Climate over the Past 1500 Years: An Improved Ice-Core-Based Index for Climate Models." *Journal of Geophysical Research Atmospheres* 113 (D23): 111.

Hsiang, S. M., M. Burke, and E. Miguel. 2013. "Quantifying the Influence of Climate on Human Conflict." *Science* 341 (6151): 1235367.

Hsiang, S. M., and A. S. Jina. 2014. "The Causal Effect of Environmental Catastrophe on Long-Run Economic Growth: Evidence from 6,700 Cyclones." National Bureau of Economic Research Working Paper 20352, Cambridge, MA, July.

Hsiang, S., R. Kopp, A. Jina, J. Rising, M. Delgado, S. Mohan, D. J. Rasmussen, R. Muir-Wood, P. Wilson, M. Oppenheimer, K. Larsen, and T.

Houser. 2017. "Estimating Economic Damage from Climate Change in the United States." *Science* 356 (6345): 1362–69.

IPCC. 2014a. *Climate Change 2014: Synthesis Report. Contribution of Working Groups I, II and III to the Fifth Assessment Report of the Intergovernmental Panel on Climate Change*, edited by the Core Writing Team, R. K. Pachauri, and L. A. Meyer. Geneva, Switzerland: Intergovernmental Panel on Climate Change. https://www.ipcc.ch/report/ar5/syr/.

IPCC. 2014b. "Summary for Policymakers." In *Climate Change 2014: Impacts, Adaptation, and Vulnerability. Part A: Global and Sectoral Aspects. Contribution of Working Group II to the Fifth Assessment Report of the Intergovernmental Panel on Climate Change*, edited by C. B. Field, V. R. Barros, D. J. Dokken, K. J. Mach, M. D. Mastrandrea, T. E. Bilir, M. Chatterjee, K. L. Ebi, Y. O. Estrada, R. C. Genova, B. Girma, E. S. Kissel, A. N. Levy, S. MacCracken, P. R. Mastrandrea, and L. L. White, 1–32. Cambridge, UK: Cambridge University Press. https://www.ipcc.ch/site/assets/uploads/2018/02/ar5_wgII_spm_en.pdf.

IRENA. 2019. "Renewable Energy and Jobs: Annual Review 2019." International Renewable Energy Agency, Abu Dhabi, June. https://www.irena.org/-/media/Files/IRENA/Agency/Publication/2019/Jun/IRENA_RE_Jobs_2019-report.pdf.

Kahn, M. E., K. Mohaddes, R. N. C. Ng, M. H. Pesaran, M. Raissi, and J.-C. Yang. 2019. "Long-Term Macroeconomic Effects of Climate Change: A Cross-Country Analysis." National Bureau of Economic Research Working Paper 26167, Cambridge, MA, August.

Kelley, C. P., S. Mohtadi, M. A. Cane, R. Seager, and Y. Kushnir. 2015. "Climate Change in the Fertile Crescent and Implications of the Recent Syrian Drought." *Proceedings of the National Academy of Sciences of the United States of America* 112 (11): 3241–46.

Lenton, T. M., J. Rockström, O. Gaffney, S. Rahmstorf, K. Richardson, W. Steffen, and H. J. Schellnhuber. 2019. "Climate Tipping Points—Too Risky to Bet Against." *Nature* 575: 592–95.

Linden, E. 2019. "How Scientists Got Climate Change So Wrong." *New York Times*, 8 November. https://www.nytimes.com/2019/11/08/opinion/sunday/science-climate-change.html.

Lüthi, D., M. Le Floch, B. Bereiter, T. Blunier, J.-M. Barnola, U. Siegenthaler, D. Raynaud, J. Jouzel, H. Fischer, K. Kawamura, and T.

Stocker. 2008. "High-Resolution Carbon Dioxide Concentration Record 650,000–800,000 Years before Present." *Nature* 453: 379–82.

Markkanen, S., and A. Anger-Kraavi. 2019. "Social Impacts of Climate Change Mitigation Policies and Their Implications for Inequality." *Climate Policy* 19 (7): 827–44.

Moore, W. H., and S. M. Shellman. 2004. "Fear of Persecution: Forced Migration, 1952–1995." *Journal of Conflict Resolution* 48 (5): 723–45.

Moss, R. H., J. A. Edmonds, K. A. Hibbard, M. R. Manning, S. K. Rose, D. P. Van Vuuren, T. R. Carter, S. Emori, M. Kainuma, T. Kram, G. A. Meehl, J. F. B. Mitchell, N. Nakicenovic, K. Riahi, S. J. Smith, R. J. Stouffer, A. M. Thomson, J. P. Weyant, and T. J. Wilbanks. 2010. "The Next Generation of Scenarios for Climate Change Research and Assessment." *Nature* 463: 747–56.

National Research Council. 2002. *Abrupt Climate Change: Inevitable Surprises.* Washington, DC: National Academies Press.

Ramstein, C. 2019. *State and Trends of Carbon Pricing 2019.* Washington, DC: World Bank.

Riahi, K., D. P. van Vuuren, E. Kriegler, J. Edmonds, B. C. O'Neill, S. Fujimori, N. Bauer, K. Calvin, R. Dellink, O. Fricko, W. Lutz, A. Popp, J. Crespo Cuaresma, K. C. Samir, M. Leimbach, L. Jiang, T. Kram, S. Rao, J. Emmerling, K. Ebi, T. Hasegawa, P. Havlík, F. Humpenöder, L. Aleluia Da Silva, S. Smith, E. Stehfest, V. Bosetti, J. Eom, D. Gernaat, T. Masui, J. Rogelj, J. Strefler, L. Drouet, V. Krey, G. Luderer, M. Harmsen, K. Takahashi, L. Baumstark, J. C. Doelman, M. Kainuma, Z. Klimont, G. Marangoni, H. Lotze-Campen, M. Obersteiner, A. Tabeau, and M. Tavoni. 2017. "The Shared Socioeconomic Pathways and Their Energy, Land Use, and Greenhouse Gas Emissions Implications: An Overview." *Global Environmental Change* 42: 153–68.

Rignot, E., J. Mouginot, B. Scheuchl, M. van den Broeke, M. J. van Wessem, and M. Morlighem. 2019. "Four Decades of Antarctic Ice Sheet Mass Balance from 1979–2017." *Proceedings of the National Academy of Sciences of the United States of America* 116 (4): 1095–103.

Schwalm, C. R., S. Glendon, and P. B. Duffy. 2020. "RCP8.5 Tracks Cumulative CO_2 Emissions." *Proceedings of the National Academy of Sciences of the United States of America* 117 (33): 19656–57.

Shahbaz, M., and A. Sinha. 2019. "Environmental Kuznets Curve for CO_2 Emissions: A Literature Survey." *Journal of Economic Studies* 46 (1): 106–68.

Stern, D. I. 2017. "The Environmental Kuznets Curve after 25 Years." *Journal of Bioeconomics* 19 (1): 7–28.

Strobl, E. 2011. "The Economic Growth Impact of Hurricanes: Evidence from U.S. Coastal Counties." *Review of Economics and Statistics* 93 (2): 575–89.

Tol, R. S. J. 2018. "The Economic Impacts of Climate Change." *Review of Environmental Economics and Policy* 12 (1): 4–25.

Way, M. J., A. D. Del Genio, N. Y. Kiang, L. E. Sohl, D. H. Grinspoon, I. Aleinov, M. Kelley, and T. Clune. 2016. "Was Venus the First Habitable World of Our Solar System?" *Geophysical Research Letters* 43 (16): 8376–83.

Weart, S. 2003. "The Discovery of Rapid Climate Change." *Physics Today* 56 (8): 30–36.

Wood, C. A. 1992. "Climatic Effects of the 1783 Laki Eruption." In *The Year without a Summer? World Climate in 1816*, edited by C. R. Harrington, 58–77. Ottawa: Canadian Museum of Nature.

Wouter Botzen, W. J., O. Deschenes, and M. Sanders. 2019. "The Economic Impacts of Natural Disasters: A Review of Models and Empirical Studies." *Review of Environmental Economics and Policy* 13 (2): 167–88.

Named Endowments

The CFA Institute Research Foundation acknowledges with sincere gratitude the generous contributions of the Named Endowment participants listed below.

Gifts of at least US$100,000 qualify donors for membership in the Named Endowment category, which recognizes in perpetuity the commitment toward unbiased, practitioner-oriented, relevant research that these firms and individuals have expressed through their generous support of the CFA Institute Research Foundation.

Ameritech
Anonymous
Robert D. Arnott
Theodore R. Aronson, CFA
Asahi Mutual Life Insurance Company
Batterymarch Financial
  Management
Boston Company
Boston Partners Asset Management,
  L.P.
Gary P. Brinson, CFA
Brinson Partners, Inc.
Capital Group International, Inc.
Concord Capital Management
Dai-Ichi Life Insurance Company
Daiwa Securities
Mr. and Mrs. Jeffrey Diermeier
Gifford Fong Associates
Investment Counsel Association
  of America, Inc.
Jacobs Levy Equity Management
John A. Gunn, CFA
John B. Neff, CFA
Jon L. Hagler Foundation
Long-Term Credit Bank of Japan, Ltd.
Lynch, Jones & Ryan, LLC
Meiji Mutual Life Insurance
  Company

Miller Anderson & Sherrerd, LLP
Nikko Securities Co., Ltd.
Nippon Life Insurance Company of
  Japan
Nomura Securities Co., Ltd.
Payden & Rygel
Provident National Bank
Frank K. Reilly, CFA
Salomon Brothers
Sassoon Holdings Pte. Ltd.
Scudder Stevens & Clark
Security Analysts Association
  of Japan
Shaw Data Securities, Inc.
Sit Investment Associates, Inc.
Standish, Ayer & Wood, Inc.
State Farm Insurance Company
Sumitomo Life America, Inc.
T. Rowe Price Associates, Inc.
Templeton Investment Counsel Inc.
Frank Trainer, CFA
Travelers Insurance Co.
USF&G Companies
Yamaichi Securities Co., Ltd.

Senior Research Fellows

Financial Services Analyst Association

For more on upcoming Research Foundation
publications and webcasts, please visit
www.cfainstitute.org/en/research/foundation.

Made in the USA
Coppell, TX
27 May 2021